AFTER THE THEFT
OF THE SACRED

American Indian Literature and Critical Studies Series

AFTER THE THEFT OF THE SACRED

EXPERIENTIAL RELIGION IN INDIGENOUS WRITING

REGINALD DYCK

UNIVERSITY OF OKLAHOMA PRESS : NORMAN

Publication of this book is made possible through the generosity of Edith Kinney Gaylord.

Chapter 4 of this book was previously published, in a slightly different form, as "Simon Ortiz's Poetry of Crisis Ordinariness During a Rosebud Reservation Winter" in *Great Plains Quarterly* 37, no. 1 (2017), published by the University of Nebraska Press.

After the Theft of the Sacred: Experiential Religion in Indigenous Writing is Volume 75 in the American Indian Literature and Critical Studies Series

Library of Congress Cataloging-in-Publication Data
LCCN #2025037357
ISBN 978-0-8061-9651-0 (hardcover)

To Kaori

I believe that what most threatens the American Indian is sacrilege, the theft of the sacred. Inexorably the Indian people have been, and are being, deprived of the spiritual nourishment that has sustained them for many thousands of years. This is a subtle holocaust, and it is ongoing.

N. SCOTT MOMADAY,
MAN MADE OF WORDS

CONTENTS

ACKNOWLEDGMENTS

"I wasn't there," Joy Harjo's narrator concludes in "Deer Dancer," one of the great poems of Indigenous religious experience. I wasn't there either. This is both a strength and limitation for Harjo's narrator and for myself. My access to Native religious experience is mainly through texts, literary accounts in particular. The analysis in the following chapters is an effort to notice and clarify the rich range of religious reports that contemporary Indigenous literature offers. Despite my intent to write descriptively rather than evaluatively, I necessarily write out of a particular range of experiences. I have tried to follow Robert A. Orsi's caution: Studies of religion should not moralize but should be moral in their "cultivation of a disciplined attentiveness to many different ways people have lived with their gods and to the things, terrible and good, violent and peaceful, they have done with the gods to themselves and to others" (*Between* 203). My dad once told me that his mother, farming in Saskatchewan in the early twentieth century, would offer meals to Indians (First Nation persons) when they came to her door. I now wonder, did my grandmother think about the conditions that had brought them there? Did she recognize the political and cultural power dynamics of those encounters? Did she think about whose land her husband was plowing? Is there any chance that she might have, as Simon Ortiz's speaker in *from Sand*

Creek insists, "listened and listened and learned to sing in Arapaho"? I doubt it. I wonder if I have.

Like most scholars, I have depended on the kindness of strangers, others who through their essays and books have expanded the depth and range of knowledge and insight available to interpreters of Native literature. Many works have shaped this project but especially those by Bonita Lawrence, Neal McLeod, Greg Sarris, Kirk Dombrowski, Robert A. Orsi, Diane Glancy, and Charles Taylor.

I have tried to balance the distinctiveness of Indigenous religious experiences with their commonalities with other religious traditions, particularly in their post-contact iterations. My goal has been to avoid the limitations of Indigenous exceptionalism (an understandably strategic position) and the conceptual violence of accounts that fail to recognize the specificities of Native nations' history and culture.

Various university, public, and private libraries and librarians have facilitated my work. OhioLink, a governmental system for democratically sharing books and journals among not only university by also public libraries, has been invaluable.

Friends and family, too, have offered essential help and encouragement. When someone writes the book *Friendship in the Time of COVID*, Alan Katchen deserves his own chapter for all his phone calls. On our walks downtown to the Mercantile Library, Marc Loy and I discussed so many topics, including the intellectual work we both were doing. Throughout my scholarly career, my brother, American history professor Stan Dyck, and David Summers, my friend and English Department colleague, have engaged with me in endless, wide-ranging, thought-provoking, and sometimes fools-rush-in conversations that often had religious centers or subtexts. My now deceased parents led sincerely religious lives and taught me much. My wife, Kaori Fujishiro, supported and taught me as well. I owe a special debt and offer grateful thanks to them all.

My interactions with two Native writers, Greg Sarris and Robert Davis Hoffmann, have been productive pleasures. I am honored to have worked with them in the republication of their books. Both do important work as literary writers and engaged tribal members. Thank you to Liam O'Loughlin and Craig Burgdoff for their comments on an earlier draft of chapter 2 and to Gloria Still and two anonymous reviewers for their helpful comments on earlier drafts of chapter 4.

INTRODUCTION

INDIGENOUS CONTINUANCE AFTER THE THEFT
OF THE SACRED

Some years back I received a reviewer's report that stung me: "The author argues that we Indians need to include spiritual practice . . . into everyday life and literature and implies that is the answer to American Indian problems and challenges within the modern world. I don't buy that. First of all, it smacks of the essentialist notion that all Indians are 'spiritual' or should be if they are real Indians."

I was taken aback. I did not think I had been so prescriptive. I did recognize, however, that particularly as a non-Native scholar, I needed to rethink my assumptions about Native religious experience. And for the reviewer, I clearly had touched a painful spot that had larger implications. "[A] return to traditional practice," they wrote, "particularly spiritual practice, is a backlash, a way to assert identity in the one free place it is most allowable." What I and others had taken as a form of revitalization was here reduced to a strategic reaction to a sense of powerlessness.[1] Scott Richard Lyons (Ojibwe/Dakota) in *X-Marks* similarly questions common assumptions about Indigenous spirituality by challenging the idea that "Native people are obsessed with spirituality and traditions to the exclusion of nearly everything else in our lives" (146). And novelist Ray Young Bear (Meskwaki) has his alter ego Edgar Bearchild assess the situation for his tribe: We were "[l]ulled into believing we were highly spiritual" (*Remnants* 89).[2] The assumption of spirituality, and its associations with Mother Earth and the Creator, also lends support to stereotypically seeing Indigenous peoples as the Other to the West's materialism and secularization (McClure 132).

Critical analysts can also be lulled, in more ways than one. My reviewer offered one caution. Religious studies scholar Robert A. Orsi offers a nearly opposite one: "The modern world has assiduously and systematically disciplined the senses not to experience sacred presence; the imaginations of moderns are trained toward sacred absence" (*Between* 12). Native studies scholarship is not immune to this disciplining (see chapter 1). Daniel Heath Justice (Cherokee) implicitly acknowledges this when he states that although he had emphasized "cultural context and history" for understanding Cherokee literature, he had "failed to adequately address one of the most significant dimensions of that context: the spirit world" ("Relevant Resonance" 71–72).[3] This disjuncture, the spirit world as most significant and yet easily overlooked, alerts us to the challenges for scholarship on modern Indigenous religious beliefs and practices.

Addressing these two cautions, essentializing religious experience or missing it altogether, *After the Theft of the Sacred* engages contemporary Native literature as it imaginatively re-creates the variousness and complexity of Indigenous beliefs and practices. A key context for these two cautions is what N. Scott Momaday (Kiowa) has trenchantly called "the theft of the sacred." He writes, "I believe that what most threatens the American Indian is sacrilege, the theft of the sacred. Inexorably the Indian people have been, and are being, deprived of the spiritual nourishment that has sustained them for many thousands of years" (Momaday, *Man Made* 76)

His novel *House Made of Dawn* bears witness to these words. The theft involves both the content and conditions of belief. In contrast to the modern imaginary, renowned Iglulik *angakoq* (shaman) Aua summed up the Inuit aboriginal apprehension of the cosmos: "All our customs come from life and turn towards life; we explain nothing, we believe nothing" (qtd. in Merkur ix). With this, Aua expressed to Danish explorer Knud Rasmussen the distinctiveness of the pre-contact aboriginal socioreligious experience.

Today we commonly find assertions similar to the first part of Aua's statement. Yet the latter part, neither explaining nor believing, now seems literally unimaginable. Momaday's "man made of words" is a man made of imaginings, reasonings, and justifications. We cannot stop explaining; it is a fundamental aspect of the modern condition. And it is hard to imagine anyone living within the modern social imaginary (see chapter 1), Native or non-Native, stating "we believe nothing" in the unselfconscious sense Aua means. A cosmos saturated with spiritual beings and powers was such a given that belief was unnecessary for pre-contact aboriginal people, as it is for us with, say, electricity or gravity. For most today, spiritual belief requires choice and thus explanation.

Despite the theft Momaday identifies, his novel does conclude with continuance: Abel's choice to struggle to integrate himself into the tribe through its ceremonial running. This continuation of tradition, however, is not a replication of the past but rather a negotiation with it. Abel's running is not the same as his grandfather Francisco's. This is hardly surprising since material and spiritual conditions had changed. The continuance of tribal religious traditions, everyone understands, involves adaptation. Many writers focus on adapted beliefs and practices. The chapters of *After the Theft of the Sacred*, however, address the changing nature of belief itself, a more fundamental disjuncture that calls for a different form of continuity.

The disjuncture within continuity that I address here is not the commonly addressed one between Native and Western/Christian ways of apprehending the cosmos. Rather it is the disjuncture between the premodern or aboriginal and the modern social imaginary or common conceptual horizon.[4] The following chapters reckon with a range of beliefs and practices in a time when few experience the givenness of spiritual realities that Aua did. Many characters, individuals, and communities experientially believe that the material world alone fills the cosmos; others adapt various traditional Native beliefs to their present needs. Many adopt and adapt Christianity in one of its many forms. Others, like Momaday, replace the sacred as traditionally understood with the power of imagining, a necessary antidote to centuries of devastating colonialism (Teuton, *Native* 1). These options, and Indigenous literature reveals others, are marked by an uncertainty of spiritual apprehensions, or at least a sense that these apprehensions are a choice that others do not make. This sociocultural reality is foreign to the experience Aua expresses. Nevertheless, adaptations do sustain continuities. Writing about Algonquins in Ontario, Bonita Lawrence (Mi'kmaw) explains, "The reality is that complex technologies of adaptation are required for societies to flourish on the land" and reports on the ways these people have sustained traditional lifeways even as their identity has become more complex and shifted in focus from band level to "a more monolithic identity as Algonquins" (*Fractured* 30–31).

Literature is part of ongoing Indigenous efforts to imagine individual, communal, and tribal/national continuance after the theft. I agree with urban anthropologist Sherry B. Ortner when she states, "Novelists, or good ones anyway, are the traditional ethnographers of their own cultures" (20).[5] Coast Miwok/Kashaya Pomo writer Greg Sarris, in his preface to *Grand Avenue*, asserts what many Native writers must feel: "The stories I have written are firmly based in history and everyday reality" (viii). Joy Porter further states that literature offers "truths" unavailable in historical accounts because it has "a different relationship to historical 'facts' and a different consciousness of the past itself" (39). Terms like "everyday" and "consciousness" suggest the lived or experiential realities that literary writers can capture. Writing within a First Nations context, Sam McKegney elaborates a further role for Native literature. Not only can it "archive cultural knowledge," but it also "refracts cultural knowledges through lived experience, imagination and identifiable sociopolitical goals in the pursuit of contemporary health and alternative futures" (410). Literature has significant work to do in the project of revitalization.

Yet authors are interpreters not transcribers of experience, and literary critics are thus second-order interpreters. This puts literary critics in a similar position to ethnographers, as Ortner's assertion suggests. Luke E. Lassiter explores this problematic in *The Power of Kiowa Song: A Collaborative Ethnography*. He explains that his challenge is to "*elaborate* instead of *reduce* the complicated experience that my consultants talk about" (8, emphasis added). Here Lassiter offers an important corrective for literary critics as well, although there are times when reduction or abstraction is a useful analytical tool. Part of the elaborative work of literary interpretation, and the purpose of this book, is to clarify the experiences depicted in Native literature by illuminating relevant contexts and providing useful interpretive strategies. Regarding contexts, Melanie Benson Taylor (Herring Pond Wampanoag) insists that Native American literary works cannot "be removed from the fluid and often messy dynamics of their imbrication in US national politics" (Introduction 3). One might add US religion and economics as well as popular and literary cultures. Similarly, Benson Taylor explains that "Indigenous literatures cannot be defined in any simplistic, static, or sovereign way" (Introduction 2–3). Thus the interpretive strategies of *After the Theft of the Sacred* involve reading both with and against the grain as they use intrinsic and extrinsic methods and theories.

Part of the power of literature is its relation to lived reality. As an abstraction or distillation of that reality, it can reveal people's religious horizons, the structure of their religious feelings, and what they imagine and assume their beliefs and practices to be. This book analyzes the ways authors, communities, and characters read the signs of the spirits—that is, the ways they consciously and unconsciously apprehend or make sense of a more-than-material cosmos. Shaped by tribal, intertribal, and individualized religious traditions, their apprehensions are also inescapably shaped by the modern social imaginary. In different ways, each of the following chapters reckons with the broad, uneven, and complex shift from an aboriginal or premodern social imaginary, in which apprehensions of a spiritual–material cosmos were a given, to the modern one, which has become pervasive not only in Western society but also in Indian Country.[6] Native characters and communities struggle to reimagine their traditions and maintain themselves religiously within an individualizing cultural context resistant to communal sustenance and discipline as well as to experiences of sacred presences. Beliefs and practices are always an interpretive negotiation among various force fields, as contemporary Indigenous literature demonstrates and the analysis here develops.

After the Theft of the Sacred analyzes this literature ethnographically (while recognizing that aesthetics broadly speaking is a part of this ethnography) to understand the contexts and processes through which authors and their characters make sense of religious experiences, both formal and informal,[7] which are more various than usually understood. In contrast to common popular as well as scholarly generalizations about Native spirituality, the analysis here finds Native literary reports often filled with doubt, disappointment, and uncertainty, marked more by longing than fulfillment. For example, when one of Susan Power's (Standing Rock Sioux) characters calls on the ancestors for help, they are found sleeping or maybe just "peeking at us from behind their hands but wouldn't look and wouldn't answer" (102). And for others, religious belief and experience is mostly irrelevant. The experiences presented in contemporary Indigenous literature, these chapters argue, are much messier, more complicated, more partial, often frustrating, often darker, less communal, and less pervasive than what most explanations presume. As characters engage what seems to many of them a fractured rather than unified cosmos, they have difficulty finding even glimpses of the more-than-material world. And the encounters they do have are not necessarily life-enhancing. Contemporary Indigenous literature suggests that doubt, uncertainty, disappointment, longing, and leaps of faith are not just Christian structures of feeling and that the difficulties in religious apprehension are not caused only by their colonial contexts. Yet characters experience both spiritual absence and presence. Many experience various forms of continuance that enrich and guide their lives.

Addressing these complexities as experiential beliefs rather than abstract or dogmatic ones, the present analysis situates them within what is often considered a time of crisis within Indian Country. Many depict this crisis as resulting from continuing colonialism, including Christianity, or from personal and communal failures. However, difficulties in spiritual apprehension can result from the nature of the cosmos itself and so reach back to the ancestors, some Native literary works suggest. For example, James Welch's (Blackfeet/Gros Ventre) *Fools Crow* depicts the pre-contact healing prayers of young Mik-api going unanswered by Blackfeet spiritual powers (386). And ceremonies have always been needed as mediations because sacred beings are often otherwise inaccessible. Recognizing both colonial and cosmic difficulties, the chapters here analyze the impact of secularization,[8] the challenges in recognizing and writing about sacred presences, the trauma religions that emerge from crises as well as from "crisis ordinariness," and the complex role of tradition in Native revitalization efforts. All of these involve the problematic of interpretation: reading the signs of the spirits.

As my reviewer attested and contemporary Indigenous literature affirms, many Indians are not engaged ceremonially or even perceptually with cosmic realities. However, many are, as the research cited below indicates. Indigenous literature attests to the same: Religious beliefs and practices in their various forms continue to be important. Using a range of contexts and perspectives, *After the Theft of the Sacred* analyzes Native North American literary works to better understand the lived religion of individuals, communities, and tribal nations in Indian Country.

Reckoning with Native religious experiences within the modern social imaginary is a neglected but important problematic that this book addresses. Within it the experience of Native secularization should not be surprising. Many works of contemporary Native literature are set exclusively in the material world. In others, spiritual experiences in the present are depicted as inner and immanent rather than transcendent. This is the case for much of Louise Erdrich's (Turtle Mountain band of Chippewa) fiction—for example, *Love Medicine* and *LaRose*. At times, transcendent presences and experiences are reported to have taken place in the past. We see this in the different experiences of the narrator and his uncle in Welch's *Winter in the Blood*. Yet "[t]he gods were not turned back at the borders of the modern. The unseeing of the gods was an achievement; *the challenge is to see them again*" (Orsi, *History* 252, emphasis added). Native literature takes on this challenge as it includes characters resisting secularization. Diane Glancy's (Cherokee) Grandmother in the play "The Woman Who Was a Red Deer" registers this sensibility when she exclaims, "I don't like this world any more. We're reduced to what can be seen." Her more modern granddaughter also struggles, but in different ways, to find religious fulfillment in a secularized present (4, 18).[9]

Indigenous religious experiences cover a wide range of engagements for literary critics to consider. Think, for example, of Momaday's *House Made of Dawn* with its Eagle Watchers Society; Father Olguin and the Feast of Martyrs; the Pecos Bull dance ceremony; the Right Rev. John Tosamah, who anoints himself "Pastor and Priest of the Sun"; Ben Benally as the modern urban Night Chanter; and Abel's concluding participation in the community's ceremonial running. Greg Sarris's novels, discussed in chapters 5 and 7, similarly include a compendium of religious experiences. Think also of the nearly detribalized powwow characters at the end of Tommy Orange's (Cheyenne and Arapaho) *There There*, who in various ways reach for more-than-material apprehensions in a time of crisis. Or *Firekeeper's Daughter* by Angeline Boulley (Sault Ste. Marie Tribe of Chippewa Indians), a young adult novel that translates the traditions of the author's tribe into the modern world of drugs and violence as well as friendship and communal support. As Boulley notes, "There is a wealth of diverse experiences" (490), even in a community relatively effective in sustaining its traditions.

These diverse experiences also include a sense of spiritual absence and abandonment that results in religious doubt and longing for more. Material conditions can make spiritual apprehensions more difficult. For example, the character Carson Two Red Foot in Young Bear's *Black Eagle Child* enigmatically explains that poverty has negatively shaped his family's religious experiences: "Hunger along with depression provided a gathering for this dark ugliness. The control of the supernatural" (168–69). Earlier in the novel, Ted Facepaint states, "So there I was, buried in the desert, a half-naked 'skinjin,' surrendering to the cosmos with a smirk" (138). Enigmatic spiritual apprehensions such as these are part of the breadth of Indigenous literary religious experiences.

Another important reckoning is with the disjuncture between Native literature's experiential depictions of Native religions and common theological explanations. Orsi finds this disjuncture in common explanations of religion in the United States, "a nation in which religion has been so wildly creative and innovative, where there seems to be no end to the fecundity of religious imaginings or to their violent and disruptive consequences, the public discourse of 'the religious' instead presents faith and practice in ameliorative and consensual terms. Nothing happens in the space of the sacred, nothing moves, nothing changes, nothing ever spins out of the control, no one is ever destroyed there." He rejects this public discourse by asserting, "Yet no one has ever seen anything like this in the real world" ("Everyday" 11–12). The literature considered here does depict the moving, changing, spinning, and destroying qualities Orsi finds in US religions although within a significantly different context. Yet these depictions are likewise mostly at odds with formal explanations of Native religions.

The experiences within *House Made of Dawn*, Sarris's novels, *There There*, and *The Firekeeper's Daughter* do not fit well within explanations that focus on the formal belief structures of the pre-contact era and so miss their present experiential iterations (see Niezen xiii). Daniel Merkur's *Powers Which We Do Not Know: The Gods and Spirits of the Inuit*, for example, is thoroughly theological, which is valuable in its own right but is not experientially revealing. Joseph Epes Brown's *The Spiritual Legacy of the American Indian* similarly leaves modern religious experiences, the actual "legacy," unaddressed. Suzanne J. Crawford's introduction to Native religious traditions does focus on present specificities, including the demands and difficulties of performing ceremonies. However, she does not consider the experience, with all its diversity and difficulty, of actually apprehending "the reality and material presence of spiritual beings" (39). Her abstract explanation does not bring up the religious doubt and uncertainty that infuse many Indigenous literary accounts. None of these writers reckons with the ways the modern social imaginary has impacted Native religious experiences of belief, including the various ways communities and individuals have responded to it.

A further reckoning within the problematic of apprehending Native religious experiences is the relationship between the past and present. Part of the challenge of translating tradition is that while traditions change, sometimes "rapidly and radically," they are sustained through a conviction of continuity (Satlow 133–34, but also see the full chapter). For example, Leanne Betasamosake Simpson's (Michi Saagiig Nishnaabeg) book title *As We Have Always Done* suggests an unbroken continuity with precolonial practices.

However, the meanings or experiential apprehensions for what Indigenous people continue to do inevitably change as material conditions, historical circumstances, and social imaginaries change.[10] Addressing changing religious practices and meanings that arise from the shift in social imaginaries is a challenge for Native revitalization efforts. Sean Teuton (Cherokee), indirectly recognizing the shift, describes an "indigenous world alive with unseen spirits" but then inserts a contemporary difference by stating that these spirits "*were thought to* produce and govern the survival of all life in the universe." He then creates a seemingly impenetrable demarcation: "This is the indigenous world before whites came." One senses a longing as he adds that in the world of the aboriginal imaginary, "kinship and worship kept the world alive, mysterious, and satisfying" (*Native* 13, 14).

Intensifying the difference in imaginaries is a sense among many that the present religious crisis giving urgency to revitalization efforts at the same time makes them more difficult. Craig Womack (Oklahoma Creek-Cherokee) states that "the deplorable situation in Indian country is a spiritual crisis" ("A Single Decade" 9). Taiaiake Alfred (Kenien'kehaha'/Mohawk) similarly argues that because Indigenous peoples are alienated from their land and traditions, they "are living through a spiritual crisis" (qtd. in Lyons, *X-Marks* 112). In *Spirit Wars* Ronald Niezen, writing out of his experience with Cree communities in northern Quebec but encompassing a broader scope, further states that "the historical background of 'social pathology' in native communities often reveals radical instability in the human relationship with the spiritual world." (4). These concerns raise questions about the role of religious experience in Native revitalization. To what extent does the recovery of belief in an enchanted or more-than-material world need to be foundational for or even part of these efforts? In his posthumously published *The World We Used to Live In: Remembering the Powers of the Medicine Men*, Vine Deloria Jr. (Yankton-Standing Rock Sioux) argues insistently that supernatural help is required to heal the spiritual crisis at the root of the material problems facing many Native peoples today.[11] For him, the dividing line between past and present imaginaries can and must be breached; Native peoples can spiritually do as they have always done.

It is within this crisis that Deloria's book calls for a particular relationship between past and present religious experiences. He begins by critiquing present conditions in Indian Country, using the past as the standard to judge present well-being: Native beliefs and practices have been so undermined, even on traditional reservations, that many are letting go of ceremonies and live "in increasing and meaningless secularity" (xvii). His critique is harsh: "The mystery is largely gone." His prescription is straightforward: "Our ancestors invoked the assistance of higher spiritual entities to solve pressing practical problems, such as finding game." What follows is a book full of examples of past supernatural encounters that solved people's problems. Deloria takes seriously these past experiences as he calls for a re-enchantment of the Native world he cared so deeply about. Yet the relationship between past and present is troubled, and the problem of translation is not addressed. Significantly, none of the supernatural stories he tells are set close to the present time.[12]

This disjuncture between past and present is reflected in Deloria's own experiences, which are notably absent from *The World We Used to Live In*. Reflecting on Vine Deloria Jr.'s life, Philip J. Deloria (Dakota Sioux) notes in the book's preface that his father "was a man of complications and contradictions." He gently asks how his father's engagement in politics and law, both secular, fit with his "vehement insistence on the power and validity of indigenous (and, indeed, all) spiritual experience. . . . Why was he not a more active participant in the spiritual life of Indian people? These are not unfair questions." (xiii). The conclusion Philip Deloria offers is that his father argued for Indigenous spirituality "without engaging substantially in its practice" (xiv). The disjuncture between past and present religious experiences that Vine Deloria Jr. decries thus marked his own life. Maybe the closest he came to a public confession of religious experience was in a plenary session of the 1996 American Academy of Religion annual meeting, ten years before *The World* was published. His title, "Origins: Physical Reality and Religious Belief," brings together material and spiritual realities but in a conspicuously different register of belief than his later book. Deloria stated, "I have been in ceremonies. I have talked to spirits. . . . And I can't deny those experiences. They're as real to me as anything in the world." However, he then adds a clarification so unlike the confidence he expresses in *The World We Used to Live In*: "I don't believe that people having spiritual experiences are necessarily deluded. . . . People have experiences. They may misinterpret what an experience means. But the experience, as related in a narrative straightaway, is a valid experience" (*For This Land* 16). The phrases "real to me," "[not] necessarily deluded," "may misinterpret," and "valid experience" suggest that Deloria at that point accepted that religious experiences are difficult to recognize, interpret, and evaluate. This is because uncertainly and doubt are inherent within them. In part the cause is the modern individualization of religious experience, which Deloria contrasts with the tribal orientation of the book's stories. The disjuncture in his address between certainty about past experiences and uncertainties regarding present ones suggests some of the challenges for religious apprehensions within the modern social imaginary. It also suggests challenges for critical interpretations of these apprehensions.

Finally, difficulties in grasping spiritual realities past and present are caused not only by human limitations. Young Bear asserts, "As with everything imperfect, revelation would arrive in a bungling 'Keystone Cops' manner" (*Remnants* 230). Gods as bunglers. Difficulties translating spiritual realities into everyday experience, at least some Indigenous literary writers assert, are not only caused by colonization; nor is it only about the limited capacities of the human recipients. It is within the nature of the cosmic situation that revelation gets distorted.

Disjuncture as well as cosmic continuity mark much contemporary Indigenous literature that engages Native traditions. This calls for a reckoning with secularization, the diversity of Native religious experiences, their divergence from common theological abstractions, the relationship of past and present, the impact of religious crisis, and the cosmic challenge of connecting spiritual and material realities.

Often enough, critical writing within Native studies works to repair these disjunctures by asserting a distinction between religion and spirituality. Within the crisis noted above, this distinction has had considerable salience, "religion" being the term associated with Christianity as a colonial imposition and "spirituality" being associated with Native traditions (e.g., Garroutte 19, n. 1). Native studies scholars are not alone in this; many in religious studies find the term "religion" suspect.[13]

Ronald Niezen, rejecting the adequacy of the term "religion," asserts, "*Spirituality* describes indigenous traditions and conceptions of sacred power with potential moral implications for all aspects of life, while *religion* refers to organized worship brought to indigenous communities by colonizers" (xvi). This binary suggests that Native beliefs and practices have been and continue to be experientially encompassing, while Christianity, at least as a missionary enterprise, is only formal and institutional.[14] Both definitions are inadequate. Anyone who has spent time in evangelical church services, for example, recognizes how little they involve formal worship and how much they focus on exhorting followers to put their beliefs into all their everyday experiences. And to ignore the formal practices and structures of belief within Indigenous apprehensions of the sacred would mean missing the role of ceremonies in religious life. Further, the insistence on this distinction leaves no means for considering, as Niezen's *Spirit Wars* contradictorily yet astutely does, the religious adaptations that developed from contact between Indigenous and Christian people. Contemporary Native literature provides considerable evidence of this, most obviously with the Native American Church.

Lee Irwin similarly rejects the term "religion," in his case because of its association with the post-enlightenment distinction between the sacred and profane. Thus "religion," he argues, fails to recognize the interconnectedness of all life. This unity is a common enough claim about traditional Native apprehensions of the cosmos. It is then assumed, without explanation or support, for present Indigenous experiences. These contemporary experiences can appear to engage a unified cosmos while actually excluding more-than-material realities generally identified as "the sacred." This slippage is evident, for example, in the memoir of Beatrice Mosionier, author of the novel *In Search of April Raintree*. She defines "Indian spirituality" as understanding the cosmos as a whole and humans as part of "Mother Earth." This has implications, she explains, for harvesting, childrearing, the need for adaptation, human relations, and the need for tolerance of others' beliefs (148). Unlike aboriginal cosmic apprehensions, here no spirit powers and supernatural interventions have a place. Within this not uncommon understanding of spirituality, human or profane relationships are at the center as values have replaced supernatural powers. This is the apprehension Lipsha experiences in *Love Medicine*, as does the narrator of *Winter in the Blood* and many other modern characters. The point here is not to judge these experiences as inauthentic but rather to note that the vagueness and slipperiness of the term "spirituality" limits its usefulness for understanding the disjunctures and continuities within modern Native religious experiences.

Irwin extends his claim by associating spirituality with "authentic participation in values and real-life practices" (3). For him spirituality is an evaluative criterion for identifying good or authentic beliefs and practices. Yet he struggles to establish criteria for making judgments. Irwin recognizes that present Native spirituality cannot be understood as reconstructing the past, yet he does not set forth an alternative standard. In centering values, Irwin makes an existential judgment of authenticity: Spirituality is "a pervasive quality of life that develops out of an authentic participation in values and real-life practices meant to connect members of a community with the deepest foundations of personal affirmation and identity" (3). This is a dilemma for any group believing in more-than-material experiences and needing definitional boundaries in troubled times: defining the real thing or authentic spiritual self within socioreligious imaginaries. The concept of authentic spirituality, somewhat vaguely understood, can be reassuring, but it is also fraught with potentially harmful consequences. In a somewhat different context, Lyons calls authenticity a "language game[] designed for Indians to lose ("Actually" 303). Orange addresses the problematic of authenticity for urban Indians in his novel's prologue. He challenges accusations that they are "citified, superficial, inauthentic, cultureless refugees" as he argues somewhat cryptically that "what we are is what our ancestors did. How they survived. We are the memories we don't remember" (10).

Both Niezen and Irwin identify Native experiences of the more-than-material world as being spiritual as opposed to religious. And one must

acknowledge that religion is often understood as theological conceptualization and institutional practice established and controlled by the
religious elite. Yet the distinguishing capability of the term "spirituality" for Indigenous beliefs and practices is questionable. Today even
the most religiously committed US person claims to be spiritual rather
than religious (Orsi, *Between* 185–86), for the same reasons Niezen and
Irwin identify. The term "spirituality" resonates with the times because
it suggests an authenticity grounded in the authority of personal inner
experience rather than abstract dogma or organizational commitment
(Taylor, *Secular* 299). Thus it is beyond seemingly stultifying analyses,
which would undermine the intimate, experiential quality of "authentic
spirituality." This is why Irwin finds Native spirituality not amenable to
theory or analysis (2). Within this now hegemonic definition is a blindness to the role of social structures and discourses in shaping individual
experience, a significant deficit.

Aboriginal apprehensions of the cosmos generally include the belief that
all parts of the cosmos are filled with spirit or spiritual power, that the cosmos is alive with constant communication among its parts (e.g., Evers and
Molina 18). This does distinguish Indigenous conceptions of the cosmos
from Christianity. However, this animistic apprehension seldom registers
within contemporary Native literature. An exception is hunters ceremonially offering pollen or tobacco to animals they have just killed. It is
often seen as a mark of their Indigenous authenticity. More common is a
disjuncture within an imagined continuity of a unified cosmos. This is the
experience, for example, of Stacie Shannon Denetsosie's protagonist/nar-
rator in the story "Dormant." It begins, "I was taught from a young age that
the earth was sacred. Yet, every two weeks or so, I'd back my little truck up to
the edge of the Divergent Dam and throw our garbage into the gorge below"
(3). This invocation of sacredness disrupted, however, seems more ecologi-
cal than animistic, and the rest of the story depicts a thoroughly material
world of pregnancy tests and John Wayne DVDs. The ending enigmatically
loops back to the seemingly sacred earth: "the alkaline soil where nothing
would grow unless we gave ourselves to the earth. Our blood, salt, iron,

and placenta" (18). This reaches for but does not quite engage the aboriginal apprehension of a unified cosmos.

"Spirituality" is as much a borrowed term as is "religion," and the baggage it carries in the non-Native world does not stay there when the term is used to distinguish Indigenous conceptualizations. Its associations with New Age religions and, more broadly, with post- or post-post-secularism (see chapter 7) certainly complicate its applicability to Native experiences. Orsi, with a descriptive and inclusive approach to religious studies, uses the term "religion" because he sees "spirituality" used as an exclusionary term, a means of establishing a hierarchy of good and bad beliefs (*Between* 187–88). The concept of authenticity is at the heart of this problem. He further sees "spirituality" generally understood as "unbound by history and cultural contingencies" (*Madonna* xxxiii–xxxiv). Inner experience, it is often assumed, transcends the uncertainties and complexities of historical contingency.

Orsi rejects this understanding in his effort to contextualize individual and communal experiences that are nevertheless structurally conditioned. For him, using the term "religion" does not mean disregarding inner experiences but rather recognizing the ways these experiences are necessarily shaped by historical and contemporary conditions. Individual as well as communal and tribal religious experiences are not freestanding. While Orsi recognizes the term's negative associations, his definition of religion focuses on people's lived experiences. It is "the totality of their ultimate values, their most deeply held ethical convictions, their efforts to order their reality, their cosmology. This could be called their 'ground of being,' but only if this is understood in a very concrete, social-historical way, not as a reality beyond their lives, but as the *reason* that, consciously and unconsciously, structured and was expressed in their actions and reflections. More simply stated, *religion* here means 'what matters'" (*Madonna* lxi).

Religion engages the agency of both humans and the gods, who "can be negotiated and bargained with, touched and kissed, made to bear human anger and disappointment" (*Between* 74).[15] This engagement is evident, for example, in Glancy's deer dance play, discussed in chapter 3, and Robert Davis Hoffmann's (Tlingit) *Raven's Echo*, discussed in chapter 6.

The question is how to use terms as tools sensitively and effectively. Each term, "religion" and "spirituality," is a conceptual model, an argument, and not just a description. Within the debate over terms, the tendency is to reify the two as opposites rather than engaging them as historically constructed, contingent discourses. *After the Theft of the Sacred* is intended, to the extent possible, to be descriptive and analytical rather than evaluative.[16] With the goal of more fully grasping the wide range of experiences that contemporary Indigenous literature engages, socially sanctioned and not, it uses the term "religion." The term is also not without its complexities and limitations, but then no term is cross-culturally and historically adequate; nor is language itself. There are no universal categories, but some terms are more useful than others. However, it must be recognized that usefulness is a matter of standpoint and values.

Despite the historical association that Irwin rightly identifies, I use the term "religion" as Orsi conceptualizes it. I use the term "spiritual" to make a distinction from the *material* world, sometimes also calling the spiritual realm the more-than-material world, in recognition of the immediacy of our bodily experience. While the aboriginal socioreligious imaginary apprehends a unified cosmos, Native literature registers modern characters and communities struggling to experience the undifferentiated cosmos of the ancestors. For them it is not a given as it had been for the Iglulik shaman Aua. It is hard to think of any contemporary Native character other than Tayo in *Ceremony* who directly experiences the cosmic wholeness usually associated with the pre-contact past (see chapter 2).

Orsi encapsulates his approach to religion with the concept of *lived religion*, now a significant tool within religious studies.[17] He explains it as an experiential strategy: "The study of lived religion . . . is concerned with what people do with religious idioms, how they use them, what they make of themselves and their worlds with them, and how in turn people are fundamentally shaped by the world they are making as they make these worlds" (*Madonna* xxxvii).[18] The concept of lived religion emphasizes human agency in cosmic meaning making as individuals and communities choose and then engage (not merely follow) religious practices developed within their cultural environments. It reckons with the ways religion is individually lived out, even in ceremonies, while also recognizing that these experiences are socially and thus conceptually structured. Lived religions are the maps characters and communities consciously and unconsciously use to engage (to various degrees and in various ways) inherited traditions, teachings, beliefs, and practices. The concept of lived religion addresses a different problematic from systematic theologies like Alfonso Ortiz's classic *The Tewa World*, with its schematic explanation.

A dialectical methodology can capture lived Indigenous religions as it reckons with the various and always changing social structures that shape religious experience and recognizes that lived religions are always in process (*Madonna* lxi–lxii). Working to apprehend the web of relations that make up Indigenous religious experiences, the following chapters analyze Indigenous literary works as ethnographies of material and spiritual experience. By recognizing the ways Native religious beliefs and practices shape other aspects of characters and people's lives, *After the Theft of the Sacred* aims to explicate how they use religion and not just believe in it. In this sense, claims that Native religion permeates all of life ring true, but this is neither exceptional nor always positive. The dialectical analysis used here looks for relationships between material and spiritual realms as they change through time and are shaped by Native and non-Native cultural and social systems in which they are inevitably enmeshed. This method engages the past as it impinges on the present while also suggesting possible futures.[19] Thus, when considering literary depictions of sweat lodge ceremonies or powwows, for example, one needs to understand their religious meanings as part of changing systems of culture that are tribal, intertribal, and pan-Indian but can also be individualistically improvised and are inevitably shaped to some degree by non-Native audiences, practices, and conceptualizations. Indigenous religious practices are rooted in particular histories, shaped by present contingencies, and imply future possibilities.[20]

Fundamental to this book's analysis is the understanding that religions are never innocent—that is, outside of the contingencies of everyday reality (Orsi, *Madonna* xxxvii–xlii). They engage certain interests, take place within specific contexts, and emerge from specific histories. Within these specificities and others, only certain practices or experiences are culturally sanctioned, desired, or mandatory (Vásquez 8). Issues of power come into play as communities judge the legitimate range of religious practices. In *Ceremony* we see the negotiations for legitimacy that outsider Betonie must engage in whereas the Eagle Society as a historic part of the community has unquestioned authority (109, 238). Communal processes of legitimation are one way that everyday religious experiences are disciplined. For example, as Tayo's spiritual ordeal concludes, he must report to the elders (238). This disciplining, here depicted positively, can also be cruel in its exclusions. Orsi notes, "Meaning making is wounding" (*Between* 144). The middle section of Sarris's *Watermelon Nights* illustrates this with the Bole Maru, a religious response to desperate times. As a means of social coherence for survival, its leader, Big Sarah, practices physical and psychological violence against those who resist its norms (154, 168). One sees a similar process of legitimization in *House Made of Dawn*. Abel's absent father has the status of a cultural "outsider," which made his family "foreign and strange" (11).

Religion is often understood as a cultural force that binds people together; however, it can also work to dissolve those bonds (Orsi, "Everyday" 13). This is the religious power of belonging and exclusion. Anthropologist Kirk Dombrowski registers this tension within a rural Alaska Tlingit village. Various Christian churches and traditional culture groups construct rival meanings for spiritual presences. In a Pentecostal church, one person testified that "people who [practice 'Indian dancing'] don't know that by bringing spirits into the town like they do that it affects the whole town" (152). With contrasting meaning, "Culture-group members point out that dancing allows them the same sort of communion with fellow participants and the spirits of past ancestors that church members claim for their own gifts of faith" (154). These cosmic meanings are asserted, as Dombrowski shows, within particular economic and political and not only religious contexts. Each offers healing for some, wounding for others. Indigenous religious experiences, including revitalized traditional ones, are shaped by the class positions and concomitant needs and desires of leaders and participants, chapter 7 argues. Reckoning with these interests calls for self-reflexivity and analytical perspicacity.

A lived religion approach focuses on the ways everyday experience is shaped by the range of available "religious idioms," including those that are historically part of a particular culture and those not explicitly or conventionally considered as such (Orsi, "Everyday" 7). For Indigenous religious experience, these idioms include the practices of other tribes, developments in pan-Indian or intertribal religious expression, and Christianity as both an insider and outsider structure of belief and feeling. George E. Tinker (Osage) comments on "fundamentalist and evangelical Indians who have, relatively speaking, simply capitulated to Euro-White norms of religious discourse" ("American Indian Theology" 177). This may not be the only or most convincing explanation for a reservation billboard that states, "Jesus Christ Is Lord of the Crow Nation." Nevertheless, Mark Clatterbuck in *Crow Jesus: Personal Stories of Native Religious Belonging* quotes a frustrated white pastor: "If given a choice between church and a powwow . . . they'll choose the powwow every time" (5, 12). An experiential approach calls attention to "improbable intersections, incommensurate ways of living, discrepant imaginings, unexpected movements of influence and inspiration existing side by side" (Orsi, *Between* 9). This seems true on the Crow Reservation. We also see all these seeming incongruities in the various, often contrasting ways that one family in Erdrich's *Love Medicine* practices Catholicism: Think of Marie as an ambitious younger and then a devout older woman, her daughter Zelda, and Nector as a young and old man. Or think of engagements with Anishinabek traditions: Fleur, Lipsha, and Lulu (with her talk of two-leggeds and four-leggeds), for example. This necessary attention to practice takes us beyond commonly legitimized religious understandings and can help reveal what official histories and theologies miss or mask.

Neal McLeod's (James Smith Cree) "Cree Poetic Discourse" provides a model for addressing the relationship between past and present beliefs and practices, their disjunctures and continuities. McLeod advocates an improvisational approach to Indigenous religious experiences.[21] "Cree poetic consciousness rests on the notion that a narrative can never exhaust its possibilities," McLeod insists, "as there are always new embodiments and new interpretive locations" (115). McLeod is clearly not an originalist. Further, he notes that while this Indigenous consciousness is grounded in tradition, it is also "a radical questioning" of it (117). He guards against using tradition in ways that do not reckon with changing material conditions.

Implicitly acknowledging a shift in social imaginaries, McLeod approaches religious belief and practice experientially rather than propositionally. Similarly, he does not see religion as innocent. Engaging traditions for McLeod involves something analogous to what jazz musicians, painters, and dreamers do: riff on established patterns without being bound to a score (111). This is religion that creates a Native, specifically Cree, space within the modern social imaginary while communally resisting this imaginary's individualizing impulses. Human improvisation is inescapably enmeshed in the interpretive problematic. McLeod presents a readerly way of interpreting the signs of the spirits. His essay references Hans-Georg Gadamer (113), and the texture of his analysis is shaped by Gadamer's historically oriented hermeneutics. McLeod uses this phenomenological or experiential approach not to understand Native traditions social-scientifically but rather to apprehend them through experiential relationships. "Process" is a key term in his dialectical methodology (109). Within the context of the modern imaginary, process is depicted in many contemporary Native literary accounts as being more individual than communal. Think of Landreaux in Erdrich's *LaRose* or any of the characters in *There There* or Caroline laFavor's (Ojibwa) novels. In contrast, McLeod calls for improvisations that are communal and thus disciplined rather than free-form.

McLeod's position is clarified early in the essay as he honors but critiques Vine Deloria Jr.'s religious analysis. One problem is Deloria's "negative sculpting"—that is, defining Indigenous knowledge in contrast to Christianity and thus describing what this knowledge is not rather than what it is (110). However, both McLeod and Deloria emphasize the need to resist modern secularism by connecting humans to the spiritual parts of the cosmos— that is, "tapping into the Great Mystery" (McLeod 111, 109; see also Deloria, preface to *The World*). Yet the nature of the cosmos that they strive to tap into and thus their strategies for renewal are fundamentally different.

In *The World We Used to Live In*, Deloria insists on transcendent or supernatural experiences as the means of spiritual healing, whereas McLeod calls for an immanent spiritual response to modern disenchantment.[22] Deloria's book full of examples make clear that he here understands spiritual experiences as having a direct, supernatural, transformative impact on the material world. His section headings include "Unusual Predictions," "Making Plants Grow," and "Changing the Nature of a Storm." Similarly, Robert Warrior (Osage) explains, "Though certainly not always the case, much of . . . traditional practices and specialized knowledges are based in spirituality and require a high level of belief in what is usually understood as the supernatural and the extra-worldly" ("Native Critics" 203).[23] McLeod's poetic discourse instead engages an immanent apprehension that is "open to something beyond" (Taylor, *Secular* 544). This open immanence does not limit experiences to the material world but creates an interpretive rather than direct relationship between traditional and present religious practices.

In advocating an improvisational, immanent approach, McLeod addresses these practices differently from Deloria, who presents prescriptions: Read the stories as models for accessing in the present the spiritual powers they describe (214). McLeod instead gives guidance for the necessary improvisations that "recreate, although imperfectly," traditional religious practices (109). By using the term "imperfectly," McLeod acknowledges that the pre-contact Cree world is a model no longer directly experiential within modern conditions. And yet his essay is not shaped by a sense of religious decline, unlike Deloria of *The World We Used to Live In*. McLeod instead embraces the improvisational possibilities of the present, which are grounded in the past but not defined by it. His is a restless, dialectical position that does not offer the comfort of certainty that fundamentalisms, Native and non-Native, do. Within the modern social imaginary, McLeod recognizes the fluid nature of Indigenous religious apprehensions as individuals and communities respond to various material conditions.

Linda Hogan's (Chickasaw) *Solar Storms* figures this shift in cosmic apprehensions from givenness to improvisation while at the same time chart-
ing experiential continuities. Within the four-generation family of women
risking a difficult canoe journey, only the oldest experiences the givenness
of the aboriginal imaginary.[24] Dora-Rouge is guided by the ancestors in a
world that includes spirits and forces independent of her perceptions. Angel,
three generations younger, begins the journey as a sympathetic but modern
outsider to traditional Native understandings. She senses the flatness of
cosmic apprehensions that are closed to more-than-materialist experiences.
Her positively depicted religious journey does not bring her into the cosmic
imaginary that Dora-Rouge experiences. Rather Hogan depicts Angel coming to inhabit an open immanent religious discourse similar to McLeod's.
Connecting to the tribal traditions in which Dora-Rouge has her being,
Angel comes to find the world meaningful in ways not available within her
previous materialist outlook. Most striking about her journey is its inter-
nalization, which places her within the modern social imaginary. Although
guided by her elders, she herself imagines meanings for what she sees. And
the farther from the town of Adam's Rib she gets, the further inside herself
she journeys. She enters a world of "seemed" and "as for me," with its improvisational interpretive possibilities. Angel has what Charles Taylor calls an
"expressive outlook": Her religious experiences speak to her personal spiritual development (*Secular* 486). And yet that personal expression emerges
from tribal structures of belief and practice. Approaching what used to be
called God Island, she recognizes, "Something lived there. . . . I would call
it God." Here she is the one doing the naming and the defining: "God was
everything beneath my feet," she states (169–70). Angel improvises her own
lived religion: "Personally, I didn't like the notion of returned souls. I believed
in newness, in the freedom of a beginning outside the past, outside history"
(257). For her, this seemingly naive immanent apprehension comfortably
coincides with her scientific understanding of nature (179). This is a form
of apprehension unimaginable within a pre-contact world and yet emerges
from it. It thus differs from Dora-Rouge's cosmic apprehensions, including

her confident bargaining with the river so that the group can navigate its terrifying, seemingly impassable rapids (193–95). If the bargaining seems a modern adaptation, the certainty does not.

Yet *Solar Storms* imagines an experiential commonality among the four characters' cosmic apprehensions. Angel observes, "The four of us became like one animal. We heard inside each other in a *tribal* way" (176–77, emphasis added). McLeod's Cree poetic discourse similarly embodies a foundational connection between past and present religious beliefs and practices because the latter are grounded in "culturally specific metaphors" and "the languages of the ancient pathways of Indigenous thinking" (110). As with Angel's expressive religion, the grounding here is language or discourse, with its culturally mediated interpretations quite different from the seemingly unmediated access Hogan imagines Dora-Rouge having. McLeod explains that "tapping into the Great Mystery," a provocative metaphor itself, involves poetic or creative thinking that apprehends through "metaphorical discourse, composed of symbolic and poetic descriptions of our world and our experience" (109). In acknowledging language as mediator of spiritual apprehensions, McLeod differentiates world and experience. To state this in starkly Saussurean terms, religious experience as language is about absence rather than presence. However, McLeod's Cree poetic discourse would be better understood as the ongoing search for communally satisfying and sanctioned spiritual interpretations that use past tribal apprehensions as discourses needing to be refigured within new contexts. This is McLeod's guidance for addressing the absence that Deloria recognizes is an inevitable part of the human religious experience of apprehending a more-than-material world.

McLeod further refines the interpretive process: "Cree poetics link human beings to the rest of the world through the process of mamâhtâwisiwin, the process of tapping into the Great Mystery, which, in turn, is mediated by historicity and wâkôhtowin (kinship)" (109). These two, McLeod explains, are part of this inescapably mediated religious interpretive experience. The first, historicization, is a process that assumes that knowledge, including religious knowledge, is contingent and so always in need of adaptive reinterpretation. The second, kinship mediation, suggests that this contingent knowledge is always relational rather than abstract or individual. Thus it is always experienced within particular contexts and communities, which makes it a disciplined rather than an open interpretive process. For McLeod then, Indigenous beliefs and practices need to be ongoing, community-sanctioned, experiential processes rather than either authoritative proposi-tions of the religious elite or individualistically determined constructs. They are "narrative imaginations [that] expand the interpretive possibilities of the sacred story" (117). McLeod does not state this, but he implies that interpre-tive uncertainty is an inevitable part of this experience. As the following chapters show, this is a common spiritual experience (and frustration) within contemporary Native literature.[25]

Part of the interpretive relation to tradition that McLeod develops is the role of ceremonies in spiritual apprehension. Almost in passing, he provides a deep-structural explanation of ceremonies in Native religious life. He notes that some individuals are *ê-mamâhtâwisit*, "spiritually gifted . . . they know something that you will never know." In Cree stories this gifted "elder brother was the first ceremonialist, trying to link living beings in this dimen-sion to the force of life beyond our conscious reality" (112). Ceremonies are necessary mediations between two realities. The cosmic distance needing bridgework is suggested by "beyond our conscious reality," and the spiritual uncertainty of the process is implied in "trying to link." This understanding acknowledges that ceremonies are material signs requiring interpretation to grasp the spiritual realities they invoke. They do not offer direct access to more-than-material realities. When Paula Gunn Allen (Laguna Pueblo) explains that "the purpose of a ceremony is to integrate" (62), the implication is that the separateness of the material and spiritual worlds is an experiential reality as old as ceremonies themselves and not just a consequence of colo-nialism and modern alienation. Similarly, Larry Evers and Felipe S. Molina (Yaqui), discussed in chapter 3, acknowledge this experiential distinction when they use the terms "double world," "equivalences," and "verbal equa-tions" to describe the ways Yaqui deer songs bridge two realities (7). The Lakota name Wakan Tanka (Great Mystery), which McLeod in his Cree explanation also uses, similarly registers the difficulty in accessing spiritual reality. If there was no spiritual absence in human experience, there would be no need for ceremonial signs. This was as true for those living within the aboriginal social imaginary as for those in the modern one.

Like ceremonies, stories are culturally imagined and improvised "poetic pathways" that are ongoing processes, "always open to re-examination" (McLeod 113). Rather than the givenness of the premodern or aboriginal imaginary, spiritual fluidity and creativity are central to McLeod's reading of traditional stories. One senses in his essay the struggles with disjuncture and continuity inherent in creating spiritual interpretations. In his use of jazz as a metaphor to explain this Indigenous process of interpretation, McLeod grasps for a nontraditional language to translate his Cree religious experience into a critical essay. This translation of experience into explanation is one more step in the process of tapping into the Great Mystery.

Native studies scholars, myself included, have tended to acknowledge the Great Mystery but then leave out the mysterious in their literary explications and cultural explanations. Literary authors often do the same. Many of their characters, as the following chapters demonstrate, miss the experience of mystery. Longing is a common religious structure of feeling within much Indigenous literary writing. As chapter 1 argues both abstractly and experientially, this problematic is central to the modern social imaginary as it is lived in Indian Country. It is an affective structure needing to be reckoned with. The following chapters do that through a range of perspectives and analytical constructs. They explore the various reports Native literary writers have created about the ways characters and communities read or choose not to read the signs of the spirits. David D. Hall, in *Lived Religion in America: Toward a History of Practice*, notes that while the history of theology is well studied, "we know next-to-nothing about religion as practiced and precious little about the everyday thinking and doing of lay men and women" (vii). This is no less true for Native religious experiences. However, engaging the lived religions expressed within contemporary Indigenous literature offers a way of addressing this lack. This diverse body of poetry, fiction, drama, and essays depicts characters' individual and communal experiences of religious joys, frustrations, satisfactions, doubts, and hopes. Religious experiences take place in the material world as they engage the cosmos. The chapters that follow investigate the various worldly contexts within which Native characters and communities practice their religion.

The first chapter addresses the changing conditions that shape the possibilities and nature of Indigenous belief. Charles Taylor's conceptual framework of two social imaginaries, aboriginal or traditional and modern, provides a heuristic for understanding various ways literary characters and communities now experience Indigenous traditions and sacred presences. Native writers have developed various strategies for including these presences; most reflect modern skepticism. Bracketing, othering, reducing, and symbolizing are all literary responses that strip sacred presences of their experiential reality. However, some novels engage the reality of sacred presences while recognizing that they are experienced contingently and contextually.

The next chapter addresses the interpretive problematic developed in chapter 1 by focusing on ceremonies as mediators between material and spiritual realms. This problematic is shaped by the desire for religious continuity after the theft of the sacred. The ceremonies in Silko's *Ceremony* and Young Bear's *Black Eagle Child* embody contrasting ontologies and spiritual apprehensions. *Ceremony* reassuringly assumes a porous cosmos in which characters find the material and spiritual realms intertwined and their signs transparent. This has made the novel enormously appealing: The social situation is disturbing, but the spiritual realm offers reassuring innocence. Characters in *Black Eagle Child* find contingencies central to all religious encounters; they experience uncertainties, misapprehensions, bafflement, and yet also meaningful encounters with sacred presences. The two novels' different religious apprehensions shape the forms of individual and tribal healing they imagine.

The steps in this interpretative contrast include historicizing the novels' publications, analyzing the nature of their ceremonies, framing these experiences within the aboriginal and modern social imaginaries, and considering the implications of their narrative forms and structures. It also reckons with the nature of literary interpretation itself as innocent or experienced.

Chapter 3 further develops the interpretive problematic within contingent religious experiences by comparatively considering the spiritual apprehensions within deer dance works by Joy Harjo, Linda Hogan, and Diane Glancy. Each expresses the longing and elusiveness that seem an intrinsic part of modern Indigenous religious experiences. However, difficulties in spiritual apprehension here are not only the result of Western colonialism or modern secular culture. Nor are they caused only by personal or communal failures. The need for ceremonies itself suggests that spiritual–material challenges have always been a part of cosmic apprehensions. Ceremonies, like stories and language, are mediated efforts to make spiritual presences available in the material world. They require imagined belief, what Craig Womack calls "a leap of faith" that goes beyond reason. The different poetic styles of the three deer dance works embody the different levels of confidence and comfort that characters achieve in their spiritual imaginings.

The next chapter engages that imagining by asking, How does Native religious experience *feel* to an Acoma speaker struggling through a bleak Rosebud Reservation winter? The traumas of crisis ordinariness are central to Simon Ortiz's *After and Before the Lightning*. The uncertainties of the previous chapter are now explored within a complete collection of poems that more directly engage materially particular contexts. The urgency is similar, but the outcome is more in doubt. The speaker's distance from his Southwest homeland and traditions, the everyday traumas of continuing colonization, and a modern secular culture that questions the possibility of religious experience all create a profound spiritual unease. *After and Before the Lightning* offers no ready resolution to the problematic of spiritual uncertainty. Only "our eagerness blooms."

"Trauma has become a major signifier of our age." Chapter 5 explores its effect on Indigenous religions. Trauma narratives offer a way for Native peoples to make sense of the insidious effects of historical and ongoing colonialism. Using Sarris's two richly ethnographic novels, *Grand Avenue* and *Watermelon Nights*, this chapter expands the concerns of the previous one by analyzing five characters' personally adapted yet communally engaged trauma religions.

Faced with profound tribal disruptions, Big Sarah leads and Elba marginally participates in the revivalistic Bole Maru religion related to the Ghost Dance. As urban (relatively) middle-class characters of the next generation, Iris and Faye respond religiously to intergenerational trauma. Iris, alienated from her mother Elba's spiritual apprehensions, experiences religious and cultural isolation. In contrast, Faye's religious and social struggles take place within family and community. However, her social ambiguity underpins her religious insecurity. Only Nellie offers a trauma religion grounded in tribal traditions but positively adapted to a troubled present. Sarris's reckoning with what has been stolen and what remains, the conclusion explains, has implications for Indigenous religious and cultural revitalization.

The darkness or theft of the sacred within Sarris's novels has to do with colonial domination and the resulting internalized oppression. Robert Davis Hoffmann's poetry collection *Raven's Echo*, the focus of chapter 6, depicts a cosmic darkness unparalleled in modern Indigenous literature as the speaker in Book 1 confronts the world Raven has created. This is tricksterism taken with ontological seriousness. Shifting the focus from the cosmos to Tlingit life in Southwest Alaska, Book 2 develops as a neotraditional reconstruction project. It addresses the problematic of place within the modern social imaginary. *Raven's Echo* presents "an ethnography of a problem" as it poetically engages a shifting Tlingit lived religion that confronts inherent cosmic darkness while reconstructing modern religious meanings that respond to cosmic but also material concerns.

The religious continuities and disjunctures within shifting social imaginaries is a guiding concept for *After the Theft of the Sacred*. Chapter 7 more insistently investigates the implications by raising Bonita Lawrence's ethnographic questions: How far can traditions be improvised and still remain valid, and what are the standards for evaluation? In contrast to Neal McLeod's communal improvisational neotraditionalism rooted in Cree tradition, discussed in the introduction, Lipsha's healing ceremony in Louise Erdrich's *Love Medicine* is much more free-form and individually devised, as are the improvisations in many modern Native literary works. This becomes clear when Lipsha's ceremonial improvisations are contrasted with the practices of the now shunned traditional healer Fleur Pillager. Secularity, as defined by Charles Taylor, affects believers and unbelievers alike as choice rather than givenness becomes central to their religious experiences. John A. McClure's explanation of post-secular improvisation provides a framework for analyzing the continuities and disjunctures both rural and urban Indigenous characters experience as they strive for spiritual fullness. The question of validity for their various forms of religious engagement underlies this analysis.

Once one starts looking for depictions of religious experiences in contemporary Indigenous literature, one finds them almost everywhere. Tommy Orange's *There There* engages the problematic of religious belief within a distinctly urban, pan-Indian cultural geography. Yet it addresses and extends many of the themes of *After the Theft of the Sacred* as it addresses both disjunctures and continuities: interpretive difficulties, the paucity of spiritual experiences, the availability and uses of traditions, urban fragmentation, tribes as identity constructs more than communal experiences, cosmic and social alienation, and the challenges of secularization and post-secularity. The novel captures a fractured Native urban community, even as various forms of kinship continue to sustain characters. "The city made us new, and we made it ours," Orange asserts. The city and religion are often seen as antithetical; *There There* tests this assertion. Three qualities stand out: spiritual uncertainty, the particular difficulties in constructing urban religious meanings, and the personalization and improvisation of communal traditions within the Indigenous marketplace of religious options. The ethnographies of *There There* and other novels considered in *After the Theft of the Sacred* map the considerable range of modern Indigenous religious experiences that sustain, but sometimes weaken, characters and communities.

1 APPREHENDING SACRED PRESENCES

CONDITIONS OF BELIEF WITHIN CHANGING SOCIAL IMAGINARIES

Apprehending and interpreting sacred presences is a fraught project within any structure of belief. Meskwaki novelist Ray Young Bear's character captures the dilemma:

> . . . there rose a choir
> of barely audible voices. For less than
> a second I heard music before the wind
> carried it away.

However, this reassuring although ephemeral aural glimpse into the spirit world is quickly undercut:

> . . . It could have been
> children beating the hell out of a junk car. (*Black Eagle Child* 218–19)

This is materialism with a vengeance. Readers are left wondering if the cryptic messages are from a more-than-material reality or just a spiritual sheen willed onto a dreary, poverty-stricken everyday world.

Within the post-theft interpretive problematic of reading the signs of the spirits, terms vie for predominance: the "spirits" themselves or the "reading" of their signs. Young Bear's novel *Black Eagle Child* engages the question of interpretive foundations with Junior Pipestar, the above listener and narrator. In his search for origins, he meets traditionalist Jack Frost (214, 217), whose ironic name suggests the evanescence of the culturally mixed meanings he is passing on to his new apprentice. Because Frost is ambiguously identified as "a credible healer and clairvoyant," we wonder how seriously (and in what hermeneutic register) to take a Native elder whose name alludes to western pop culture. While Pipestar's self-assumed name suggests traditional authenticity and cosmic connectedness, he concludes the explanation with his interpretive trademark "I would never know" (220, 219). This interpretive uncertainty is fundamental to the novel as a whole. Readers are caught in at least a double bind. We are not sure if we should trust the irony-inclined narrator: Is Pipestar mocking readers' readiness to believe in "a quest for identity, / a longing for origins" (214)? And we wonder if we as readers or Pipestar himself should trust his oddly named mentor dressed up in 1839 regalia. Is he actually bearing witness to the ancestors and not just caught up in a nostalgic fantasy? Frost is the one who insists that the sounds are more than material; should we trust that his depictions of spiritual beings exist outside of his mind and language? Interpreting the signs of sacred presences is a complex process that can be as unsettling as it is unsettled. This is true not only for a novel like *Black Eagle Child*, which forces readers to reckon not just with spirits but with the reading of them. We should bring the same concerns to novels like Leslie Marmon Silko's (Laguna Pueblo) apparently transparent novel *Ceremony*. This chapter takes on this task as it addresses the interpretive problematic for both novels.

The above questions and the analysis that follows engage the interpretive problematic of reading the signs of the spirits. The challenges that inhere in human efforts to find or construct religious meaning for our lives are necessarily also in the texts we read, the two being inextricably related. Both involve, the analysis here assumes, an "interpretive commitment" to collective discourses even as we recognize individual choices: "Our lives derive meaning . . . not as solitary embodied texts but as moments in living traditions," Jay L. Garfield explains in "Philosophy, Religion, and the Hermeneutic Imperative." As a result, our meanings are "always the collective achievement of the community in which that life is lived and of the tradition through which that community understands itself and by which its members can understand themselves and each other" (100). Indigenous apprehensions expressed in literature are no different. Individuals can only draw on the discourses available within the conceptual habitus. For Indigenous characters and communities, translating past traditions into present practices is not only or predominantly individual, even for characters whose religious strategies are improvisational (see chapter 7). Nor are religious apprehensions innocent—that is, developed outside of worldly relations of power. Understanding the experiential transmission of religious traditions calls for a dialectical interpretive strategy that pays attention to both individual and collective interpretive efforts as well as the ways these efforts are enmeshed in past, present, and future (seventh-generation) human processes. Engaged in religious experiences or not, most Native characters live in the shadow of their traditions, which include apprehensions of the cosmos. The central concern here is the various ways authors of literary characters and communities experientially translate Native traditions as their characters, through agency mediated by structures, embrace working interpretations of self, culture, and cosmos.

The problematic of reading the signs of the spirits suggests two interpretive paradigms. The difference is a matter of emphasis. Starting with "the spirits" means recognizing them as fundamental realities at least somewhat knowable. The spirits really, literally exist. This does not mean that the spirits are beyond interpretation. Spiritual experiences are mediated, but the signified and signifier are inherently if often mysteriously linked. In the premodern world, people mainly perceived spirits, gods, ancestors, demons, and other supernatural beings as unquestionably an active part of their world. The boundary between the material and spiritual realms for them was porous.

The second paradigm, which focuses on reading or interpretation, has become predominant in the modern West and beyond. This, however, does not mean that religion no longer plays a significant role in culture and society. Human interpretation is at the center of modern religious experience even as it reckons, in quite various ways, with belief in the spirits and their supernatural interventions in human life. Signs become stand-ins for something longed for or imagined but no longer unselfconsciously accepted as given. If believed in, the spirits are believed in by choice. Edwin Black in Tommy Orange's *There There* registers this form of cosmic apprehension: "The trouble with believing is you have to believe that believing will work, you have to believe in belief" (62). Within the modern social imaginary, discussed in the next section, spirits are apprehended and experienced through such thick layers of mediation—political, cultural, familial, personal, and more—that believing can come to seem an internal performance rather than a cosmic engagement.

Robert Warrior recognizes the consequences of beginning with reading rather than with the spirits when he observes, "One of the problems of the modern condition is its loss of the impulse to seek direct, unmediated religious experience" (*Tribal Secrets* 72). The impulse is troubled within the modern social imaginary because confidence in the possibility of an "unmediated religious experience" is generally lacking. Modern ways of apprehending the world, including spiritual apprehensions, no longer automatically interpolate a person into a cosmos of spirits. Warrior too, as a contemporary Native academic, is caught up in the focus on reading, and thus his intellectual history does not resolve the problem he identifies. Diane Glancy's play "The Woman Who Was a Red Deer" expresses this dilemma. The Girl states that her Grandmother told her that the spirit deer (Ahw'uste, but maybe the Grandmother herself) had wings; "[y]ou couldn't see them, but they were there." Nevertheless, *"you had to decide* what they meant." In the next section, the Grandmother states that Ahw'uste "was only there for some people to see," and "[s]he had wings, too. *If you thought she did. She was there to remind us*—you think you see something you're not sure of. *But you think it's there anyway.*" Then with a sarcastic, epistemologically exasperated tone, the Girl responds, "Maybe Jesus used wings when he flew to heaven" (6, 7, emphasis added).

This last comment ironically engages an almost canonical way of resolving, one might say evading, this interpretive bind: asserting a contrast between Native and Western conceptions of the cosmos. The former is depicted as grounded in the relatedness of all beings and the wholeness of the spiritual–material cosmos, while the latter is predicated on an ontological material–spiritual dualism. We see this contrast asserted in, for example, Paula Gunn Allen's *The Sacred Hoop* (55, 57, 61), Marilou Awiatka's (Cherokee) *Abiding Appalachia* (57), Susan A. Miller's (Seminole) "Native America Writes Back" (11), and Craig Womack's (Oklahoma Creek-Cherokee) *Red on Red* (90). If the cosmos is unified, these writers imply, then there can be no disjuncture between what is falsely demarcated as the material and spiritual worlds. While this Native–Western binary may be conceptually reassuring and at times strategically useful, it is not experientially convincing, most Native literary writers imply.

While Vine Deloria Jr. regularly engaged this Western–Native binary, he also added a significant experiential confounder. Implicitly making a contrast with Western dualistic beliefs, he writes that within a Native understanding of material and spiritual worlds, "there could be no discontinuity *except in the manner in which we experience life*" (*The World* 86, emphasis added). Deloria here acknowledges that in our very humanness we readily misapprehend the spiritual world by seeing it incompletely. We cannot help it. We accept the material world as our home because of its immediacy, and thus we have difficulty experientially (as opposed to conceptually or rhetorically) engaging spiritual realities, even within the practice of Native ways of knowing. Religious studies scholar George E. Tinker similarly acknowledges an experiential divide by addressing the Otherness of the spiritual dimension of reality ("Spirituality" 122). This is quite different from addressing the Creator, a now commonly used appellation. Certainly, the perceptual disjuncture between material and spiritual worlds is intensified by modern Western spiritual alienation, now a global phenomenon, but Deloria does not add this qualifier. Even if one reads him as implying this, he still clearly sees that apprehending spiritual reality within our present condition is a challenging interpretive venture that requires more than an assertion of Native difference.[1]

Characters and communities' beliefs and practices, their lived ways of interpreting spiritual realities, are developed within historically situated social conditions. As Indigenous movements revitalize tribal traditions, including religious practices, they face the challenge of reckoning with the ways changed social conditions affect the nature of religious recovery. While practices may be revived, the conditions of belief that gave them life have historically shifted. Groups and individuals striving to engage a cosmos animated by the spirits face the problematic of reconciling premodern or traditional Indigenous structures of belief with modern ones. After setting forth a framework for understanding this shift, the analysis and examples that follow suggest various ways this problematic is addressed in a range of Native literary works.

Charles A. Taylor has developed the concept of "social imaginary" to address the horizons that shape people's ways of apprehending the world. He explains the term as "not a set of ideas; rather it is what enables, through making sense of, the practices of a society." This includes its sense of moral order. It is "the ways in which people imagine their social existence, how they fit together with others, how things go on between them and their fellows, the expectations that are normally met, and the deeper normative notions and images that underlie these expectations" ("Modern" 91–92, 106). Laura Bieger, Ramón Saldívar, and Johannes Voelz further explain, "The imaginary is not separate from reality, an addendum or a surplus. . . . The real itself depends on the existence of an imaginary. We cannot understand the reality of the real without mediating it through the imaginary." However, a particular apprehension of reality is not individually accepted as real. It is not imagined individually. Rather apprehensions of reality "draw[] on already existing forms and patterns—imaginaries—that have an important social function." By creating group coherence while adjusting to shifting social situations, imaginaries, "enable and condition subjectivity" (xi).

Imaginaries are social in two ways: commonly shared and about society (Taylor, *Secular* 323). They are the "common understanding that makes possible common practices and a widely shared sense of legitimacy." Imaginaries embody ordinary people's understanding of the everyday ways in which their world works, as expressed in "images, stories, and legends" ("Modern" 106). To this list I would add literature.[2] A group's social imaginary is its sense of appropriate social expectations and norms, including religious ones. As habitual ways of apprehending the cosmos, imaginaries facilitate and legitimatize common religious practices ("Modern" 106).[3] As a result, practices enabled by particular social imaginaries make the most sense within their historical situation (Warner, VanAntwerpen, and Calhoun 20–21). However, social imaginaries, like cultures in general, are discourses shifting at various rates in response to many different force fields. Remnants remain in diverse ways and degrees, depending on social conditions.

Taylor's acknowledged focus is Western Christendom. However, like Orsi's "lived religion," with necessary adaptations his concept of "social imaginary" offers a useful framework for considering literary expressions of modern Indigenous religious experience. In *The Secular Age*, Taylor analyzes the ways that apprehensions of spiritual realities have intersected with material densities, which then have shaped the profound shift in the conditions of belief within Western societies. This shift in conditions of belief has affected Indian Country as well. However, a process that took Europeans centuries to absorb was often rapidly forced onto Indigenous societies, evoking responses of both resistance and accommodation. It is important to recognize that tribal nations as well as individuals within them experienced this process differently. Nevertheless, Taylor's explanation of the two basic social imaginaries provides a heuristic for clarifying the challenges that communities and characters experience in translating religious traditions into modern practices.

"Why was it virtually impossible not to believe in God in, say, 1500 in our Western society," Taylor asks, "while in 2000 many of us find this not only easy, but even inescapable? . . . How did the alternatives become thinkable?" (*Secular* 25). Similarly, we might ask why Ella Deloria's (Yankton Sioux) *Waterlily* depicts no characters having doubts about the efficacy of the Dakota Sun Dance ceremony while in D'Arcy McNickle's (Salish Kootenai) *The Surrounded*, Archilde can only apprehend the Salish dance as "*almost* real enough to make it *seem* like a spirit come from the grave" (215, emphasis added). Because the two novels are set on different sides of the colonial divide, the conditions of belief described in them are drastically different. Kwame Anthony Appiah (Asante) has recognized a similar shift in the traditional Asante religion. The relationship between spiritual beings and their followers had been "as relations between persons" (114). Within the time of traditional cosmic apprehensions, there were individual doubters, he explains; the traditional imaginary did not have complete and uniform acceptance. However, the preponderance of believers "naturalized" the accepted forms of religious experience (129). That has changed.

The premodern, traditional, or aboriginal imaginary envisions a fixed cosmos enchanted with spirits and supernatural forces that exist independently of those who experience them (Taylor, *Secular* 346–47). Belief in gods or spiritual beings seemed undeniable even if people experienced them with varying intensities. Nature itself is understood to express spiritual presence and cosmic design. Structures of society could not be imagined without their being grounded in a reality beyond human agency. Premodern or aboriginal religions were generally collective in sensibility and practice. Individuals were engulfed in social and cosmic belonging, a necessary condition for sustaining the group's ritual, magical experiences (*Secular* 25–26). Kathleen DuVal notes in *Native Nations* that "Native North Americans lived pretty much like everyone else in the 1100s through 1500s," including their belief in the everyday intersecting of spiritual and material worlds. Globally, as in North America, people looked to the sky not just to track time but to find "portentous signs." Events did not happen randomly for societies living within the aboriginal social imaginary. They happened for a reason, even if the reason was not known (3–4, 7–8, 84). Sean Teuton, while acknowledging a wide range of belief systems in the precontact Indigenous world, usefully sums up the aboriginal cosmos: It was "alive with unseen spirits" who sustain and order "all life in the universe." Aboriginal Americans access their power "through Prayer, ritual and ceremony." Their "survival depended on properly meeting these spiritual obligations." Further, "spiritual leaders mastered oral narratives that reviewed and affirmed the people's sacred covenants with the spirit world." Thus "kinship and worship kept the world alive, mysterious, and satisfying" (*Native* 13–14).[4]

The shift from the premodern to modern imaginary, if experienced not only as loss, certainly entailed profound losses. It must have felt to many as a "theft of the sacred." Native peoples living within the premodern imaginary experienced an enchanted cosmos "in which spiritual forces impinged on porous agents, in which the social was grounded in the sacred and secular time in higher times," Taylor explains. He then states, "All this has been dismantled and replaced by something quite different" (Taylor, *Secular* 61). This is certainly an overly categorical assertion about a disenchanted cosmos, yet disenchantment is a significant structure of feeling within many, maybe most, contemporary Indigenous novels.

"Enchantment" and "disenchantment," terms from Max Weber (155), are further developed by Taylor in relation to social imaginaries. In the enchanted world of the ancestors, the self is porous, open to spiritual and moral forces rather than self-contained. Human and nonhuman forces are not distinct but are "bound together by relations of hierarchical complementarity." This hierarchy means that spiritual forces have "the power to impose a certain meaning on us" (*Dilemmas* 290–91). Taylor's generalized explanation fits with, say, the understanding expressed in Deloria's *The World We Used to Live In*, Larry Evers and Felipe S. Molina's *Yaqui Deer Songs*, and Daniel Merkur's *Powers Which We Do Not Know: The Gods and Spirits of the Inuit*. This premodern social imaginary gradually lost experiential resonance and so was slowly transformed into the now dominant, disenchanted post-Enlightenment social imaginary. Native peoples, however, experienced a considerably different trajectory. And as Leigh Schmidt importantly notes, there remain "unresolvable struggles of enchantment and disenchantment" (qtd. in Vásquez 119). This is particularly evident in Native literature that engages characters' efforts to situate themselves within changing forms of cosmic apprehension. James Welch's characters in *Fools Crow* and *Winter in the Blood*, for example, experience this shift in socioreligious imaginaries but within quite different temporal and social contexts.

Since contact with Europeans, Native people's social imaginaries, including the ways they apprehend the spiritual world, have inevitably and complexly changed, but in different ways and degrees because of different material conditions. Rosalyn R. LaPier (Blackfeet, Red River Métis) addresses this shift in cosmic apprehension in *Invisible Reality: Storytellers, Storytakers, and the Supernatural World of the Blackfeet*. Using family members as informants as well as archival sources, she explains the worldview of the "buffalo Indians," those at the turn of the twentieth century who had lived much of their adult lives before the reservation was established. Their traditional Blackfeet experiences included alliances with supernatural beings. They accessed supernatural power. The supernatural realm was "omnipresent," "permeated their daily lives," and "defined their existence" (43). LaPier concludes from their many recorded stories, as well as ones she personally heard from her grandmother and others, that "it was rare for a Blackfeet not to have an alliance with a supernatural entity" (28). The turn of the twentieth century forced Blackfeet Indians to make "a rapid social and economic shift" from hunting and gathering to reservation life (136). The consequences for religious experiences were significant as the older generation, "accustomed to a close and intimate relationship with a large area the size of Montana," had to adapt to a more "limited connection to much smaller ecosystems" (136). As people's relation to place narrowed, their apprehensions of the cosmos also changed. In a book published in 1910, when the reservation had come to dominate Blackfeet life, Piegan religious leader Brings Down the Sun explained a consequence of this shift: "At one time animals and men were able to understand each other. We still talk to the animals just as we do to people, but now they seldom reply, except in dreams" (qtd. in LaPier 138). This newly attenuated relationship was part of the shift from an aboriginal Blackfeet socioreligious imaginary to a modern one.

Richard Dauenhauer and Nora Marks Dauenhauer (Tlingit) reckon with changing social imaginaries among Tlingit people. They identify one of the key components, the shift in the transmission of structures of belief, which "will rely increasingly on explicit instruction, teaching, and explanation, rather than on implicit or intuitive transmission through models of conventional behavior." The result of this pedagogical shift instigated by the shift in imaginaries is that "confusion will no doubt continue." The changes have resulted in "a fundamental reorientation in the thinking and social organization of most Tlingit people" ("Evolving" 278, 253; this is further developed in chapter 6). The Dauenhauers conclude, "What seems to be evolving on the spiritual level is a blend of generic worldviews: generic pan-Christianity and generic Native American, with important features from both sources" ("Evolving" 272).

Because Indigenous tribes, communities, and individuals have experienced a religious transition specific to their own circumstances, their experiences within the modern socioreligious imaginary have varied. Michael Angel's *Preserving the Sacred* investigates how the Ojibwa Midewiwin ceremony has undergone several socioreligious transitions shaped by changing social, economic, political, and cultural conditions. This study is a clear example of how one group experienced the transition to the modern imaginary by holding on to religious practices but adapting them to changing material conditions.

As *Preserving the Sacred* documents how the ceremony and its structure of belief continued changing, it models a reckoning with the transitional stages in the shift from one socioreligious imaginary to another experienced by particular Indigenous groups. For example, Angel explains that because the Ojibwas were "geographically scattered and culturally diverse," the changes took various forms, with only a few instances of open rebellion (ix–x). Also, their transition was influenced by their traditional value structure, which was more individualistic than that of neighboring tribes. They had a tradition of openness to "new beliefs and practices" that came to them through visions and dreams (27). However, their "ethic of generosity, reciprocal sharing, and consensual decision making" and their "affinity with their natural surroundings" put traditionalists in conflict with Methodist converts (122). Some came to believe in the Christian God but as part of their Ojibwa understanding of the cosmos (126). Yet even when Christian Ojibwas held on to their Midewiwin beliefs, their worldview changed "radically" (121). Analyzing the various ways that Christianity shaped Ojibwa religious beliefs—for example, the concept of heaven and hell as future rewards—Angel observes that changes came for all "as the Ojibwa developed, in relation to both their Aboriginal and Euro-American neighbors" (24, x). Yet despite missionary efforts, many held to their "traditional worldview" (125), even if the nature of their believing inevitably was in process. Recent scholars generally accept that the rise of Midewiwin beliefs and practices "reflected a change from a dependence on dreams and visions, to a reliance on inherited knowledge, as a means of accruing power in Ojibwa society" (10). Angel here recognizes a significant epistemological shift that links changing religion and social power.

This historical analysis of a transitional period importantly recognizes the Midewiwin as "a religious institution" or structure within society (viii). It analyzes the ways material conditions affected Midewiwin ceremonies and religious culture. For example, there was a shift in instruction from pictographs on birchbark scrolls to those drawn in sand and dirt as memory aids. Also, initiations became less rigorous: Visions were not required and some never had their guardian spirit appear (151–52). Further, acceptance lessened as some followers came to feel "abandoned by the spirits." Some turned to Christianity "in an attempt to ensure security and survival" (121).

Nevertheless, Midewiwin beliefs and practices continued, if changed; this is the message of *Preserving the Sacred*. It recognizes that there has been considerable variation in teachings and practice as well as "variability of meaning in Ojibwa symbols, songs, and narratives." Further, "meanings were not precise, even for the initiated" (173, 147–48). This religious flexibility helps sustain community cohesion and continuity (Cohen 14–16). In the 1970s and 1980s, Angel reports, a new generation turned to elders to learn about old ways and to rediscover their "unique world view." This led to a revival of ceremonies, often among urban and middle-class professionals who experience no contradiction between Midewiwin beliefs and their contemporary lives (174). If "the Midewiwin has lost its central role in Ojibwa communities," it remains meaningful to groups and individuals (184). In this way traditional religions continue, adapted to new conditions of belief.[5] The shift in the way belief is experienced is an important part of Indigenous transitions to the modern socioreligious imaginary.

Indigenous novelists have been attentive to the transitions from one social imaginary to another that communities and characters experience. In doing so they face the interpretive problematic discussed above. A recent novel like Yup'ik writer Mia C. Heavener's *Under the Nushagak Bluff* captures a relatively isolated community's changing social and religious experiences as a fishing village is increasingly invaded by canneries, airplanes, alcohol, imported food, and missionaries. For example, Agnes Girl no longer sews fur clothing for the whole village as her mother, Marulia, did, and subsistence living is increasingly difficult. Religiously, only one elder is left who may be a shaman and is able to interpret material conditions and spiritual omens. Yet no one believes he has the supernatural powers of the old shamans. More-than-material realities linger in characters' talk of little people and as a threatened structure of feeling. Agnes Girl faces the challenge of teaching her daughter Ellen demanding traditional work skills but also ways of being. She recognizes that Ellen will also need the skills that the missionaries teach while strongly wanting to keep her daughter away from the social and religious indoctrination of Sunday School. The encroachments of cannery life also threaten.

In the face of new capitalist-colonial conditions so amendable to the modern social imaginary, Agnes Girl struggles to sustain subsistence work and the sense of being it requires. She dies a symptomatically alcoholic death. Ellen, living the cannery life of store work and "dirty" casual sex, nevertheless still experiences meaningful material and spiritual continuities. Seemingly counter-intuitively, direct and regular supernatural experiences occur only in Ellen's section of the novel. Although described in realist terms, they are experienced in a different register. The depicted spiritual recovery too facilely breaks down the cosmic "dialectic of proximity and distance," and thus the narrative here seems marked by "performativity and autoreflection" or self-consciousness (Smola 4, 3). With these unprecedented supernatural interventions in material life, the author creates a comfortably conjured traditionalism drained of mystery or horror or sacrifice. It can seem like a Native novelistic cliché. This is quite different from the neotraditionalism in Robert Davis Hoffmann's *Raven's Echo*, which engages this transition in imaginaries in a similar setting, Tlingit villages across the Gulf of Alaska (see chapter 6).

Momaday's phrase "the theft of the sacred" evokes the colonial cause of this loss of givenness and the resulting religious confusion. Taylor calls it the "fragilization of religious positions." He cautions, however, against understanding this change simply as a declension; only seeing losses means ignoring the complexities of this socioreligious transformation (*Secular* 595). The two imaginaries Taylor identifies provide a heuristic for grasping the ways modern Indigenous literature makes sense of new spiritual and material realities. It is important to recognize, however, that imaginaries overlap, change at different rates, and shift in meanings. The specificities of particular tribal and individual situations must be reckoned with. Neither imaginary is monolithic, although important generalizations can be made.

The modern imaginary is anthropocentric and individualistic as it envisions a flattened, material universe offering no certain meanings because life's fullness comes from within ourselves rather than from experiencing transcendent realities (*Secular* 15). The modern social imaginary is fundamentally secular, as Taylor carefully defines this term.[6] Yet he rejects the idea that the change in social imaginary was a shift from belief to unbelief. Rather it was a change in "the conditions of belief" that affects both unbelief and belief (*Secular* 8). Belief in spiritual or more-than-material realities is available within the modern social imaginary, but it is no longer a given or even the most readily available option. Belief and unbelief are optional "lived conditions" in the marketplace of beliefs (*Secular* 8). Choices are necessarily made with the recognition that many other equally sincere people are making different choices (*Secular* 3). As part of this secularization, religion became personalized and expressive rather than communally or tribally sanctioned and experienced. This is "believing without belonging" (Grace Davis, qtd. in *Secular* 514), as religion came to focus on individual fulfillment through a bricolage of beliefs.

Believing and belonging are varied and changing practices. Often differences are experienced generationally, as younger characters struggle to engage Indigenous traditions while living within the modern social imaginary. For example, in Momaday's *House Made of Dawn*, both Francisco and his grandson Abel participate in the tribal ritual of running as an experience of communal believing and belonging. However, the structure of belief that shapes their experiences is significantly different. Francisco remembers participating in the "race for good hunting and harvests" and recalls its consequences: That year he killed fourteen deer (7). For Francisco, spiritual realities materially affect his experience of belonging to place. The novel's prologue depicts Abel also ritually running, yet "he seemed to be standing still, very little and alone" (1–2), a quite different experience of belonging. In the final section, the novel's circular structure returns the reader to this scene, now depicted as a communal event. Nevertheless, it becomes clear that this running involves a shift in dispensation. Francisco dies, and Abel, after instructing the priest to bury his grandfather, rubs himself with ash and runs to join the other participants. "He was running and there was no reason to run but the running itself and the land and the dawn appearing" (185). If he is running for "hunting and harvests," it is symbolic, individualized, and interior. It is also fragilized. This shift in imaginary has, not surprisingly, resulted in less religious continuity between generations (Taylor, *Dilemmas* 256).

The disjuncture between past and present apprehensions of the cosmos is further developed in Welch's *Winter in the Blood*. Both Yellow Calf and his grandson are cut off from tribal living and support. The grandfather can sustain his aboriginal religious experiences individually because of his rural isolation and remembered past. His urban grandson cannot quite believe in the relatively porous cosmos his grandfather experiences. Yellow Calf understands "most" of the conversations of the deer, and they "mostly" understand him, but his grandson is skeptical (67–68). To his grandson's inability to believe or belong, Yellow Calf responds, like the Inuit shaman Anu discussed in the introduction, "It wasn't a question of belief, it was the way things were" (155). Because the givenness of the grandfather's enchanted world is unavailable to his grandson, the healing he finds has immanent spiritual meaning that provides him with an inner readjustment. The instigating event is individually imagined and personally expressive. However, the psychological healing inspired by his grandfather is cosmically disenchanted.

Louise Erdrich's *LaRose* also depicts the challenge of adapting traditional practices of the aboriginal social imaginary within a reservation community that no longer holds tribal ceremonies and has no elders to instruct the younger generations. (Characters instead turn to a Catholic priest or a freelance Indigenous ceremonial practitioner.) No character in the novel lives within an enchanted world, even in memory. Yet traces remain as adapted tribal practices provide forms of continuance for some. Landreaux Iron, after accidentally shooting his neighbors' young son (his nephew) and as an alternative to getting drunk, gathers his wife and his son, Emmaline and LaRose, into the family sweat lodge. Their songs "invit[e] in the manidoog, aadizookaanag, the spirits" as the parents struggle over the decision to follow a traditional practice and give their son to their neighbors as a replacement for the one killed (11). Mainly Landreaux's decision, it is an agonistic one that seems unprecedented in modern times and so is made without the support of present social mores. He does turn for help to his friend Randall, the local "medicine man," who understands the troubled context for Landreaux's decision: "Loss, dislocation, disease, addiction, and just feeling like the tattered remnants of a people with a complex history . . . so much fucked-upness wherever you turn." Randall reassures him by explaining the history of elders battling demons, yet it is a fragilized reassurance as he puts the burden of belief solely on Landreaux: "Accept their words if they feel right" and later "You gotta take on faith you did right with LaRose" (22, 51–53). Within this individualized leap of faith, Landreaux experiences, as best he can, a form of believing that offers rightness, strength, and solace. (See chapter 3 for a discussion of "a leap of faith.") Although tradition guides Landreaux's religious life, his experience is devoid of ritual and magic, and his healing is personal and interior. No longer living in a traditionally porous cosmos, the self is now boundaried from the supernatural and so has become its own source of moral order (*Secular* 27). Yet Landreaux struggles against this disenchantment with the tribal and personal resources available to him.

In this and other Erdrich novels, supernatural occurrences do take place in the present. However, the events described seem more like the literary devices of fantasy writing than the lived experiences of people within the reservation and tribal nation to which she belongs. An example is Maggie's acceptance of an owl into her body and the razer cuts she has to show for it (221). This seems incongruous with the general tenor of this and Erdrich's other reservation novels. Supernatural events also can be psychological experiences literalized, as when LaRose talks with his dead friend Dusty (211).

With much more confidence than the authors of the above-mentioned novels give their protagonists, Sasha taqʷšəblu LaPointe's (Coast Salish) contemporary memoir *Red Paint* depicts her experience of contemporary material and spiritual belonging. Although the subtitle of her book, *The Ancestral Autobiography of a Coast Salish Punk*, suggests both disjunctures and continuities, she records her satisfying experiences of individualized, personally expressive yet tribally inflected healing within a distinctly contemporary urban setting. Experientially, LaPointe's family is her tribe. The book's prologue registers a shift in imaginary and nature of belief as the Salish ancestral religion has become "something protected, something private" (8). Red paint is a trope of continuity for LaPointe's account: "I come from a long line of dancers who wore red paint" (209). However, the individualized, internalized quality of her tribally originated experience is acknowledged when she describes her punk performance wearing the red paint as "my own ceremony, my way to honor the ancestors. I would never dance in the longhouse, but I would find my own ritual of healing." Individualized and yet connected, she uses the paint to acknowledge and share in "the wounds we carried in our bodies, through generations" (215). LaPointe's experience, like those of the above protagonists, fits with Taylor's understanding of the modern socioreligious imaginary: "To take my religion seriously is to take it personally, more devotionally, inwardly, more committedly" (*Dilemmas* 216).

Key to the interpretive framework of *After the Theft* is the nature of spiritual presences. This framework may also be useful for Indigenous revitalization projects. Within the premodern or aboriginal social imaginary, supernatural interventions into the material world are accepted as givens. However, the modern conceptualization of transcendence elides this everyday givenness as it sets those interventions apart from "the compromises and equivocations" of social and political experience (Orsi, *History* 68). Within the modern context, the term "supernatural" refers to a separate realm of experience. Further, the modern socioreligious imaginary, focused on internal experience, tends to register experiences of spiritual presence as immanent rather than transcendent—that is, "without making any appeal to some supernatural or supra-historical force or entity such as God, the Holy, or the sacred," explains Manuel A. Vásquez (323).[7] Taylor helps clarify this modern religiophilosophical situation by differentiating immanence that is closed or secular from immanence that is open to more-than-material experiences. (See his chapter "The Immanent Frame" in *A Secular Age*.) Like Taylor's "open immanence," Vásquez's phrase "transcendence within immanence" identifies a way of negotiating "the duality of other-worldly transcendence and this-worldly immanence" (324). I understand his use of the term "duality" as experiential rather than ontological. He further explains, "I see transcendence as diverse, contextual and intra-historical material expressions of the immanent frame's openness, fecundity, and complexity" (348, n. 1). It is this multivalent form of transcendence, more than material (or psychological) while not traditionally supernatural, that *After the Theft* reckons with.

Linda Hogan's novel *Power* engages the problematic of interpreting sacred presences within shifting imaginaries. In the beginning, narrator and protagonist Omishto states that she does not believe in the "magic" of the Panther Clan, although she does find the belief attractive. She lives in a different world, she asserts, from her traditionalist friend and mentor Ama Eaton. Omishto has been disciplined, but not completely, by family, school, and the Catholic Church. Her experiences gradually pull her away from these force fields and toward Ama's place outside of town and isolated in nature. There she comes to accept what Ama perceives, that "the other world is visible. It lives beside us in trees and stone." Only within this traditional socioreligious imagining does Omishto come to realize that Ama's shooting the panther can be understood not as an environmental threat but as a sacrifice to reestablish a balance that would reunite humans and gods "fitted together in the same realm" (189–90). Yet the novel imagines the sacred presence of the cat only within nature, where the modern social imaginary encroaches but is not hegemonic. Urban sacred presence seems an oxymoron here and in many works of Indigenous literature (see Conclusion).

Paying attention to both disjunctures and continuities of Indigenous religious experiences, the literary analyses in *After the Theft of the Sacred* recognizes the diversity of Indigenous religious apprehensions. This recognition challenges the secular story of modernism and its imaginary, but it also questions the binary of Native versus Christian–Enlightenment conceptualizations and practices. Unlikely intersections of beliefs occur as unexpected influences are braided together (Orsi, *Between* 9). Taylor finds an unprecedented pluralism of outlooks, which creates a "mutual fragilization" that includes the easy movement among religious options (*Secular* 437). We see both strengthening and fragilizing adaptations taking place in the communities that Native literature depicts.

The modern world has been thoroughly "disciplined" to disregard sacred presences (*Between* 10, 12). Reckoning with them within the modern social imaginary can be a challenge for academic literary critics as well as literary writers. In her thoughtful commentary on the critical anthology *Reasoning Together*, Kristina Fagan (Labrador Métis) addresses the conundrum of engaging spiritual realities in Native academic essays.[8] She explains that Enlightenment reason, the dominant academic mode of inquire, is "secular and skeptical." And it is materialist: "Spiritual claims sit uncomfortably in the reason-based essay form" (97). Traditional stories "are of course deeply spiritual." However, instead of reading them for their "literal, spiritual truth," the authors in the anthology abstract them as "a source of ideas" (97). This reduces religious experience to theology and so fails to reckon with practices that engage more-than-material realities. That is, it leaves no room for the spirits except as tropes.

This is exactly the dilemma Robert A. Orsi addresses: "The study of religion is or ought to be the study of *what human beings do* to, for, and against the gods really present—using 'gods' as a synecdoche for all the special suprahuman beings with whom humans have been in relationship in different times and places—and *what the gods really present do* with, to, for, and against humans" (*History* 4, emphasis added). For Orsi as for Fagan, religion is about gods and humans interacting in the world, and not just a set of ideas or figures of speech, as is often assumed within the modern social imaginary. This absence creates "a double intellectual tragedy here." The exclusion of sacred presences means that academic apprehensions of reality are only partial. Also, because these presences are excluded, they are unable "to enlarge our understanding." What is needed is "an empiricism of the visible and invisible real" (64–65, 42, 58).

Fagan's response to this dilemma emerges from her understanding of the ways spiritual realities intersect with experiential apprehensions. Commenting on Womack's concluding essay, she agrees that "empathetic imagination" is needed to "think about spiritual realities, and connect to our ancestors and to the others with whom we share this world" (99). Imagination, here a form of faith that establishes a basis for believing, is too often unrecognized. Rational apprehensions have hegemonic status. "Empathetic imagination" (with its focus on experience and emotion) has been disciplined. Earlier in her essay, Fagan quotes Jeanette Armstrong (Okanagan): Indians "have ceded not only vast territories of land, but also the territories of the imagination and of voice" (221). Spiritual apprehension that includes both reason and imagination can help take back the ceded territories, Fagan asserts.

While Orsi's research focuses on a particular form of Catholicism, he suggests that his concerns are relevant to other cultures (*Between* 2). His concluding chapter of *Between Heaven and Earth* can be read as a disciplinary manifesto that elaborates Fagan's concern about the common Native studies approach to religion. Fagan calls on Native critical work to engage "experience, emotion, [and] imagination" so that it can apprehend more of the cosmos than reason alone can. Like Fagan, Orsi cautions that analytical tools have "hidden normativities." The academic norm most concerning to Orsi is the modernist story or secularization thesis, which "only barely masks its prescriptive edge" (*Between* 6, 9). Even while insisting that the holy should not be reduced to a sociological or psychological phenomenon, however, he recognizes that it is a part of "culture and history. . . . The 'holy' is a construction; it is a made thing" (98). That is, the holy or "the Otherness that is the Sacred Mystery," to again use Tinker's term, is more than material but is always experienced within particular material conditions. Dialectical thinking is needed to hold onto both aspects of sacred presences.

Orsi does this by calling attention to people's lived religion, including their experiences of spiritual presences. As an empathetic observer of religious experience, Orsi writes descriptively rather than prescriptively as he explicates the conditions of belief that shape individual and community religious experiences. Thus his analysis resists the almost inevitable claim within religious studies that certain practices are legitimate, authentic, or traditional while others are not (7, 9). Similarly, my purpose here is not to evaluate religious practices but rather to question slippages within literary and analytical practices.

Many Native novels include supernatural occurrences depicted in a realist mode, despite the fact that, as Orsi observes, "in an intellectual culture premised on absence, the experience of presence is the phenomenon that is most disorienting, most inexplicable" (*History* 64). Since most modern literature is similarly premised on spiritual absence, it would seem that readers give Native literary works a special dispensation as they have come to expect depictions of supernatural incursions into the material world. These incursions often involve various forms of bracketing so that spiritual presences are often neither "disorienting" nor "inexplicable."

One way that contemporary Indigenous literature and literary scholarship have addressed the interpretive dilemma of sacred presences is by bracketing "questions about the ontological realness of religious phenomena" (Orsi, "Problem" 84). Fiction itself as a genre can be a form of bracketing when religious experiences like Tayo's in *Ceremony* are not reckoned with as ethnographically grounded but rather as authorially imagined accounts satisfying to audiences but incongruous with, for example, the memoirs authors have published (see chapter 2). Readers themselves may participate in this form of bracketing as they confer canonical status on Native novels that include experiences out of place in other literatures or in their own experience. This can indicate a difference in Indigenous experiences, but it can also be othering as a form of bracketing.

In some works, the supernatural is experienced only by special minor characters, particularly elders, who report encounters with sacred presences in the past. Younger characters, more central and modern, offer them respect but do not share their experiential belief. *Winter in the Blood*, discussed above, is an example. Part of what makes, say, Carole laFavor's detective novels Natively modern is that protagonist Renee LaRoche recognizes the traditional spiritual realities experienced by her grandmother while at the same time liberalizing them for herself. For example, the narrator of *Evil Dead Center* vaguely states, "Ren figured she needed all the spiritual help she could get," yet she does not receive the supernatural assistance that Gram describes (74).

Indigenous experiences of spiritual presences can be further bracketed as exoticized plot devices, giving them a status similar to ghosts in gothic novels (see Anderson's "Native Horror, Fantasy, and Speculative Fiction"). For example, David Heska Wanbli Weiden's crime thriller *Winter Count* cracks its case through a sweat lodge ceremony vision.

Another narrative strategy for taming spiritual presences is to bracket ontological issues by slipping without explanation or notice from the supernaturalism of the past to a psychological or symbolic register more acceptable in the present. Lipsha, Erdrich's character in *Love Medicine*, humorously disenchants the supernatural love medicine of the past as the modern reservation community embraces his bumbling psychologized healing. When writing about earlier generations experiencing "the twilight time," the transition from one social imaginary and lived religion to another, Erdrich more ambiguously creates situations that could be either supernatural or psychological. An example in *The Painted Drum* is Anaquot hearing her dead daughter's voice and also Ziigwan'aage knowing someone else had been with Anaquot when she came to her house (136, 147). Erdrich's deft writing keeps these accounts just this side of fantasy as she uses the language of supernatural traditionalism while draining it of the kind of power that Deloria describes in *The World We Used to Live In*. Appiah addresses a related form of bracketing, that of demythologizing religious beliefs by changing literal meanings to symbolic ones. (114–16). He makes the issue personal: "The question how much of the world of the spirits we intellectuals must give up (or transform into something ceremonial without the old literal ontology) is one we must face: and I do not think the answer is obvious" (135).

The implications, however, are not just personal. Orsi makes a related observation concerning the critical or academic reduction of sacred presences: "By confining the gods to the inner life of individuals, to the edges of the modern, to the corners of the human mind, and to the past of the species, theorists of religion [in various disciplines] contributed to the constitution and legitimation of the modern state and . . . citizen" (*History* 40–41). This is a challenging question for Native nations. The problematic of spiritual presence and absence seems an unavoidable consideration for revitalization movements, scholarly analysis, and literary production.

Engaging the experiential realness of sacred presences is thus a significant challenge for both literary writers and critics. The analyses of this and the next section explore various ways Native literary writers have imagined experiences of spiritual presences and the degrees to which these encounters have been imbued with supernatural, symbolic, or psychological meanings. Within changing material circumstances, each work wrestles with the tension between enchantment and disenchantment in the modern world.

Welch's *Fools Crow* depicts the historical transition from the premodern to modern social imaginary that results from the Blackfeet people's increasing confrontations with the US Army, traders, and settlers. We see how Welch depicts givenness giving way to a leap of faith. As the protagonist becomes an adult, traditional society is fracturing and becoming increasingly fragile as the tribe begins losing faith in their elders (354), their ceremonies (367), themselves as a tribe (371), and the spirits as aids in desperate and disorienting times (359, 368). Yet the novel concludes with a vision of an enchanted cosmos in which, "All around, it was as it should be" (390). Karl Marx's famous statement "All that is solid melts into air" provides a troubling but relevant analytical perspective on this transition (Robert C. Tucker 476). Many characters in *Fools Crow* experience the dreadful sensation of their solid pre-contact world melting away. Yet Welch imagines that a traditional apprehension of the cosmos is still available to Fools Crow, even in the face of the devastations caused by modern military, cultural, and political imperialism. However, it must now be chosen as a leap of faith, and readers' knowledge of the Blackfeet future (its early twentieth-century history) clashes with the novel's hopeful conclusion.

Even as Fools Crow experiences visions and other supernatural reassurances, he struggles to come to terms with his friend Fast Horse, who loses faith when his cosmic apprehensions become secularized as he experiences the underside of US modernism. This multifaceted and nearly incomprehensible growing hegemony creates for him an alienated structure of feeling. He rejects his tribe's socioreligious imaginary, its way of making sense of the cosmos, because it no longer makes sense of his experience. Within the same historical and cultural context, however, Fools Crow remains part of the community and faithful to traditional cosmic apprehensions. Yet Fast Horse as a spiritual nemesis challenges the givenness of Fools Crow's beliefs. Characters like Fools Crow must reinvigorate their belief in an enchanted world under new conditions that seem inimical to that belief. The novel's concluding vision seems an act of will or a leap of faith on the author's part as his character challenges readers' historical knowledge.

Orange's twenty-first-century *There There* presents a considerable shift in material conditions and spiritual apprehensions from *Fools Crow*. Only one incident in the novel seems supernatural: Young Orvil finds spider legs mysteriously embedded in his own leg. It baffles him and his family, even after checking with more traditional relatives and doing a Google search. Finding no explanation, Orvil's brother sums up their apprehension: "That's fucked up" (125). The novel itself presents no better explanation of this apparent supernatural intervention, and the issue loses relevance as the violence at the powwow dominates the conclusion. Experiences like Orvil's, and a similar one reported by his great-aunt, might have been traditionally understandable, but in a world saturated with the modern socioreligious imaginary, they have become unreadable signs of the spirits. Writing about the aboriginal world,

Taylor asserts, "Our peasant ancestors would have thought us insane" for going to movies to experience terror. It was real to them because the gods are not necessarily or always looking out for our good, and they need to be propitiated (*Dilemmas* 220–22). In accounts given to Knud Rasmussen, Inuit shamans describe their travels in a porous cosmos that includes active supernatural beings. They depict conflict and danger at least as prevalently as peace and harmony. (See *Intellectual Culture*, particularly chapter 5.) Greg Sarris in *Grand Avenue* also acknowledges the mixed nature of supernatural powers as he contrasts his most bourgeois character Steven Penn's bland moralizing reduction of traditional stories with his father's stories of supernatural terror used in a class-climbing family rivalry (186–89, see also Dyck, afterword to *Grand Avenue* 215–19). Novels may provide a fantasy of enchantment only through a safely filtered—that is, generic—reading experience of terror. However, they may also reveal the sense that something is lacking in post-transcendent contemporary experience and that a turn to tradition may adaptively work to heal characters' spiritual emptiness.

As noted above, literary depictions of Indigenous religions have a particular position within the modern social imaginary. Magical or more-than-material experiences are accepted, even expected, by many readers of Native literature and "connoisseurs" of Indigenous culture. For many, these experiences are part of the genre's attractive Otherness. Supernatural literary experiences can also be read as tropes of authenticity, creating another way of reading the signs of the spirits: symbols with no spirits to signify. This is reading within a truly disenchanted world. Similarly, magic realism also engages an enchantment that is disenchanted. Certain Native novels that include contemporary supernatural experiences engage magic realism rather than magic itself. Leanne Howe's (Oklahoma Choctaw) *Shell Shaker* is an example, but works by Thomas King (Cherokee) and others also fit.

Shell Shaker imaginatively integrates traditional and contemporary religious experiences in a way that creates a challenging interpretive situation. The novel's parallel constructions of Choctaw life in the 1730s–1740s and the 1990s come together as the novel's murder mystery is supernaturally "solved." In an *American Literature* essay, Monika Barbara Siebert takes up the novel's interpretive challenge as she analyzes its last two chapters, both undated and outside of everyday experience, as the novel's two historical realities supernaturally intersect. Shakbatina, a character from the 1700s, aids her modern descendent Auda Billy in assassinating the corrupt tribal leader Redford McAlester, who is the embodiment of 1700s Choctaw leader and betrayer Red Shoes. Shakbatina states that although she died a couple of centuries earlier, she is the one who actually pulled the modern trigger. Siebert explains that Shakbatina's story challenges both Auda's own confession and the explanation the tribal court accepts. Both are rational materialist accounts. Shakbatina is given the final word, yet her story is "viable only if readers share Choctaw cosmology," Siebert argues (104). This narrative strategy is Howe's effort, Siebert claims, to "fundamentally retrain[] those contemporary readers who are willing to examine and potentially suspend their customary reading practice" (99). This not uncommon interpretive move of unifying aboriginal and modern spiritual apprehensions is, however, hermeneutically troubling.

Although Siebert implies that "shar[ing] Choctaw cosmology" is more than a readerly convention, she does not explore the relationship between text and world that she posits. Failing to reckon with the shift from a traditional to a modern socioreligious imaginary that has thoroughly affected the novel's modern characters (and the earlier ones to a lesser degree), she reifies Choctaw conceptions of the cosmos. Shakbatina, key participant in supernatural experiences, begins the novel by echoing Ishmael's famous opening for Melville's *Moby Dick*—"*Ano ma Chahta sia hoke oke.* Call me Shakbatina"—and then repeats this Choctaw and English phrase at the beginning of chapter 9, a pivotal chapter. Ishmael is a modern character for whom material reality is not just a pasteboard mask covering a fundamentally spiritual cosmos; it is all there is. Although he prays with South Sea Islander Queequeg, he cannot "share" the traditional cosmology of his friend's aboriginal socioreligious imaginary. It is a gesture of religious pluralism that does not reach beyond the material world. *Shell Shaker* is no different.

The allusion to Ishmael also alerts readers to Howe's self-conscious, playful narrative style in *Shell Shaker.*[9] Within it Choctaw religious practices share spiritual space with astrology, tai chi, psychic readings, herbal teas, and a lost Atlantis. The supernatural return of Shakbatina takes place within this self-consciously cliched context. *Shell Shaker* is an inventive postmodern pastiche, a gesture cosmology for a disenchanted world, a religion of Jacques Derrida's "perhaps" (see chapter 2). It would be absurd to look for similar events in Choctaw newspapers or personal memoirs, the novel implies. The novel's religious practices and supernatural experiences are ironic commentaries on the present, not reports of a more-than-material cosmos.

Comments like "shar[ing] Choctaw cosmology" mystify rather than clarify. Supernatural events in the novel's present are depicted as absurd or magic realist, a perspective unimaginable within a traditional Choctaw cosmological imaginary. As characters prepare a feast, for example, the dough being mixed in Oklahoma is transubstantiated into Mississippi mud. Howe offers an interpretive clue to events like this on her website Why I Write. Commenting on her 2013 collection of stories and memoir, the site states that they "depict, with wry humor, the contradictions and absurdities that transpire in a life lived crossing cultures and borders. The result is three parts memoir, one part absurdist fiction, and one part marvelous realism." This last phrase reminds us that the bread-into-mud event reads like the miraculously multiplying frybread scene in Alexie's *Reservation Blues* or the priest's ability to levitate when drinking hot chocolate in Gabriel García Márquez's *One Hundred Years of Solitude.*

Howe's choice of the term "marvelous" rather than the more common "magic," however, is ontologically slippery in ways that seem to reassuringly bridge the disjuncture between past and present without reckoning with the interpretive problematic involved. The term "marvelous realism" was developed, although not originated, by Afro-Cuban writer Alejandro Carpentier. His seminal essay "On the Marvelous Real in America" originally introduced *The Kingdom of This World*, his novel of the Haitian Revolution. Carpentier explains that "the marvelous begins to be unmistakably marvelous when it arises from an unexpected alteration of reality (the miracle) . . . an unaccustomed insight that is singularly favored by the unexpected richness of reality. . . . To begin with, the phenomenon of the marvelous *presupposes faith* (86, emphasis added). In stories of Haitian slave revolts, Carpentier finds this faith in the "unexpected richness of reality" that crosses the material–spiritual divide. Historically and in his novel, material conflicts are transformed into spiritual warfare as, for example, the leader Macandal is miraculously transformed into a fly and escapes as his body is being burnt at the stake. An event meant to teach slaves the high cost of rebellion is instead transformed into a liberating Voudou religious experience that inspires further rebellion (45–47). This is clearly not Carpentier's world but one he wants readers to "share." The presupposed faith on the reader's part is not in the Voudou that characters stake their lives on. Rather this shared faith is an acknowledgment that the Haitians of the revolution experienced the cosmos fundamentally differently from Carpentier and his modern readers. The novel's marvelous realism allows readers to imaginatively apprehend or share, to a degree, others' imaginary while living outside of it.

This is not what *Shell Shaker* expects from its readers. The distinction between marvelous and magic realism offers a useful tool for more carefully interpreting Native texts that engage supernatural figures and events. There is considerable difference between the "marvelous" of Carpentier and the "magic" of Márquez. Magic in *Shell Shaker* is a form of narrative defamiliarization to wake readers up from a reassuring realism. The novel calls on readers to share a historically informed, contemporary, disenchanted Choctaw cosmology that still has continuities with the traditionally enchanted one, at least in memory. The final undated chapter can be read as a cosmic triumph only if the "past and present collid[ing] into a single moment" is read as marvelous rather than magic (222). I do not think the novel, with all its irony, sustains this interpretation.

Reading the literary signs of spirits after the theft of the sacred requires careful attention to the ways that shifting languages, genres, and social imaginaries shape depictions of supernatural experiences. Both writers and readers can disenchant that world through various forms of bracketing. However, reading against the grain can also call us to reckon with the kind of revitalization work various literary texts can participate in. Un-disciplining and redisciplining are needed to interpret the cosmos of those characters and communities who do live in a porously bounded material and more-than-material world. With that, reading the literary signs of the spirits can engage us more perceptively in recognizing the range of Indigenous religious experiences (as well as secular ones) and in reckoning with the differences and continuities between traditional and the various contemporary religious expressions. Appiah insists that even though contemporary expressions may be symbolic in their adaptation, they can still embody a traditional belief in actual spirits—that is, in "the ontology of invisible beings" (112–13).

2 TWO CEREMONIES, TWO LIVED RELIGIONS

LESLIE MARMON SILKO'S *CEREMONY* AND RAY A. YOUNG BEAR'S *BLACK EAGLE CHILD: THE FACEPAINT NARRATIVES*

Ceremonies are ritual readings of sacred presences. As noted in the introduction, ceremonies are necessary mediations between the material world, with all its contingencies, and unchanging spiritual realities. Shaping ceremonial meanings is the common desire for continuity between past and present practices, for resting the weight of experience on a foundation of tradition. This desire makes it difficult to reckon with altered, even invented traditions as it puts their ontological status in question. This difficulty can be addressed, though not necessarily resolved, through literary reports of sacred presences, particularly the narrative strategies authors use to engage them. This chapter works through the relationship of ceremonies to the more-than-material world by means of two literary case studies. The quite different religious apprehensions depicted in Leslie Marmon Silko's *Ceremony* and Ray A. Young Bear's (Meskwaki[1]) *Black Eagle Child: The Facepaint Narratives* delineate the forms of individual and tribal healing the novels engage.

Ceremony extends the Laguna Pueblo ceremony Betonie performs for Tayo to include his summer-long encounter with the supernatural figure Ts'eh. The first part of this extended ceremony is descriptively immersed in material reality, yet its rituals imply a spiritual reality beyond it. The encounter with Ts'eh is similarly described in the realist, materialist register even as events extend beyond its usual grasp. Here Silko depicts material and spiritual realities seamlessly converging in the modern world. The ceremony that opens *Black Eagle Child* is one of the most detailed ceremonial descriptions in contemporary Native literature. What follows it is a scattering of transcendental interventions occurring in the midst of everyday experience. The novel begins with young Edgar Bearchild agreeing to participate in a peyote ceremony because he feels socially abandoned when not invited to a drinking party. While this sets a satiric tone, most of the description is quite earnest. The shifting tone is part of the novel's negotiation of tradition and modernity. At the ceremony Edgar is confused from the beginning. He sees that the altarpieces rest on a mat that reads, "THE LORD LOVES AND WATCHES OVER THIS HOUSE" (13). Because of his inexperience, Edgar fails to recognize that he is participating in a syncretistic Native American Church ceremony. This is not an auspicious beginning for a religious journey; its humanness is all too evident. Edgar's experience suggests the often ambiguous nature of spiritual encounters. This experiential ambiguity pervades *Black Eagle Child* just as religious clarity and certainty are the structure of feeling for *Ceremony*.

Robert A. Orsi rhetorically asks, "But what religious experience is innocent?" ("Problem" 90). The term "innocent" contrasts with "experience," the latter term as interpretively complex as the former seems straightforward. Experience distinguishes the ceremonial depictions and supernatural engagements of *Black Eagle Child*. In contrast, *Ceremony* constructs Tayo's ceremonial encounters, this chapter argues, as occurring innocently outside of disturbing material contingencies even as the need for the ceremony results immediately if not ultimately from the traumas of material life. This innocence is part of the novel's powerful appeal, a reason for its wide readership. *Black Eagle Child* is much less reassuring. The religious experiences within *Ceremony* are transcendent or supernatural. They take Tayo out of everyday social reality.[2] Edgar's experience is categorically different. Rather than a supernatural encounter, he experiences spiritual immanence. Although later in the novel he does have what seem to be transcendent experiences—for example, when he sees the supernatural strobe light—they are uninterpretable (184).

Novels are arguments, among other things, making implicit normative claims. This essay works to make those claims explicit. *Ceremony*, I argue, is a reassuring song of transcendent innocence, while *Black Eagle Child* is a baffling song of immanent experience punctuated with inexplicable transcendent interruptions. The two novels offer quite different theodicies: explanations as justifications for the way the cosmos works. In *Ceremony* metaphysical evil is ultimately the cause of suffering and thus must be confronted spiritually rather than materially. One might say that *Black Eagle Child* is an antitheodicy. It seems to lack a metanarrative but rather offers micro-explanations for a broad range of experiences that do not add up to a coherent story. Not just mysterious, the cosmos is baffling to the novel's main characters. This is the novel's structure of feeling.

The steps in developing this interpretation include historicizing the two novels' publication, analyzing the nature of the ceremonies depicted, framing the experiences within the social imaginaries of enchantment and disenchantment, considering the novels' differing narrative forms and structures, and reckoning with the nature of literary interpretation itself as innocent or experienced. The endgame is a clearer grasp of the different ways these two novels negotiate the material–spiritual interpretive problematic discussed in the introduction.

The multiple differences between the two novels are shaped by their particular historical moments. When *Ceremony* was published in 1977, Red Power was achieving its high point as American Indian Movement (AIM) warriors, with considerable controversy, replaced the vanishing, drunken, or even invisible Indian as the dominant Native image in US culture. More broadly, the modern Indian movement was giving Native peoples new hope for the fulfillment of treaties and self-determination in general. The 1975 Indian Self-Determination and Education Assistance Act provided a basis for even broader tribal changes (Wilkinson 177, 197). Charles Wilkinson summarizes the new generational outlook: Tribes had "earned the right to be heard and knew how to make the most of it" (205). So did Silko. By this time more than half of Native Americans lived in cities, but "they had begun looking back over their shoulders." It was with more than nostalgia, David Treuer (Anishinaabe) explains. In a "never-quite-extinguished sense of personal and cultural identity vested in Indian practices," they found hope in a time of violence from within and without (*Heartbeat* 293). *Ceremony* embodies this hope even as it acknowledges profound troubles within Indian Country. The novel engages traditions in a way that links present possibilities to a reassuring mythic reality still alive in the cosmos. In the following decades, no other Native novel would depict the seamless intersection of material and spiritual worlds and the spiritual certainty that *Ceremony* presents. The generally unremarked uniqueness of this novel clearly did not diminish its popularity within and outside of the academy.

 Black Eagle Child, published in 1992, was a complicated marker of resistance to the Columbian Quincentennial. This was a quite different time from the 1970s. The two federal legislations that most changed Indian Country at this time were the 1988 Indian Gaming Regulatory Act and the 1990 Native American Graves Protection and Repatriation Act. While these created significant changes, historian James Wilson argued at the time that "the Native Americans' world has . . . become more contradictory and confusing than at any time in the last 500 years." The complexity "defies analysis" (410). One feels the same about Young Bear's novel.[3] Its seemingly unstructured narrative fails to lead to thematic wholeness or a convincing sense of closure. *Black Eagle Child* is an unsettling novel for a world that is not only fundamentally unjust but also experientially baffling. The reassuring unified structure of *Ceremony* could not serve Young Bear in these new times.

 The two novels also have different cultural geographies. *Ceremony* is set in the Laguna Pueblo, which is more isolated, cohesive, and able to sustain traditional ceremonies than Young Bear's tribe is. The Meskwaki home is in the middle of Iowa cornfields and small towns. Although the goal of the leader who established (purchased) this tribal home in 1856 was to maintain an isolation that could sustain the tribe's religion, that dream died with the failures of later generations, *Black Eagle Child* explains. Not surprisingly, then, the peyote ceremony of the Native American Church, a comparatively new hybrid religion, draws on both traditional, neotraditional, and Christian rituals.

The death of innocence is the beginning of interpretation. Neal McLeod finds in this understanding important possibilities. His "Cree Poetic Discourse," discussed in the introduction, argues that because religious narratives are processes rather than objects, "there are always new embodiments and new interpretive locations" (115). From this premise he concludes that "Indigenous poetic consciousness does not simply involve a glorification of tradition but rather *a radical questioning of tradition*, albeit one that is grounded in it" (117, emphasis added). Silko's novel creates no space for "radical questioning," as it sustains its religious innocence apart from a world infected with witchery. In contrast, *Black Eagle Child* embraces the radical questioning that its sense of contingency requires. Although working within a framework similar to McLeod's, Young Bear constructs a less hopeful, more troubled lived religion.

The novel's only ceremony is the peyote ritual of the Native American Church, an adopted and adapted Meskwaki practice going back to before 1920 (Maroukis 109) but not time immemorial.[4] Its depiction is troubled because its mid-teen narrator has little framework for understanding his ceremonial experience. Also disturbing are some of the participants, who lack innocence in a different sense: At least one is an apparent pedophile; another sold sacred tribal objects to museums; some agreed to the Western education that broke down the tribe's protective isolation; others are alcoholics. They are part of a group of Meskwakis, or Red Earth People, who are members of the Well-Off Man Church and believers in Star-Medicine ceremonial experience: "our sacrament, which is after all / our sole means of spiritual communion" (14). Young Bear gives a detailed depiction of a ceremonial engagement with the more-than-material world.

First the ceremonial drum is carefully prepared. Then the grandfather recites the tribe's origin story, bringing tears to the old people: "There exists a past which is holy and more close to us than ourselves." When the peyote is passed around, Edgar is gently mocked because he has difficulty eating it.

Yet soon he finds "[t]he medicine's / effect was unbelievable but thoroughly / convincing" (31). As the all-night ceremony progresses, he comes to take it more and more seriously. During a break, Edgar helps one of the leaders go for blessing water to a nearby sacred bend in the river. Edgar notes that no one knew if this water "healed or destroyed," and he is afraid "of disturbing some lumbering deities" (21, 32). When the ceremony resumes, the Deer Man, "varnished antlers glistening / in the dull electric light," performs his ritual with a fawn. Readers apprehend the ceremony through Edgar's peyote-shaped young eyes (36–38). Becoming disoriented to everyday reality, Edgar experiences a perceptual shift: "Me, a solitary and powerless speck of dust; / He, a powerful giver of medicine" (39). This embodies Young Bear's philosophy of "cosmic insignificance" (Afterword 256). Visions and confessions follow and then abruptly stop; sparks from the meteorite also stop. "Once again we were in its realm of nothingness" (40).

"Throughout my ordeal I had been horrified," Edgar states retrospectively. This religious emotional response, common to the aboriginal sensibility, occurs in *Ceremony* only in material situations, like Tayo's response to Emo bringing out a bag of human teeth (56). For Edgar, religious experiences are as mixed as material ones; he is horrified at the otherness that has entered his everyday experience yet also thankful for the songs he received "to 'see' with." An old man concludes, "We have made it," but the last gesture goes to Edgar's friend Ted Facepaint, who farted and then "gave me a wink" (42–43). That wink engages the central problematic of the novel, the difficulty in interpreting the signs of the spirits. Robert Dale Parker sees Young Bear's irreverent sensibility as "ironic and slippery" while also recognizing that his "writing [is] more thoroughly from within a Native culture than any other Native American literary writer I know of" (102). For readers, *Black Eagle Child* has enough slapstick humor and satirical distancing amid its earnestness to make room for the second interpretive thoughts of a wink.

The ceremony in Silko's novel does not. Her brilliant, earnest writing and unselfconscious narration create a seemingly transparent immediacy in depicting the interpenetrating material and spiritual worlds. This immediacy develops from Silko's philosophy of language as expressed in her essay

"Language and Literature from a Pueblo Indian Perspective," first published two years after *Ceremony*. She begins, "Where I come from, the words most highly valued are those spoken from the heart, unpremeditated and unrehearsed" (48). This is the effect her style and narrative structure create. Even if this is a Romantic or Emersonian dream rather than a recipe for a novel, the essay nevertheless presents her vision of true language and stories distinguished by their unity, wholeness, connectedness, transparency, and directness without mediation. Language and thus stories are grounded in an unquestioned past, which gives them authenticity and communal authority. *Ceremony* similarly presents ontological and epistemological certainty even as its social events are deeply disturbing. Silko's novel is premised on the accessibility of the spiritual world. Failures of apprehension are human failures, not difficulties within the nature of spiritual interpretation itself. Young Bear, in contrast, uses his craft to open up the cracks and disjunctures through which doubt enters. Packed into *Black Eagle Child* are social analysis, medicine man traditions, tribal and personal histories, mythic storytelling, meta-theologizing, and depictions of conflicts and betrayals that are not simply explained as cosmic evil. The parts of this collage do not intertwine to create a reassuring wholeness or transparent innocence.

Sharon Holm skeptically makes the point that for Silko, "land not only generates stories but also author(ize)s them as cultural identity." As a result, *Ceremony* ultimately presents "a particularly untroubled, almost unmediated, spiritual relationship between words and place" (244). Holm references Robert M. Nelson's comment that the novel's basis for identity is not the social world but the land or place. She sees this "dishistoricizing" strategy as shaped by the development of Native literary studies as well as the environmental and countercultural movements of the 1970s and 1980s. All look for a redemptive relationship with the land. As noted above, *Black Eagle Child* came out of a later, more skeptical time. Not surprisingly, then, the mediated quality of religious experience is foregrounded rather than its transparency. The spiritual world is opaque and confusing even as it is enticing. Speaking of the summer ceremonies that Edgar attends at Pine Ridge with his family, he explains, "Possessing various interpretations of the prayers, songs, and rituals was inevitable." Uncertainty is in the nature of things because interpretation is inescapable. Edgar criticizes those Meskwaki fundamentalists ("exactness / was touted as the only form of communion") who refuse to recognize the inevitability of change and instead insist on the illusion of authenticity as a defense against and a cover for the "disarray" of tribal spiritual life (60).

Understanding ceremonies as the primary bridge between the material and spiritual worlds (Geiogamah 22), we can see *Ceremony* as one model of cosmic engagement and *Black Eagle Child* another. *Ceremony* presents a cosmos that, in spite of all its material devastations, is fundamentally orderly and stable rather than contingent and capricious. Thus it is directly knowable. Overseen by the Great Mystery, the cosmos nevertheless becomes comprehensible through stories and ceremonies. Tayo's personal struggles are enveloped in the larger story of witchery overcome (for now) within an ultimately unchanging cosmos. At key moments, spiritual reality intersects seamlessly with material lives because the boundary between them is not merely porous but open. This openness makes the traditional stories and ceremonies immediate and integral to the contemporary life of the novel. Spiritual reality as ultimate reality is the guarantor of meaning in the material world. Because of this, Tayo "cried the relief he felt at finally seeing the pattern, the way all the stories fit together. . . . He was not crazy; he had never been crazy. He had only seen *the world as it always was*" (229, emphasis added). But who among us lives in a world like this and can make this claim?

Young Bear's troubled protagonist never finds this hermeneutic resolution. For him it is one thing to have a spiritual encounter, another to interpret it. For the cosmic apprehensions within *Black Eagle Child*, an authoritative narrator as perceiver of the spiritual world is unimagined and unimaginable. Human characters are inherently incapable of such reliability through no fault of their own; it is in the nature of the cosmos. Also, the historical context of the novel makes the interpretive process even more difficult. Yet although characters face disenchanting circumstances, some still deeply believe in a spiritual reality they struggle to apprehend. Examples include

Edgar's grandmother, who gives him a stone protector as he goes to college, and healer Rose Grassleggings. Yet their religious understandings offer little certainty even if the cosmos is to a degree apprehensible through ceremonies and the interpretive practice of belief. Although Tayo also at times struggles to interpret the signs of the spirits, his impediments are different. Tayo needs spiritual healing to repair the ruins; the interpretive difficulty is in the nature of the material ruins. The devastations of everyday life make spiritual belief difficult. For Edgar the difficulties are that but more: the nature of spiritual apprehension itself. Signs are not transparent, and the available interpretive framework, belief, seems inadequate. Not surprisingly, he experiences considerable bafflement and disenchantment as a result.

Modern spiritual disenchantment is a key site of decolonial struggle for both novels. Max Weber's contrast between the enchanted world of traditional societies and the disenchantment of the modern world is useful here. Weber associates disenchantment with "rationalization and intellectualization" (155; see Fagan's comments in chapter 1). These processes strip magic from belief and establish "an internally consistent and universally applicable theodicy" (Kenneth H. Tucker Jr. 166) that is thoroughly material. As Enlightenment rationalism became the preeminent Western form of apprehension, the world came to be understood as governed by humans rather than gods (Puett 109). Charles Taylor defines an enchanted premodern world in relation to Weber's understanding of modern disenchantment: "The enchanted world . . . is a world of spirits, demons, and moral forces" that our ancestors experienced. For them "the moral/spiritual is lived . . . as immediate reality, like stones, rivers and mountains" (*Secular* 4, 12).[5] Atheism is close to unthinkable within this social imaginary.

Religion traditionally works to apprehend the world of unchanging sacred or enchanted reality. Mircea Eliade's classic work *The Sacred and the Profane: The Nature of Religion* argues that for religious people, the world "is not a chaos but a cosmos," ordered because it is a creation of gods, not humans. Michael J. Puett further explains this sense of cosmic order: "Humans do not legitimate their actions by appeals to the sacred but rather, in their attempts to create order, are in fact imitating the gods. . . . The sacred models are embedded in the cosmos and when humans construct order in their own social worlds, they do so by following these sacred models" (111). Both novels present "sacred models" in their ceremonies, which are the key site for material–spiritual interactions. Silko has structured *Ceremony* itself as a sacred model that contains characters' disenchantments within an ultimately enchanted cosmic reality. This containment is grasped at in *Black Eagle Child* but is not only unachieved but unachievable in the cosmos Young Bear has depicted.

Clifford Geertz notes that through ritual or ceremony, "the world as lived and the world as imagined" become one through a set of symbols (112). For Tayo the symbol that transforms reality from chaos to cosmos is the pattern of stars that Betonie draws in the sand and that Tayo sees again with Ts'eh (166–67). Then having escaped the violence of witchery by not attacking Emo, he again finds in the night sky "a convergence of patterns" (235; see also 229). These patterns coherently unite the material and spiritual realms for Tayo, and this transforms him. If bafflement drives people to belief, then belief makes the cosmos interpretable (Geertz 109, 100). Not the stars themselves but their transparent meaning, the pattern, allows Tayo to have confidence in his apprehension of the cosmos.

For Edgar Bearchild, bafflement never fully resolves into belief. No religious symbol can adequately reassure him because his interpretive framework for the spiritual world lacks the premodern givenness that Silko has Tayo experience. Edgar cannot unconsciously believe in an enchanted material–spiritual reality. Stars for him and his tribe are also central religious symbols: the Star Medicine and the Three-Stars-in-a-Row pattern (23, 115, 250, passim). Yet his ceremonial Star Medicine peyote experience at the beginning of the novel, the strange spiritual imaginings of his second Star Medicine hallucinogenic experience in Pomona, and the pulsing supernatural strobe light together yield no certain pattern that can assuage his confusion and sustain his belief (184–85). "Perhaps an omen" is the best Edgar's interpretive powers can offer (9). His "perhaps" resonates with what Jacque Derrida in *The Gift of Death* calls a "strategy of perhaps," in which there is "no need *of the event of a revelation or the revelation of an event. It needs to think the possibility of such an event but not the event itself*" (49, emphasis in the original). And yet because Edgar's disenchantment is never that thorough, he is not ready to settle for Derrida's "perhaps." His bafflement drives him rather than lets him coast.

Edgar experiences the cosmos much as the Girl does in the beginning of Diane Glancy's deer dance play (see chapter 3). Although neither she nor her Grandmother doubt that the cosmos is enchanted, both are frustrated with the inaccessibility or incomprehensibility of spiritual beings and immanent experiences. She finds her Grandmother's cosmos a "wordless world. . . . Not silent, but wordless." The difference is important; the cosmos is not spiritually empty for her but rather lacking in a language or system of knowledge that could make it both apprehensible and comprehensible. Thus her Grandmother's "deer noise" could mean whatever she wants it to mean but has no certain interpretation (7). Similarly, the spiritual nature of the cosmos in *Black Eagle Child* is apprehended only in strange glimpses more disturbing than reassuring. An example occurs during the peyote ceremony, when the Deer Man enters carrying a fawn in a potato sack. As the fawn pokes its head out, Edgar, because of the peyote, finds himself aboard a flying saucer. The fawn seems to have been sacrificed but only in Edgar's imagination. His interpretive powers become overloaded and so shut down. Yet the mythic interlude concludes with an ultimate affirmation: "For as long as you continue to do this, / you will receive our blessing." Edgar then apprehends the voice of the Fourth Star, who "lit the way for me; / He illuminated fully the philosophical concepts." This assurance, however, is immediately undermined by the Fourth Star's troubling words: "The asphyxiated fawn was you, / . . . fumbling in [y]our own misguided / beliefs" (38). This disconcerting interpretive dance seems a setup for failure because "We first had to be clear in / our thoughts before He could descend" (38). Although Edgar feels gratitude for the songs he received at the ceremony, he spends much of the rest of the novel struggling to gain spiritual clarity in the midst of everyday material life.

The structure of feeling for *Ceremony* is much different. Although the "ritual of witchery" is almost too powerful for the healing effects of Tayo's ceremony, in the end Tayo is able to grasp the cosmic "convergence of patterns"

(235), which reassures readers that all is right and understandable with the cosmos, in spite of its social appearance.

In their engagements with spiritual realities, both novels stretch the materialist limits of realism as a genre. It is not that one would mistake either novel's form for a nineteenth-century novel like those of Charles Dickens or Mark Twain. Yet fiction, unless read against the grain, can make more things believable than actual experience allows for. Despite the complexity of both novels' forms, they do imply a claim to ethnographically represent aspects of Indigenous experience. No critic writes about either one as fantasy literature, although Gary Eric Anderson provocatively identifies *Ceremony* as a precursor of later horror, fantasy, and speculative fiction (433). The two novels' different narrative strategies for depicting spiritual experiences, however, result in distinct forms of spiritual and thus also material, specifically social, engagements. While the narrative form of *Ceremony* creates innocent spiritual–material interactions, that innocence comes at the cost of social morality and a failure to convincingly reckon with everyday Indigenous experience. *Black Eagle Child*, as a novel of experience, develops generic challenges that reinforce the spiritual bafflement that Edgar experiences throughout the novel. Spiritual encounters do not take characters out of their unsettling social circumstances, yet they do little to help resolve the problems the Black Eagle Child community experiences.

For *Ceremony*, the unity of the material and spiritual worlds is reflected in the way mythic sections frame and so give meaning to the Tayo's material story. The "I" of the story, the storyteller, receives Tayo's story from Thought-Woman: As she "named things and / .... / they appeared." She thinks the story, and the narrator tells it (1). Because language is direct action, there is no mediation, no troubled relationship between signifier and signified, and thus no need for interpretation. No death of the author or authority. We instead have the most reliable of narrators. This narrative strategy is established with the opening page of *Ceremony*. The next page shifts from the origins to the uses of stories. They are spiritual weapons in a war over which explanation (spiritual or material, Native or Western) will structure characters' understanding of the cosmos. Then, between pages 2 and 3, comes a fall, the human failure to hold onto the stories as spiritual weapons in the hermeneutic struggle for cosmic hegemony. The spiritual world has not changed, but humans' apprehension of and participation in it have become fractured and out of balance. Healing ceremonies are now needed to restore the efficacy of the stories. Page 4, "Sunrise", reassures readers of their outcome. The novel can conclude with "Sunrise" because witchery has devoured itself "for now" (242–44). The storytelling that opens the novel is now complete as the mythic story has subsumed the realist one.

Yet this is done at a cost. Writing about Navajo healing songs, Geertz explains that they are about "human, and so endurable, suffering powerful enough to resist the challenge of emotional meaninglessness raised by the existence of intense and unremovable brute pain" (105). That is, songs or ceremonies make life bearable by helping individuals and communities experience a theodicy of cosmic meaning for human life. Yet often there is "the disquieting sense that one's moral insight is inadequate to one's moral experience," Geertz adds (106). In contrast to this unsettled, contingent, and experiential if clearly outsider assessment of religious experience, Tayo's initial disquiet can be resolved because the moral map provided by his ceremonial experience elides social realities, "the brute pain" that nearly kills him. It is not, of course, that *Ceremony* does not engage social realities; they permeate much of the novel. Because of this it is easy to overlook the fact that nothing socially has changed or even been challenged by the end. The novel's thick social texture implies a critique; however, characters take no social action, and the novel implies none.

The most troubling example of the novel's social–moral engagement is its response to Emo, who receives neither punishment nor healing. We are left to imagine that he will continue to damage or murder others. Because his witchery will now be practiced far from home, Tayo makes the morally flippant quip—California is "a good place for him" (242)—when moral seriousness is needed so that witchery as a cosmic explanation does not engender social quietism. Yet part of the power of *Ceremony* is its ability to depict troubling material conditions and then set them aside as spiritual healing repairs individual and cosmic fracturing.[6]

The moral action of the novel comes to its climax as Tayo watches Emo torture and murder his friend and scapegoat Harley. Tayo's triumph is in submissively doing nothing. While this makes sense within the novel's spiritual apprehension, should we nevertheless ask the question: Did Silko create the right response to the novel's moral conflict within the social realm? Tayo took a screwdriver with him as a premeditated weapon (235). Did he miss his moment, usually a required event for fictions engaging cosmic battles between good and evil? The old trope of redemptive violence, however, hardly seems appropriate here, and the question may seem an affront. The novel rejects the material resistance appropriate to realism and fantasy, instead presenting violence as a "deadly ritual" that would implicate Tayo in the cosmic witchery (235). Yet his passivity seems out of sync with the times.[7] The activist confrontations of the decade leading up to *Ceremony*'s publication include occupations of Alcatraz, the *Mayflower*, Mount Rushmore, the Bureau of Indian Affairs headquarters, and the village of Wounded Knee. Tayo is clearly not meant to be an AIM warrior; nor does the novel support political confrontation.

Silko stated in 1976 that while she sympathized with the movement, "there's no subtlety to their view. They oversimplify the world." They are "simply another political group" (Seversted 7–8). Yet there is an opposite simplicity to her novel's world as characters are given no conception of political resistance. The one exception might be Tayo's stealing back the stolen cattle, but that is a long way from challenging the system (as imagined, say, in *Almanac of the Dead*). *Ceremony* establishes its political passivity by bracketing social from cosmic reality. It accomplishes this by subsuming material stories within spiritual ones. Silko sets the mythic stories apart by separating them on the page and centering their short lines, giving them a poetic, distinctly non-realist status. At the same time, conceptual parallels between the two realms reassure the reader of their idealist unity in a porous but hierarchical cosmos. For example, the story of Reed Woman and the drought parallels Tayo's experience of the jungle rain and the New Mexico drought, just as the conclusion to Tayo's journey is reassuringly followed by the successful ending of Hummingbird and Fly's rescue operation (11–13, 237). Positive outcomes for the mythic stories reassure readers of the same for the realist stories. Yet those outcomes are only personal, not social.

This parallel is interrupted in the novel's most striking challenge to the limits of literary realism. This occurs when the spiritual being Ts'eh humanly enters the material world and so dissolves the material–spiritual boundary. The two realms merge. Silko presents this encounter without the graphic differentiation the novel has given mythic stories. Nor are there the usual narrative cues. As noted above, Tayo does not enter Ts'eh's world through a portal, as Fools Crow does Feather Woman's world. Nor does Ts'eh come to Tayo in a vision or dream. Their encounter, described in the language of realism, is seemingly part of everyday experience. "When transcendence breaks into time," Orsi observed, "the transcendent is bound to become dirty." It also becomes morally ambiguous ("The Many" 15). Neither of these occur as Silko imagines this Dené–Laguna engagement between material and spiritual realities. Her depiction is innocently uncomplicated, and because of this it raises questions about experience. How many Laguna young people have had a summer like Tayo's? Do spiritually attuned Native people today experience similarly unmediated intersections? Are they recorded in memoirs—Silko's, for example? If we say that these questions are off-base, what are we asserting about the way present-day cosmic apprehensions and their literary representations work? The reassurances of *Ceremony* only seem reassuring as long as we do not ask these experiential questions. The novel's innocence offers a "compensatory fantasy" for a disenchanted world.[8] This seems a key reason why *Ceremony* is one of the most popular Native novels (Roemer 223) and is published in a "Thirtieth Anniversary Classic Deluxe Edition."

Imagined alternative realities, however, are not only compensatory fantasies, comforting escapes from troubling material conditions. Religious ceremonies call on participants to imagine more than material reality to seek a connection to spiritual reality that is healing. Even if they passively surrender within the experiences, individuals and characters who participate gain a form of control through their choice to supplicate, and so endorse, supernaturally powerful forces. Thus prayers and ceremonies can be seen as not passive but "unequivocally empowering, oppositional, or subversive" (Orsi, *Thank You* 197). Within Silko's conceptualization, the "fantasy" of Tayo's encounter with Ts'eh does empower his spiritual healing and it does oppose the solely materialist apprehensions to which most of the other characters limit themselves. While this healing and opposition certainly matter as they potentially challenge readers to spiritual reflection, Silko nevertheless leaves Tayo socially passive as a result of his spiritual encounter. Readers may be caught in the same passivity. However, if they reckon with the unchallenged and unchanged material contexts of the novel's spiritual encounters, they will find Silko's literary construction disturbingly innocent.

Black Eagle Child, in contrast, insistently and experientially addresses social realities and everyday contingencies and uses them to field test more-than-material apprehensions. Throughout the novel, tensions between the material and spiritual worlds remain unresolved. For participants of the peyote ceremony, the harsh realities of Meskwaki tribal life are not left behind when the ritual begins, as noted above. And when the blankets are taken off the windows, the "extraordinary and sacred" light of the ceremony is replaced by "harsh sunlight." Edgar feels "immense gratitude" for the songs he has received, which will help him "see" his way (43). The rest of the novel then depicts the challenges of practicing this spiritual seeing as he travels toward maturity through a difficult social landscape. He, unlike Tayo, remains troubled to the end.

Young Bear situates Edgar's spiritual experiences within his tribe's mythic and historical past in relation to its present situation.

> . . . . The clash
> between deities of the land, water, and sky
> was imminent for human beings as well.
> What our supernatural predecessors
> experienced, it was said, we would
> relive. It was part of our mythology—
> and religion. But this was 1965,
> and we were older and more stationary
> in time. (3)

Coming at the beginning of the novel, this explanation sets the stage for intersections between spiritual and material realms. This is the opposite of Tayo's experience of being taken out of the messiness of the material world in his encounter with Ts'eh. In Edgar's experiences, the cosmic realm becomes dirtied, to use Orsi's term. An example is his alcohol- and drug-induced, personally improvised Star-Medicine encounter far from home in the California foothills. He experiences a cosmic transformation similar to what he experienced in the earlier peyote ceremony. However, he is immediately brought back to a frenzied confrontation with the Pomona Police because a nearby ROTC building had just been firebombed (125–32). While the spiritual experiences of the novel are saturated with materiality, they do not much help heal the material world or offer relief from it. If the spiritually infused realism of *Ceremony* seems quietist, the material–spiritual encounters in *Black Eagle Child* do not lead to social or cultural change either. However, this is a different, alienated quietism emerging not from cosmic certainty but from doubtful hope and uneasiness. The spiritual world matters, but addressing individual and tribal conditions is also baffling to characters.

Enchantment is not an experience readily grasped within the modern social imaginary. Nor does it easily fit within the genre of realism. Yet at its heart is a tension, its "fictionality and mimesis" (Benediktssonn 122). Many Indigenous novels resolve the dilemma of genre and cosmology by bracketing the supernatural (see chapter 1). Silko's and Young Bear's novels are different. As the supernatural seemingly crashes into the material world, *Ceremony* and *Black Eagle Child* work to convince readers of the mimetic quality of these encounters. In this sense these novels, like all works in the realist genre, are arguments trying to convince readers of their depiction of the cosmos. Both novels require a leap of readerly faith as they quite differently engage the supernatural within the material world. Their different adaptations of realism, innocent and experienced, mark their different lived religions and experiential theodicies.

Critical interventions can also be hermeneutically innocent and thus raise similar concerns. An example is Sean Kicummah Teuton's reading of *Ceremony* in *Red Land, Red Power*. He calls for knowledge that is experientially grounded both materially and spiritually. Teuton challenges the critical tendency to "secularize" Native spiritual experiences or, in a form of cultural relativism, to bracket them as only Native and thus Other to everyday experience (123). Critics, he states, and I would agree, have failed to "closely" examine *Ceremony*'s "metaphysics" (121). However, his own reading of the novel also does not reckon with the ontological status of the spiritual experiences depicted. He describes Tayo's "supernatural experiences" as "mythic" but does not investigate their relationship to everyday material reality. Teuton rightly challenges readers to "reconsider the adequacy of conventional understanding of experience in *Ceremony*" yet offers no analysis of the ways its intersecting material–spiritual realities are experienced. "Like Tayo, we readers are sent into this mythic space where events challenge our own sense of reality" (155). This abstract assertion needs explaining conceptually and experientially in ways that would help readers better grasp the spiritual–material meaning of the mythic space they should enter as they engage the novel.[9] Otherwise it can easily be understood as a kind of Indigenous religious liberalism that maintains the appearance of enchantment in quite disenchanted and disenchanting ways.

Just as the two novels' different apprehensions of the cosmos are shaped by their relation to realism as a genre, these apprehensions are relatedly shaped by the way they are narratively structured. *Ceremony* shifts back and forth between "realist" depictions of everyday material and spiritual experiences and the mythic stories that frame the earthly realm in reassuring ways. The structure of *Black Eagle Child* lacks this reassurance; it seems as structurally disjointed as the spiritual–material world it depicts. Readers grasp at connections but find no unified whole and little interpretive clarity. The abrupt narrative shifts, and odd juxtapositions mirror the sporadic, inconclusive spiritual encounters characters experience as well as the material incongruities of their everyday lives. Its "collage" of genres (Young Bear's term; Afterword 255)—letters, gossipy stories, melodrama, UFO accounts, fictional memoir—as well as shifting narrators and languages—English and Meskwaki—its strange range of allusions, and its seemingly epic poetic form for decidedly non-epic experiences all create readerly uneasiness. It is a strange fictional ethnography or choreography. Slapstick descriptions juxtapose and seemingly mock ceremonial scenes. The novel often has adolescent intensity and seeming lack of control. Yet the seriousness of the conflicts and the depicted desires are not dissipated because of this. It is a profane book reaching for the sacred.

The placement of the ceremony within the narrative structure helps determine the spiritual resolutions *Ceremony* and *Black Eagle Child* reach. The ceremonial summer with Ts'eh creates the culmination of Tayo's healing; the earlier ceremony performed by Betonie is a prelude and preparation for this more transformative one. While the subsequent action offers reassurance of the ceremony's efficacy, it does not significantly develop its lived implications. The momentum of the concluding action leads us to imagine Tayo's life continuing positively, spiritually attuned to ultimate reality. The ceremony as culmination of his religious education prepares him for his one climactic moment; no room is left for complicating details of how a changed Tayo will now live in the everyday material world that has not changed. Implying the outcomes of Tayo's healing is more reassuring than working out the experiential details.

In *Black Eagle Child*, Edgar's experiences following his ceremony are explicit and detailed. The narrative choice to have the key ceremony, his first spiritual awakening, at the beginning rather than the end is one more way Young Bear gives his novel a more troubling picture of ceremonial transformations. Readers are immersed in the details of Edgar's post-ceremonial erratic and incomplete growth, both spiritually and psychosocially. The novel's structure makes it impossible to convincingly state, as Silko does for Tayo, that "[t]he transition was complete" (236). Edgar has years of everyday and spiritually distinctive experiences to live through and make sense of. The novel's conclusion, like its subtitle, does not even center on him. Its concluding chapter, oddly, focuses on his friend Ted Facepaint getting patched up at the Heijen Medical Center after a revenge beating by three depressed, cross-dressing Indians (241–42). It is a strange chapter, ending with an elder, the mother of the three attackers, brushing Ted's face with an eagle-wing fan as he imagines, dreams, or spiritually experiences himself as an eagle mending its own broken wing. This religious individualization clearly fits within the modern social imaginary. Reading the falling leaves "as a signal," he "confidently" takes flight (251). If the symbolism is rather heavy-handedly optimistic, it is called into question in many ways: its heavy-handedness itself, the obvious need for interpretation, the odd and disturbing happenings of the rest of the chapter—for example, an Indian health care worker selling "fondling rights" to handicapped patients—the apparently mocking tone in phrases like "the Morse code of an imminent celestial revelation," the remembered Nevada highway patrolman's comment "Whichever holy / star you thought we were is unquestionably / the least of your nihilistic problems" (246–48), and the odd title: "The Man Squirrel Shall Not Wake." Something more-than-material is being evoked, but its spiritual nature is hard to figure out. And Edgar Bearchild is absent from it all. There is no reassuring climax that resolves everything for him or the reader.

The point of view of the two novels works in similarly disparate ways. The narrator of *Ceremony* is acknowledged in the opening as only an amanuensis rather than a creator or even a diachronic translator having a specific, knowable perspective. This gives the novel its reassuringly authoritative air. Since the ultimate narrator is Thought Woman, the narration cannot be unreliable. The shifting narration of *Black Eagle Child* gives all interpretation a sense of fallibility. Meanings are always in doubt because they are constructed by humans interpreting spiritual realities. Even the third-person narration of the final chapter gives no more certainty to readers than Ted Facepaint himself has about what his experience means.

Related to differences in narrative certainty are differences in readers' experience of the texts. The first-person narration of *Black Eagle Child* brings the reader into the story. During Edgar's teen years, the novel has the intensity of a young adult novel gone askew. And the ceremony of the first two chapters has an immediacy of detail that draws us in. Yet bizarre incidents like the one reported in the newspaper as "A Buck Buck-Naked" (138) have an absurd quality that creates distance that allows for readerly reflection on the truth status of the narration's insights, a status that Parker, as noted above, explains as "ironic and slippery" (102). The poetic form functions similarly, engaging the reader without creating the illusion of transparency. The narration of *Ceremony*, in contrast, requires readerly submission to Thought Woman as author. The mythic framework also asserts a narrative authority that is scriptural. We neither lose ourselves in the story nor stand back and critique it but rather read meditatively, drawn in by a material–spiritual world revealed.

Thus *Ceremony*, despite its setting, takes the reader out of a troubled secularized world and into a reassuring pre-secular aboriginal social imaginary in which belief is communally certain rather than contingently individualized. One might say the brilliance of the novel's structure is that it has it both ways, a secular realism that makes the novel socially convincing while also reassuringly sacred. For *Black Eagle Child*, spiritual reality is always in doubt, both because belief is a confusing, conflicted human choice always in process and because experiencing a more-than-material reality is never assured or readily interpretable.

How to live well with the spirits in an antagonistic, materially oriented world is a key question for both novels. Each one answers with a theodicy that sets forth the nature of the cosmos that characters live in and the nature of their suffering—that is, the desires they are capable of imagining and the limitations placed on them. In the end, the world of *Ceremony* makes sense, but does making sense make sense? Is it too reassuring? This is not a question we would pose about *Black Eagle Child*. Maybe that is why it remains relatively obscure, having received barely a mention in most major critical books on Indigenous literature.

Puett's essay "Social Order and Social Chaos" offers a striking historical insight that helps us recognize the different ways the two novels explain suffering. The essay challenges the widely held and seemingly commonsensical view of religion as "giv[ing] order to an otherwise contingent and meaningless world" (109), an explanation that fits *Ceremony* well. Generally within theological accounts of traditional Native religions, belief in the timeless unity of the cosmic order has predominated (see chapter 1). However, Puett observes that many ethnographic and historical accounts of traditional societies challenge this: "Claims to cosmic order are rarely as seamless and lacking in tension as they are so often presented in our theoretical discussions" (123). *Ceremony* acknowledges that witchery has only been defeated "for now," yet its mythic story reassures readers that good will ultimately triumph in spite of intermittent battles, and thus cosmic order rather than chaos will be sustained (242–43, 237–38). Silko enmeshes Tayo in material and spiritual circumstances he cannot actively combat. His ceremonial encounters do lead to the healing activities of rescuing the cattle and rejecting the internal oppression of his fellow veterans. Yet Tayo's experiences of transcendence are not only healing but confining. Just as he is passive in the healing ceremony with Betonie and Ts'eh, he has no active role in combatting the witchery. Can this focus on individual inner peace work as a strategy for Indigenous revitalization?

In *Black Eagle Child*, the cosmos depicted through various characters' apprehensions and in the overall sense of the novel is much less static and orderly. It better fits Pruett's description as it acknowledges, as noted above, "The clash / between deities of land, water, and sky / was imminent for human beings as well" (3). Chaos is inherent in both realms, this perspective asserts. Because cosmic interventions are much more difficult to interpret in *Black Eagle Child*, they provide a less certain foundation for belief. The problem of authority presents itself in the different role elders play in the two novels. In *Ceremony* they certify the cosmic nature of Tayo's healing (128–39). As Edgar Bearchild considers the need for ceremonies to change, in contrast to tribal demands for fundamentalist "exactness," he recognizes that "disagreements / were becoming frequent among our elders. / We each held them in such high esteem that / we could never doubt their memories, / even if they forgot our own names" (60). Here belief only replaces bafflement through the acceptance of a dubious traditional authority. In *Black Eagle Child*, authority is always being culturally negotiated within changing lived circumstances. Because of this, its characters struggle between belief and bafflement, submission and self-assertion, and cosmic reassurance in the face of a chaotic social world. The result is frustration at their inability to interpret the signs of the spirits.

Ceremony is a beautiful book. It is also a troubling one when read in light of *Black Eagle Child*. Young Bear, in his novel's afterword, identifies the problematic of interpretation as fundamental to his theodicy. And yet he finds in the material world practical, helpful signs of the spirits as he references the incident that opens this chapter: "While a few possess an uncanny ability to detect watery voices rising from the lakes and rivers, the rest of us are convinced the sound is the garbled music of inexperienced vocalists pounding on a rusted truck hood upshore. While these few will always appear despondent and unpredictable, it is frequently their doting powers of healing that work and come through when modern medicines fail." (260) Despite the difficulties, Young Bear has created a lived religion that does offer some healing for a disenchanted world.

3 DEER DANCING BETWEEN TWO WORLDS

JOY HARJO, LINDA HOGAN, DIANE GLANCY

Watching deer bound across a prairie or through a woodland, we see their grace and near freedom from gravity. One easily imagines why deer are often part of Indigenous ceremonies as transitional figures between the material and spiritual worlds. Joy Harjo's poem "Deer Dancer," Linda Hogan's poem "Deer Dance," and Diane Glancy's short play *The Woman Who Was a Red Deer Dressed for the Deer Dance* all use deer dancing to imagine cosmic connections. Imagination, however, is a fragile epistemology, which easily leads to doubt as the specter haunting and yet quickening religious experience. Each of the three deer dance works reckons with doubt as well as belief as they explore experiential difficulties inherent in apprehending, seeing, and then interpreting the spiritual world with its illusiveness.

These literary reckonings take place within specific genres: a prose poem, a narrative poem with commentary, and a play made up of fragments. Irish writer Colm Tóibín, writing about the place of religion in literature, explains, "Poets have it easier than novelists because they don't have to tell us what the 'someone' who saw the ghost or visited the church did next." In contrast to poets, and Glancy as a playwright should be included, Tóibín argues that novelists must consider "perspective, context, point of view and banal issues of narrative line and credibility" (213, 214). The three deer dance works claim a certain representational freedom, as most poetry does. However, they should not be given a pass on the requirement of credibility, even if it is achieved differently, more suggestively. Poetic ambiguities can be provocations but also evasions.

Related to this interpretive problematic, Billy-Ray Belcourt's poem "Hermeneutics of the Sometimes/Somewhere" begins its interpretation of Indigenous spiritual realities in the title's vague last two words. The sixth tenet of the poem then makes a commonplace assertion about Native apprehensions of the cosmos: "the otherworldly is a category of the experience of indigeneity." Later tenets claim Indigenous "ontological fugitivity," "an ontology of ghosts," and a "theoretics of the doorway." These are a "revolutionary undertaking" that rejects modern secular disenchantment (8, 9, 10). As theological claims, however, they are not substantiated in the other poems, include one titled "Sacred." Powerful as its poems are, *The Wound Is a World* nevertheless can hardly be described as engaging even a closed immanence. If the claim for an experiential "hermeneutics of the sometimes/somewhere" here has questionable credibility, the situation is quite different for all three deer dance works. Their implied hermeneutics do actually alert us to the possibility of literary works as experiential, cosmologically revolutionary undertakings. Their credibility comes in part through the spiritual doubt they explore, something Belcourt's poems leave little room for. This absence also alerts us to the atypical spiritual apprehensions within the deer dance works.

In Joy Harjo's prose poem "Original Memory" (47), also from *In Mad Love and War*, doubt is a shapeshifter, there from "the beginning of the world," invading and pervading life. Religious doubt is not only a Christian or colonial experience. It is more fundamentally an apparently inherent component of human religious experience: the source of human creation, inventor of possibilities, caught in time but leaping beyond it to another world, the poem asserts. Humans were created out of doubt and so have their being in it. Harjo concludes her meditation with the question, "And who are we to make sense of this slit of impossible time?" And yet the pull to explain is irresistible, as the existence of so many deer dancing works attests.[1]

Religious engagements in literature are cosmically uncertain when they are experiential rather than propositional. Ceremonies, including deer dances, are imagined connections that work to assuage the uncertainties between the material and spiritual realms. They are not only models, "enactments, materializations, realizations" of belief that bring these realms together; they are also "models *for* . . . believing" so that participants "attain their faith as they portray it" (Geertz 114).

Literary deer dances as models of and for believing engage readers and characters in an enchanted ceremony meant to fuse material and spiritual realities. The purpose of the deer dance is no longer to call on spiritual help for deer hunting. The help needed today is to repair the "ruins," to use Harjo's term, of present Indian experience (1). In this new way, ceremonies, literal and literary, continue as practices of spiritual–material connectedness. Larry Evers and Felipe S. Molina's (Pascua Yaqui, Yoem Pueblo) *Yaqui Deer Songs: Maso Bwikam* provides useful commentary. The deer dancers' performance is "a parallel" to "that mythic, primal place Yaquis call *sea ania*, flower world," they explain. Deer songs depict "equivalences" or "verbal equations" that link the "double world" (7). These terms suggest that for Yaqui people, the world of the ancestors, which encompassed material and spiritual realities, continues. "The actions of the *pahkolam* [ceremonial dancers] and the deer dancer during a *pahko* [deer dance ceremony] may be thought of as reflections of experience performers have had in one of the other worlds" (Evers and Molina 45). The power of these equations and reflections is not to be taken lightly. Evers and Molina explain, "All these worlds are considered to be *supernatural* and dangerous if not approached correctly."[2]

Ceremonies are thus signs of the spirits, material markers of more-than-material realities. For Evers and Molina, Yaqui deer ceremonies acknowledge the "double world." They are human constructs or analogues for spiritual realities, however, not unmediated apprehensions. Rather they are "reflections," a play of presence and absence. "I have seen traces of this spirit but the spirit itself I have not seen. Like the sacred deer of the Cherokee, it is from everlasting . . . invisible . . . abiding in the quick of mystery," Marilou Awiakta's (Cherokee) speaker in *Abiding Appalachia* acknowledges (2).

Often difficulties in direct spiritual apprehension are explained as a consequence of the destructive impact of Western secular culture as well as personal or communal failures. Vine Deloria Jr.'s prologue to *The World We Used to Live In* dramatically makes this case. Silko's *Ceremony* and Momaday's *House Made of Dawn* are literary examples that register the spiritual devastation resulting from material destruction. As with characters in those novels, the speakers and most characters in the three deer dance works considered here share the impulse to experience more-than-material realities; however, the material conditions of continuing colonialism similarly impede that experience. Yet almost uniquely, these deer dancing works also explore difficulties inherent in the nature of the cosmos itself.

The lived religions embedded in these three works all recognize a fundamental spiritual uncertainty and inaccessibility. Apprehending the spirits in them is not just a matter of desire or commitment. The spiritual world itself is mostly opaque. Speakers and characters experiencing its inaccessibility do not doubt that the spiritual world exists, but they are troubled that their experience of it falls short of their expectations. They struggle to recognize and then interpret the signs of the spirits. Few other Native literary works engage this specific difficulty; similarly, literary critics and writers on Native religion have seldom addressed this fundamental issue.

The interpretive struggles embedded in each of the three works are shaped by various traditions: tribal, pan-Indian, and Christian. While the Hogan poems considered here are the least tribally specific, Joy Harjo's relationship to her Muskogee tribe is also complex. Craig Womack explores her negotiation of tribal specificity and a pan-tribal perspective in his argument for a tribally specific criticism. He explains, "For Harjo's artistry to be effective, Creekness is essential, even though this writer is pan-tribal in her concerns" (*Red* 224). In commenting on "Deer Dancer," he claims a "Creek specificity" for the poem (228), although the Lakota specificity seems more evident. Further, deer dances are not part of the Muskogee tradition, to my knowledge, but rather are associated with the Southwest, where Harjo has lived much of her life. While Glancy's two characters share the same tribal traditions, they experience them from different generational perspectives. Compared to the other writers, Glancy much more self-consciously and persistently has explored this problematic, surely in large part because she has taken a religious stance that is so controversial. Thus her religious perspective cannot go without saying. The dilemmas of the play are not only experienced within Cherokee religious experience, even if the play itself engages only the Cherokee cosmology. For Glancy, the problematic of spiritual inaccessibility is especially acute because of her commitment to both Native tradition and Christian belief. "It's a matter of faith in both traditions," she emphasizes (*Claiming* 95).

My analytical focus is not on the specific tribal conceptualizations of the spiritual world; the three works themselves are not that specifically related to their authors' tribal belonging. Rather, the analysis here looks at the ways spiritual experience itself is depicted. In exploring the possibilities of apprehending spiritual realities, Harjo, Hogan, and Glancy share key understandings. They recognize that their stories are not transcriptions of experience but rather interpretations. Spiritual experiences are not unmediated; neither are the reports on them. Each writer uses language, specifically English, to describe or evoke spiritual experiences. Language is a material phenomenon used to construct spiritual meanings; it is an inherently limited bridge between two realities.

As the three authors explore the problematic of apprehending the spiritual–material world, their characters express varying degrees of confidence in the apprehensions they experience. Although Harjo's speaker at the end acknowledges the constructed nature of her story, she nevertheless confidently asserts the continuing presence of the ancestors. By self-consciously imagining them, she constructs a for-her satisfactory bridge between worlds. Despite presenting the most overtly mediated spiritual apprehension, this work's speaker has the most confidence in the experiential accessibility of the spiritual world and its healing potential. Hogan concludes her poem with a more troubled material–spiritual apprehension as her speaker perceives, maybe projects, the deer finding their fur coats, their physical being, not quite fitting their spiritual selves, and the speaker finds herself distanced from them. The material–spiritual fit is uncomfortable for both deer and humans. Although the dilemma is unresolved, the longing remains gentle. The speaker has come to terms with this inevitable aspect of being human. This is a part of the rounding of human corners, Hogan's title for the poetry collection, helping humans better fit into the world as they experience it. Glancy's play extends the problematic by more insistently and stridently depicting, across generations, characters' struggles with spiritual desire and meager fulfillment. The elder Grandmother and her modern granddaughter both experience spiritual disillusionment but in different ways: the Grandmother is frustrated by her limited access to the spiritual world; the Girl is more ontologically troubled.

No direct more-than-material experience occurs in the present of these three deer dance works. Rather than experiential reports, they are meditations on possibilities. Despite the writers' acknowledgment of spiritual uncertainty, their works suggest the possibility of personal apprehension through imagined belief, what Womack, referencing Søren Kierkegaard, calls "a leap of faith" ("Theorizing" 371). Momaday asserts something similar when he discusses "the awful risk involved" in living a "life in language"— that is, imagining spiritual meanings that "no defeat, no humiliation, no suffering" could destroy ("Man Made" 93, 57). Womack acknowledges that inherent in our humanness is a "tenuous" grasp of "other realities and nonhumans." Because of this, we must use "imaginative vision" as "one of the ways we understand these relationships between humans and nonhumans." We create "meaning out of the 'raw data,'" Womack explains, by making "speculative leaps." He brings up Momaday's seminal essay "The Man Made of Words," where he finds "imaginings within imaginings" ("Theorizing" 371–73). Harjo's speaker expresses this uncertainty inherent in imagining as a strategy for knowing: "We all take risks stepping to thin air. Our ceremonies didn't predict this. Or we expected more" (8). All three deer dancing works self-consciously engage religious imaginings within the modern social imaginary as characters experience varying degrees and forms of spiritual longing and uncertainty, together with comfort and healing. Their stories are imaginative leaps of faith and hope.

Harjo's *In Mad Love and War* offers a poetic report of the spiritual consequences of Indigenous peoples' material losses. Characters in these poems have often lost their cultural rootedness, and yet in unpromising circumstances, some find spiritual renewal. Material problems are not supernaturally solved, but characters do gain awareness of worlds beyond their troubled everyday circumstances. Doubt, the darker side of uncertainty, seems here inherent in the cosmos itself. Yet the experiences of uncertainty and doubt are various. It is a consequence of Western cultural dominance, the problem of time, the impermanence of love, and the transience of existence; but it is also the basis for being human, Harjo finds. The fundamental problem (or problematic) of uncertainty remains unresolvable.

"Deer Dancer" offers thick descriptions of characters' harsh historical and immediate circumstances, which frame their apprehensions of the spirit world. The setting is a bitter winter night, with the "broken survivors" finding something of a communal home in an Indian bar. These "hardcore" can tough out a cold night with the help of alcohol and each other. Their confidence, however, falters as a beautiful woman walks in, apparently as hardcore as they are and yet so different. Her presence pushes them to self-awareness: they are "ruins" but also "Indian." The poem later plays on this double recognition when the speaker turns a pickup line into a troubling inquiry, "what are we all doing in a place like this?" Kathleen Ann Pickering's *Lakota Culture, World Economy* helps answer that question as she considers, for example, the consequences of economic and social racism that can trap Indians in bars like the one Harjo describes. The poem's reference to Buffalo Calf Woman suggests that the characters are Lakota (see Looking Horse 67–73). Pickering's book thus provides a useful context. She explains that "the imposition of a negative social identity ultimately restricts Lakotas to limited wage work opportunities on their reservations or confines them to the lower rungs of the socioeconomic ladder when they do venture beyond the reservation" (97). Something more than individual choice brought Harjo's characters to this Indian bar; their experiences have been shaped by destructive political and social conditions. Despite this, they are "survivors" (3).[3]

For all the negative stereotypes the characters represent, they embody more. Their insight (Henry Jack) and blindness (Richard and his wife) prepare us for the speaker's narrative struggle to apprehend the spiritual world (3). A traditional story of Harjo's Mvskogee tribe suggests that the problematic of spiritual apprehension is not just a contemporary concern. In it, a hunter is visited by a woman and little child. She tells him that she is the doe he had killed last year. They are attracted to each other and marry. Although warned by his deer/wife that he must not tell anyone how they met, years later the hunter does just that. Immediately the wife "took off with her white tail sticking up, and with her child, too, they went in the same way, it was told long ago" (Gouge 87–88). This story implies that a spiritually engaged life has always been precarious. Although tribally structured, it is secret, personal, and fragile. The story suggests that "long ago" people struggled with their own version of uniting the apparent incongruity Harjo's poem brings up: a woman entering the bar in "a stained red dress with tape on her heels" who is also "the deer who entered our dream in white dawn" (14). Experiencing spiritual realities within material circumstances is a cosmic but historically contingent difficulty. Seeing the more-than-material world means "stepping into thin air," stanza 8 suggests, a leap of faith. Dancing naked, her material degradation discarded, the deer/woman becomes an ephemeral sign from of the spirits, "deer breath on icy windows" (12, 9). As the deer dancer strips away material accoutrements, she embodies the spiritual connection the characters at the bar long for, "the myth slipped down through dreamtime" (13). Using the term "dreamtime" rather than "visions" suggests further uncertainties.

Abruptly, however, the concluding stanza disrupts this ambiguous reassurance: "The music ended." The song of sentimental desperation stops spinning in the jukebox. "And so does the story." Then the third staccato-like sentence presents the fundamental fact of the poem: "I wasn't there." The speaker's role, we now realize, is not as eyewitness to spiritual transformation, as implied, but

rather its creator as she imaginatively constructs the story's spiritual possibilities. With this stanza, Harjo transforms a good story lesson into an interpretive
leap. But this has been the point all along.

Unlike in Hogan's poem, Harjo's deer dance is not a mediating ceremony
but an ordinary experience turned extraordinary by fusing the material and
spiritual worlds. The traditional ritual deer dance is actualized as experience.
This experience is presented with such lived supernatural immediacy that
we as readers may reduce it to an accepted trope within the genre of Native
literature. Hopefully we instead take the poem and its author more seriously
and more deeply puzzle over the enigma of the more-than-material ritual
that is described. If we do, we then face the challenge of making an ontological meaning for the event. Before the reader has time for that, however, the
speaker's last stanza comment, "I wasn't there," knocks us off our interpretive
standpoint with the recognition that the experience might be just an urban
legend: religion as reassuring rumor. Now we must interpret not only the
meaning of the event but also its linguistic mediation. This is the position one
is in when reading traditional stories with their supernatural explanations of
the world. We must wrestle with the conundrum of whether the world worked
categorically, cosmically differently in the time when people and deer actually
spoke together. This gap between "the time of origins" (referenced below)
and the present is what Vine Deloria Jr. in *The World We Used to Live In* works
to experientially bridge. Others construct only symbolic bridges. Robert
Warrior's reading of "Deer Dancer," for example, focuses solely on its social
meanings rather than supernatural engagement ("Your Skin" 347–48). To be
fair, Warrior does not give a full explication of the poem, but the materialist
reduction he presents, not taking the supernatural descriptions literally as
Deloria does, drains the poem of its religious power. Another critical option
is to slip between these two interpretive schemas, literal–transcendental and
symbolic, without acknowledging the slippage. As noted in chapter 2, Sean
Kicummah Teuton's reading of Tayo's supernatural experiences in *Ceremony*
takes this tack of strategic ambiguity. This interpretive move places experiences of the more-than-material cosmos in the special category of "in there,"
as one of Tommy Orange's characters categorizes her ceremonial experience

(198). "In there" is a dualistic reconstruction of the aboriginal socioreligious imaginary within or parallel to the modern one, an interpretive move well-known within modern philosophy and liberal religion.

This interpretive problematic is relevant to all three deer dance works. One might argue that this hermeneutical thinking imposes a Christian schema onto an interpretive situation where it does not belong (even though some, such as Evers and Molina, discussed above, do wrestle with this ceremonial interpretive problematic). It is true that for centuries, Christian theologians have debated about the sacred presence or symbolic attribution of the communion wafer. However, dismissing this hermeneutic issue by seeing it as foreign and thus irrelevant is neither innocent nor inherently appropriate. Like any other interpretive religious experience, the Indigenous–Christian dichotomy involves a leap of faith that captures both insight and blindness (see chapter 1). Harjo's sly conclusion adds to the interpretive drama, yet it also resolves it by refusing its terms with an imagined, traditionally referenced, socially aware assertion of hope, a leap of faith that the past still lives in the present and can help create a meaningful future.

Harjo's poem embodies Momaday's understanding that "stories are true in that they are established squarely upon belief." Traditional or contemporary, they are human forms of apprehension. "Stories are not subject to the imposition of such questions as true or false, fact or fiction. Stories are realities lived and believed." They are "the realization of the imaginative experience." (*Man Made* 3, 84). Self-consciously constructing meaning within a fractured world may seem typically modernist, and it is, but this poem has an Indigenous spiritual difference. For Harjo does not, as W. H. Auden writes, "find the mortal world enough" ("Lullaby" 27). Her speaker calls on communal resources, strained though they may be by historical and contemporary circumstances, to create, maybe conjure, spiritual meaning out of the experience. The speaker finds this imaginatively constructed more-than-material apprehension enough.

Linda Hogan's "Deer Dance" is disturbing in a somewhat different way as it presents a less urgent, less materially or tribally specific, and more self-consciously reflective spiritual uncertainty. The longing for certainty is itself reassuring, and yet the troubling problematic lingers as the poem concludes with the ontological relationship between the material and spiritual realms of the cosmos. Nature in Hogan's poem is not particularized; neither are Native beliefs or tribal connections. The speaker's verbal journey of bodily experience and philosophical rumination takes us through four thematically related spiritual encounters. The poem is a teaching moment; the speaker explains, "See how" (*Rounding*), as she leads the reader to the final experience of watching a deer dance in the bush near her house, and then she creates its meaning.

"Deer Dance" is included in Hogan's *Rounding the Human Corners,* which Janet McAdams notes is centered on "this essential fact of human estrangement" (226). Indigenous spiritual concerns are subsumed within human dilemmas. The poem comes in the book's concluding section, tellingly titled "Affinity," which suggests the similarity and yet ultimate difference or distance between material and spiritual realms. Its first five poems, speakers struggle with the uncertainty and inaccessibility of the spiritual world.

"Wild" (59) begins, "This is not the horse. It is the poem, / even if it calls out for its sister" (1). Telling is translating, not being. The poem concludes by asking whether we can still speak the language of wildness that the ancestors used. Paralleling the shift from the aboriginal to the modern social imaginary, the estrangement inherent in shifting apprehensions of nature creates a significant challenge. The next poem, "Walking" (60–61), raises further uncertainties about contemporary people's relationship to "ancestors / And beautiful spirits" (19–20). The speaker is confident in her knowledge of the local material world. Yet, holding her newly born granddaughter up to see the ancestors, the speaker admits, "But I don't know what else is there" (21). In "Affinity: Mustang" (64–66), the speaker and horse share a sorrowful bond at the loss of a foal. Yet this connection is the speaker's construction, her leap of faith. "Emergence," the poem preceding "Deer Dance" (67–68), opens with another epistemological leap: "I trust what all they say" (1). The speaker then ecumenically embraces various origin stories but concludes with the Romantic trope that a newborn child, emerging into light, finds that its "blue eye / . . . will darken"—that is, will come to see less clearly as well as less hopefully.

The gentle quality of these poems, their lovely images and straightforward language, belies the disturbing questions they engage.[4] Yet for all the questioning, the speaker's language of longing is also a language of comfort. Longing is what connects the speaker to the cosmos, not direct experience, and this can seem enough. Yet this is an individualistic reassurance rather than the comfort of communal belief. Although Norma C. Wilson identifies Hogan as having "a traditionally minded Chickasaw perspective," she also explains that after her first book of poetry, Hogan's work became less directly connected to her tribe's traditions (87, 89). *Rounding the Human Corners*, as the title implies, moves further toward investigations of the human, not only tribal or Native, cosmic condition. Self-asserting individualism is destructive of community and continuity, the poems suggest, and yet the "I" fills the poems. For their speakers, the communal world seems as difficult to belong to as the spiritual one.

The "affinities" of the opening poems are further probed in "Deer Dance" (69–70) as the speaker explores, through two deer dances and two ruminations, the ways "the bodies leave their mark" as "the unseen becomes seen" (9). The deer dance of the second stanza evokes the spiritual unseen through the mediated experience of Indigenous ceremonial apprehension. The dancers perform the unseen connections between material immediacy and the spiritual world of the ancestors. The speaker engages this translation by first using the verb "show" and then "became" (16, 18). The unremarked and yet profound shift from the symbolic to the transubstantial or transcendent is an imagined leap of faith, a conceptual construct slipped in. These two forms of apprehension, the symbolic and the transcendent, have considerably different ontologies or realities.

Hogan's poem includes the only description of a tribal ceremony within the three deer dance works considered here. Very few modern Native literary works do include formal, tribal ceremonies; more common are individualized, pan-Indian ones. The description in stanza 2 concludes with a transformative, one might say "transubstantial," moment as the deer dancer danced "until he was more than human, / until he, too, was deer" (24–25).

In the sixteenth-century Western world, Michel Foucault explains, "the plethora of signs, the fact that things resembled each other, simply proved the benevolence of God and separated the sign from the signifier by only a transparent veil" ("Nietzsche" 277). This is belief without modernist skepticism and interpretive doubt. Hogan evokes a similarly reassuring aboriginal transparency. Her speaker describes the active participants, "the men dressed in black / the human women," whose participation evokes as well as embodies their belief. However, the speaker as observer seems no more present that Harjo's. Are we as readers of her ceremonial sign convinced? Do we see ceremonies as embodiments of cosmic realities or are they "interpretations that try to justify themselves" (277)? The "as if" of the poem's final line suggests the latter while only gesturing to the former.

Rituals or ceremonies can work in two ways. Their work can be to communicate: to reassure participants and observers of their belief in an orderly, meaning-creating realm beyond their actions. This requires submission to authoritative tribal beliefs. Ceremonies are also bodily experiences of agency, creating belief through experience. The meaning of the communal deer dance of the second stanza slips between the two for the speaker. The anthropological tone, attention to detail, and construction of meaning leave her an ambiguous outsider to both belief and experience.

Jon P. Mitchell explains a shift in understanding within religious studies that is relevant here. In "From Ritual to Ritualization," he explains that interpretation of rituals has shifted from an integrative communicative process encoded with authoritative meanings to a performative one—that is, to ritualization in which participants actively embody beliefs that are more than propositions but rather are experiences. Within this experience, two interpretive operations take place. First, participants "do rather than have done to them." And that doing or ritualization then involves, maybe requires, a misrecognition in that it assumes transcendent continuity for what is a "situational" and "strategic" experience (381–82). This shift is part of the uneven, often uneasy, and variously experienced change in social imaginary and in people's relation to the cosmos that the three deer dance poems embody.

Turning away from the second stanza report of a performative bodily experience, participants as agents rather than passive recipients, stanza 3 reframes the ceremony as communicative gestures. It abstracts symbolic meaning by bringing up various stories, Native and non-Native, of humans turned into animals. In explaining that none of the animals wanted to return to their humanness, the speaker expresses her modern world-weariness. It seems more a Romantic gesture than a Native act of species solidarity. Her past subjective "I would do it, too" (31) keeps her out of the experiential process. The comfort of aboriginal communal believing has been lost, and the speaker's universalizing hermeneutic effort to round the speaker's human corners cannot re-create that comfort in cosmic certainty.

The final stanza concludes the poem with the speaker observing nature's deer dance, yet she experiences it from the same detached position that permeates the poem and creates its sense of estrangement. As in "Emergence," which begins with "I trust," this deer dance transformation rests on the "as if" of the last line. For Hogan's speaker, abstracting rather than participating in "equivalences" or "verbal equations," to use Evers and Molina's terms, leaves her spiritually unfulfilled. The deer's fur, she observes, is scarred by materiality and does not quite fit; this parallels and projects the speaker's own experience of the material and spiritual incommensurability. It is a quiet but devastating conclusion unless one has comfortably settled into the modern socioreligious imaginary. One might call this reassurance a gesture spirituality or an Indigenous religion of "perhaps" (see chapter 2).

In this final stanza, Hogan's speaker projects her own spiritual uneasiness onto the deer, who keep their distance. This uneasiness is at the heart of all three deer dance works discussed here, as their speakers long to live in more than the modern socioreligious imaginary by ritually renewing aboriginal experience. Yet they all question whether modern rituals can re-create this world, with its access to the spiritual realm. Rosalyn R. LaPier, in *Invisible Reality* (see chapter 1), registers a Blackfeet historical background and present context for this interpretive–experiential problematic. She reports that her grandparents "intimately" knew the invisible world (xxxiv). The Blackfeet believed that with the help of "supernatural allies," they were able to control nature to fulfill their needs (xxxvii). Their supernatural stories were told when the Blackfeet had control of their destiny (6). Even at a later time, one reported, "His understanding of and relationship with the supernatural provided him confidence and stability in an unstable changing world" (134). However, living more thoroughly within the modern social imaginary, Hogan's speaker does not experience this social and spiritual confidence.

It is not that the "old timers" did not differentiate between everyday and spiritual realities, LaPier explains. Theirs was not a unified but rather a porous cosmos, in which "the invisible dimension was the real world and . . . the visible dimension was a partial expression of this world." The "unseen" was "known." (24–25). Stories indicate that in the past, most Blackfeet were connected to a spiritual being, and it was "often kinship relationships" that structured their social lives. Although only experienced occasionally, this nevertheless "defined their existence" (28, 31, 25). And if they kept up these supernatural relationships, they would have a good long life of health and happiness (65).

More than any other modern Native literary text, Silko's *Ceremony* imagines this experience within the modern socioreligious imaginary. Yet as chapter 2 asserts, its ontological status is far from clear. Erdrich's *Love Medicine* and *Tracks,* in the early experiences of Fleur, depict a character living within intersecting social imaginaries. However, even she in the present resorts to a material trick rather than spiritual assistance as she resists the men cutting down tribal forests (*Tracks* 222–23; see also chapter 7). We see a similar contrast in imaginaries with the one-dimensional moralizing of Steven Penn's storytelling and the supernatural terror his father's stories evoke in *Grand Avenue* (164–68).

This ontological dilemma (also considered in the introduction) challenges Indigenous literary writers and scholars who work with a certain amount of hermeneutic suspicion. In part this involves reckoning with what Robert Dale Parker calls "the emerging obstacle course of expectations for 'Native American Literature'" that its writers must contend with (128). These include the expectation of spiritual innocence. More than the other two deer dance works and most Indigenous literary works that include cosmic engagements,

Glancy's play directly embodies a hermeneutics of suspicion. The Grandmother, as a fragilized transitional character between the aboriginal and modern social imaginaries, experiences spiritual absence as much as presence. And this haunting sense of absence has shifted and intensified for her granddaughter even as she strives to overcome it.

Like Harjo and Hogan's deer dance poems, Diane Glancy's play *The Woman Who Was a Red Deer Dressed for the Deer Dance* takes up the problematic of reading the signs of the spirits, but with a significant difference. The form and style of each writer informs her religious engagement. Harjo's poem troubles us, but it also dazzles us with its puzzling yet profound juxtapositions: everyday language mixed with memorable phrases, pop culture references and complex narrative layering. We are challenged to follow conceptual leaps that can distance us from the immediacy of her characters' pain. Harjo mediates the action with self-conscious poetic strategies even as her striking language awakens us to disturbing material conditions and hopeful spiritual possibilities. The spiritual world in Hogan's poem is confidently approached through the speaker's ability to imagine its meanings rather than through transcendent apprehensions of cosmic realities. The speakers of her "Affinity" poems work through thought problems about making the unseen seen, and they find themselves alienated, unable to create satisfactory meanings that can overcome the seeming incommensurability of the material and spiritual worlds. Yet longing itself seems to reassure the speakers. Hogan's poems take us on an internal and individualized although socially recognizable journey of spiritual possibilities.

In contrast, Glancy's play develops its immediacy and urgency by directly presenting the everyday language of the Girl and her Grandmother. Because their monologues and dialogues create a dramatic world unmediated by a narrator, they express their spiritual frustrations with a disturbing directness. The play, however, is not short on complexities, as the material–spiritual problematic seems to demand.[5] For one thing, the play's two characters have the same Cherokee heritage but experience it from different generational standpoints. Glancy also depicts the ways socioeconomic conditions shape her characters' lived religions. The play considers the personal consequences when the spirits fail to help sustain characters materially or to manifest themselves spiritually, something neither Harjo nor Hogan addresses. In doing this, the play explores the issue of spiritual fragility more insistently.

No visions or supernatural transformations have taken place by the end of the play. Instead, the two characters struggle with the uncertain and fleeting quality of spiritual apprehensions. Because of their experiences, they critique the spirits. It is in the nature of the cosmos, this play suggests, that humans do not get as much help as they need. It is a cosmic setup "so we'll struggle all our lives," the Grandmother explains (15). The lesson she teaches and struggles herself to learn is that a spiritually engaged life is not about making the unseen seen but rather about learning to live with unseeing while still believing. This is at the heart of the material–spiritual problematic within Indigenous religious life, Glancy's play teaches.

Both the Girl and her Grandmother face frustrations and disappointments. At one point the Grandmother explains, "The spirits push us out so we'll know what it's like to be without them." This seems a strict lesson, but the purpose is "so we'll struggle all our lives to get back in" (15). This making a spiritual virtue out of absence and longing is a strategy for belief. In the Grandmother's concluding monologue, both a prayer to the ancestors and a lament over her hard, poverty-driven life, she exclaims, "Damned spirits. Didn't always help out. Let us have it rough sometimes" (17). Who but Diane Glancy gives readers lines like that? The Grandmother, caught between an aboriginal and modern imaginary, even wonders if the ancestors' voices are actually her own imagination (9, 17). Uncertainty and abandonment mark the Grandmother's concluding lines although not unbelief (17). If she is not the reassuring Native elder we have come to expect, her enigmatic openness does offer spiritual help that her granddaughter in the end recognizes (18). Disappointment with the spirits does not create a crisis of faith for the Grandmother as it does for her granddaughter. The Grandmother in the past has seen Ahw'uste (13), the spirit deer of Cherokee stories, and believes it has wings, even if you can't see them (8). It is an odd, seemingly contradictory spiritual apprehension that engages the troubled yet unshaken relationship between past and present religious experience. Related to this and important to her form of believing, she has experienced being part of a community of believers even though she is now alone with her beliefs (12).

The Grandmother longs for the experiences Vine Deloria Jr. describes in *The World We Used to Live In*. The Girl needs something different. She lives in a world much less sustained by communal belief, as she only knows a community of two. She must struggle in her own way, and she too finds the results frustratingly meager. The meagerness she experiences is less material than is the Grandmother's more porous sense of the spiritual and material worlds. The Girl longs for inner experience of spiritual realities rather than their material interventions. Yet intensifying her spiritual frustration is the feeling of being trapped in a material world of low-wage jobs and self-centered lovers. The final section begins with her reporting on a series of job interviews after she has been fired from a soup kitchen. Although they fail to land her employment, the encounters prompt spiritual introspection and insight. She incongruently reports to one interviewer that she has the skill to make a red deer dress. It is a "dress of words," a phrase that echoes Momaday's title "Man Made of Words." She has experienced the "psychic dislocation," the "deep psychological wound" that the essay describes ("Man Made" 54, 57). As noted above, Momaday explains that wounds like the Girl has experienced can be healed only through "the imagination of meaning" (57). Surprisingly similar is the Grandmother's explanation, "We're carriers of our stories and histories," the tribe's imagined meanings. Yet the Girl responds, "We carry ourselves." The Grandmother has imagined her belief within a tribal context even if she is alone with it now. For the Girl, belief has become individualized; she herself must carry the burden of imagining belief.

Birgit Dawes explains the differences and similarities of these two characters' religious experiences as a shift in forms of spiritual apprehensions: "This play outlines the boundaries of identity as shifting: between traditional and modern ways of life, spiritual and material orientations, mythical and positivist modes of knowledge, and—as the title indicates—between ontological and performative claims to religion" (304, 303). The experiential consequence is a communicative disjuncture between the two characters. When asked in the opening section about deer as "spirit animals," Grandmother responds with "I don't know" three times and "I forget" once (5–7). In the next section her granddaughter expresses frustration with these responses yet cannot escape her sense that her Grandmother is tied to a world beyond the material: that she can transform herself into a deer and thus knows much more than she is telling. The Grandmother remains cryptic throughout the play. She refuses to communicate information that would fit into her granddaughter's preconceived ideas. Instead she tries to evoke a deeper, experiential understanding of the material–spiritual world in which she lives.

In defensively asking her Grandmother, "Who are you besides your stories?" the Girl suggests her uneasiness with her own limited integration of the remnants of communal belief. The Grandmother reveals the continuing qualities of her world by responding, "I don't know—no one ever asked" (14). The Girl's question does not make sense to the Grandmother because of the givenness of her communally constructed beliefs. Forced to more thoroughly engage the modern secular and individualistic socioreligious imaginary, the Girl experiences the spiritual world more tentatively and tangentially. As much as she has learned about "the next world" from her Grandmother, her glimpse into it is experientially different. The Grandmother is frustrated by partial spiritual abandonment. For the Girl, the illusiveness of the spiritual world is not fundamentally about the access to it but rather the nature of it. The problem is ontological. Gerald Visenor (Anishinaabe) calls this condition "the very ruins of representation and modernity." Setting up a celebratory contrast that only partly fits the Girl's experience, he states, "We are mythic by conversation, conversion and remembrance, and the pleasure is in the contradiction" (21). There seems little pleasure in the contradictions between the Girl and her Grandmother's spiritual experiences, yet there is pride in the Girl's realization that she must sew her own red deer dress and thus construct the spiritual world through her imagination. It is her leap of faith. This seems much like what both Momaday and the speaker of Harjo's "Deer Dancer" describe, but without their confidence that the leap will take her to the other world. Fragility rather than certainty marks her leap into language.

Glancy's two characters' spiritual failures and successes come together in the Girl's concluding monologue. Here she is able to leap across socio-religious imaginaries, carrying enough of her Grandmother's communally based cosmic apprehensions with her so that she can cover her individualized, existential nakedness with a dress made of words. Her monologue suggests a key religious dilemma. She explains that her Grandmother did not teach her how to create a deer dress. The Girl herself makes the dress her Grandmother could have given her "if only she knew how" (18). Often Native accounts depict wise elders finding the younger generation unwilling or unable to grasp the traditional lessons they want to teach. Yellow Calf and his nephew, the narrator of *Winter in the Blood*, are an example; Abel and his grandfather in *House Made of Dawn* are another. These are stories of declension about a younger generation drifting away from the true faith and toward worldliness. Glancy has created a different generational story. The Girl emphasizes the Grandmother's failure, yet the play as a whole embodies a more complex assessment. The Grandmother and the Girl speak different discourses that have only partial mutual intelligibility; the result is considerable mutual bafflement. The Grandmother's frustrating incomprehension and inability to help occur not because her granddaughter lacks spiritual seriousness but because the Grandmother herself lacks the necessary social insight needed to translate the cosmic language of the spirit deer Ahw'uste into a different social discourse. That is why the Girl must sew her own dress.

The two characters' tribally related, generationally distinct lived religions engage a problematic that other writers have also reckoned with, the difficulty for elders to translate their traditional knowledge across a divide between a passing aboriginal socioreligious imaginary and the modern one that engulfs the next generation. Greg Sarris in *Watermelon Nights* depicts this genera-tional shift with the miscommunications of Elba and her daughter Iris (see chapter 5). Richard Dauenhauer and Nora Marks Dauenhauer also address this generational shift in Tlingit society. This society had been structured by clan-based "ceremonial exchange . . . at the heart of traditional spirituality and folklife," they explain. However, this clan-based social structure was challenged as Tlingit people experienced "a fundamental change in concepts of personal identity and sociopolitical organization to ways that are more congruent with Euro-American patterns." Although traditional cultural symbols and markers continue, "their perception, function and patterns of use have changed." Dauenhauer and Dauenhauer recognize this resulting in a basic shift in Tlinget ways of making sense of and then socially organizing their world ("Evolving" 254). They explain that Tlingit cultural dance groups had been clan-based and integral to that aboriginal social structure. With the diminishment of clans, however, groups are now made up of members from various clans and even non-Natives. This concerns traditional elders, who fear that new cultural practices will improperly call on the spirits, with troubling consequences ("Introduction: Form and Function" 111–12). Chapter 6 considers how this socioreligious shift in imaginary impacts the generational spiritual experiences depicted in Robert Davis Hoffmann's poetry.

Glancy's play, as an investigation into this generational socioreligious divide, can be read as a contingent response to Momaday's universalized question, "What happens when I or anyone exerts the force of language upon the unknown?" ("Man Made" 55). Language, embodying worldviews, allows the two characters to imagine meaning for their lives. Their different languages or discourses prompt them to create different if related apprehensions of the spiritually unknown. Writing within the modern socioreligious imaginary that the Girl experiences, Momaday states, "We are concerned here not so much with an accurate representation of actuality, but with the realization of the imaginative experience" ("Man Made" 88). Although in a different register, this sounds much like Harjo's conclusion in "Deer Dancer" as well as Hogan's poetic–philosophic ruminations. Glancy's intergenerational spiritual exploration reckons with the ways this modern language differs from the one spoken by previous generations as communal givenness must be translated into the language of religious individualism. For her work and that of others, the shift is as much about the basis of authority as it is about the content of traditions that are translated.

At the end of the play, as the Girl takes over the job interviews by asserting her own imagined sense of the world, she actualizes for herself what she had wanted from her Grandmother. She now has become the one who sees the next world through a crevice (18) and, like her Grandmother, understands that a glimpse is all that is offered. For all their differences, this remains as a cosmic constant. The Girl now finds this enough, even though Ahw'uste never directly enters her world. She is able to "hear" the deer, she thinks, and create a dress made of imagination. The ontological uncertainties of this conceptual dressmaking, however, alert us to the inherent instability of her spiritual experience.[6] Her lived religion is created within the modern, not the aboriginal, socioreligious imaginary.

"Writing is the weapon we bear as we go into the new world we did not want. It reinvents locale. It reshapes loss. Words after all have light," Glancy asserts ("Naked Spot" 278). One can imagine Joy Harjo and Linda Hogan agreeing. The terms "reinvents" and "reshapes" call to mind the struggles the speaker of Robert Davis Hoffmann's "Reconstruction" experiences in creating a neotraditional dance staff or Edgar Bearchild's religious engagements in Ray Young Bear's *Black Eagle Child*. They also parallel Harjo's speaker as she re-creates the story that she only heard by bringing spiritual imagination to bear on the material world of a dingy Indian bar. Yet Glancy complicates the interpretive situation: "Language is creator as well as trickster that robs meaning," she states ("Naked Spot," 279). This is the generally unexplored and dark corollary to Thomas King's oft-quoted and celebrated statement "The truth about stories is that that's all we are" (2). Just as the Girl questions the efficacy of the Grandmother's connecting stories to experience (13), so Glancy questions the trustworthiness of language by describing it as a trickster.

Language is unreliable because it is never the thing itself; it is a sign that signifies spiritual realities rather than embodies them (see chapter 1). In "Dance Lessons with the Spirit World," a fragmented meditation from *Claiming Breath*, Glancy states, "The word does nothing but manifest our nothingness. In fact, speech itself is a separator" (99). She does not state whether this separation is a modern phenomenon or if it was also part of the aboriginal world. She does, however, explain that healing comes through reckoning with this gap that language embodies. She concludes her meditation with a baffling but provocative assertion: "Our life is a migration of tribal separations-from, until we face the Great Nothingness, the Great Coyote & say to him who we think we are" (102). This "who we think we are" is the Girl sewing her red deer dress, Harjo's speaker imagining cosmic meanings in a tough world, Hogan writing, "This is not a horse." It is Momaday addressing "the awful risk" of a "life in language" ("Man Made" 62). It is Neal McLeod's riffing on tradition. In these modern, Indigenous lived religions, spiritual presences can only be imagined in a leap of faith.

Glancy explains that "contemporary native poetry [and by implication drama as well] carries the loss of culture, the loss of a way of life, and the bare spots that annihilation and acculturation left." ("Naked Spot" 278). Again, we imagine the other two authors agreeing. In different ways, all of their characters have been rubbed raw by colonial experience. Along with exposing material conditions, Indigenous literature for Glancy also "carries the knowledge of *silence and shadow* outside or beyond the loss, circling back to the essence that does not die or transmute, which is survivance" ("Naked Spot" 278, emphasis added).[7] For the three deer dancing works, "silence and shadow" as a fundamental religious experience does not mean absence but rather hope that reckons with the unavailability of direct apprehensions of the more-than-material world. The "Great Nothingness," or more commonly the Great Mystery, must be imaginatively filled in with a leap of faith across the spiritual–material divide.

4 SIMON ORTIZ'S POETRY OF CRISIS ORDINARINESS

RELIGIOUS UNCERTAINTY DURING A ROSEBUD RESERVATION WINTER

The gloomy dark, a winter that has entered the spirit. I do not know. /
I have never known. / I may never know.... the galaxy shifts / ... / and
we will never quite know.

SIMON ORTIZ, *AFTER AND BEFORE
THE LIGHTNING*

How do Indigenous religious beliefs *feel* to a speaker struggling through a bleak Rosebud Reservation winter?[1] "Like sexuality, religion and spirituality also constitute intimate domains of feelings where 'traumatic events' are collectively processed and made meaningful, especially in colonial contexts," Joanna Brooks explains (25). Her concern with religious experience in a time of trauma is part of a shift within Native religious studies away from theology or abstract beliefs and "towards close analysis of lived practice" (Martin 8). This analytical approach, developed by Robert Orsi as "lived religion," emphasizes human agency by focusing on how humans use religious idioms available to them. In turn they are shaped by cultural structures of belief as they consciously and unconsciously create cosmic meanings within the material world. This approach offers a useful framework for considering Acoma Pueblo writer Simon Ortiz's poetry collection *After and Before the Lightning*.[2] The title is a Lakota phrase referring to the beginning and end of prairie winters (Patricia Smith 230–31). This poetic account expresses the experience of Native religious beliefs in a difficult context: a harsh Northern Plains winter, the speaker's distance from his Southwest home and traditions, the everyday trauma of continuing colonization, and modern secular culture that questions the possibility of even experiencing the more-than-material world.

The resulting structure of feeling the poems present is uncertainty as the speaker struggles to reconcile religious belief and experience. Reflecting on the life that falls between autumn and spring, Ortiz depicts religious liminality as the poems engage the two meanings of the term "apprehension": the act of conceptually grasping something but also the feeling of anxiety because of experiential uncertainty about the grasp. My argument is that religious apprehensions in the first sense never fully reassure the speaker's apprehension in the second. Despite the book's structure of promise of spring renewal, the speaker's experiences of religious misgivings during a Rosebud Reservation winter are not resolved. *After and Before the Lightning* is marked by a probing experiential investigation of this religious problematic as well as a challenge to generic expectations for a hopeful conclusion. What makes the book's journey distinctive is Ortiz's unflinching and unresolved exploration of difficulties in sustaining religious belief and the resulting disjuncture between belief and experience.

This religious uncertainty takes place within a specific historical context. In her essay "Thinking About Feeling Historical," Lauren Berlant uses the term "crisis ordinariness" to describe "traumas of the social that are lived through collectively" and that create "the heightened perceptiveness" of the historical conditions one is living through as a group (243, n. 5). Seldom is anything dramatic reported in *After and Before the Lightning*, only the day-to-day struggle to make sense of what people, and the speaker himself, are experiencing. The culturally and historically astute quality of Ortiz's writing creates the heightened perception of everyday religious experience that results from "the loss of the freedom to be unconscious about the internal limits to their sovereignty" (Berlant 231). That is, the speaker is forced into a questioning self-consciousness because the usual framework for apprehending experience can no longer be unconsciously invoked. The resulting necessity of finding new ways of apprehension gives impetus to this poetry of crisis ordinariness. Traditional spiritual assumptions are no longer givens in this uncertain world, even as the speaker strives to reclaim them. Berlant explains, "Amidst the rise and fall of quotidian intensities a situation arises that provokes the need to think and adjust, to slow things down and to gather things up, to find things out and to wonder and ponder. What's going on?" (231). This is the key question for Ortiz's book, its structure of feeling.

This essay's first main section sets forth the various contexts that shape the religious uncertainty the speaker experiences. Each of the sections that follow explores a section of the book. Rather than a pattern of struggle and resolution, the analysis finds themes and variations: efforts to connect quotidian experience to the cosmos, the harsh conditions of everyday life, the problem of making sense of these experiences and conditions, and, again, the struggle for finding larger meanings that offer hope in bleak circumstances. Each of this essay's expository sections finds the poems' speaker grasping and longing for answers, but in the end it is only "our eagerness [that] blooms" (126). The essay's argument about religious uncertainty concludes by contextualizing *After and Before the Lightning* with Ortiz's earlier works. *Fight Back* and *from Sand Creek* are politically engaged; the later book is more focused on religious searching. The shift is addressed by recognizing that *After and Before the Lightning* was not written during the heady 1970s and early 1980s but rather the more cautious 1990s and by considering the Rosebud Reservation within the context of global capitalism.

Charles Taylor in *A Secular Age* explains that secularization, in addition to its generalized meaning, also refers to the historical conditions that shape contemporary spiritual experiences. These include the shift from a society in which belief in God is a given to one in which belief is just an option. "Secularization in this sense is a matter of the whole context of understanding in which our moral, spiritual or religious experience and search takes place" (3). This is a relevant framework for understanding the religious struggles in Ortiz's account. Vine Deloria Jr. (Yankton/Standing Rock Sioux) addresses this problematic of religious experience in a secular world. In his posthumously published *The World We Used to Live In*, he explains that "even on the most traditional reservations, the erosion of the old ways is so profound that many people are willing to cast aside ceremonies that stood them in good stead for thousands of years and live in increasing and meaningless secularity." Deloria then sets forth a point central for my analysis: "The change of living conditions experienced by Indian people in the last century also has a great deal to do with the erosion of our spiritual powers" (xvii–xviii).

This relationship of religious experience to historical conditions is encompassed in Raymond Williams's term "structure of feeling" or "structure of experience" (132). By defining "feeling" as "meanings and values as they are actively lived and felt," he emphasizes that personal feelings, including religious feelings, are not exclusively private, even if they are experienced that way, but are formed within social structures. Individual experience is inevitably social. Williams emphasizes the dialectical or processural quality of both structures and feelings. The qualities of religious experience that Deloria reports and Ortiz explores are, within Williams's framework, neither static nor epiphenomenal but central processes that, for some, make up Indigenous identity or sense of being within particular historical moments.

Away from his Acoma Pueblo—with its dramatic sandstone cliffs and canyons, desert terrain and heat—Ortiz writes out of his temporary residence on the Rosebud Reservation during a winter that is bitter materially and spiritually. Ortiz writes experientially although not confessionally. Rather than a summing up of Ortiz's Native worldview or life story, this book is a reflection on a dark time in his life (personal conversation, March 30, 2012). And yet the feelings or experiences expressed in the book are socially and culturally structured. The experiential religious journey through a prairie winter has representational or community significance. The individual trauma involved is part of a communal crisis ordinariness.

The winter "was forever—or at least it felt like that," Ortiz reports as he distinguishes between "legend or story" and the "reality" of what he lived through (xiii). This is a surprising and significant distinction because it acknowledges the difficult challenge of bridging belief or traditional apprehensions. This, for example, includes reconciling "Mother Earth, She Cares" with the sentiments stated in this essay's epigraphs. The dates that order the book, from November 18 through March 21, keep the reader focused on day-to-day experience, "a reality that could not be denied" (xii). Yet the speaker struggles to find a larger meaning for that experience. The poems map the speaker's effort to construct an understanding of "where I was in the cosmos" (xiv).

Often enough, writers assert that from a Native perspective, the distinction between material and spiritual realms are misconceived. The Native cosmos is a unified whole that brings together earth and sky, the seen and the unseen, ancestors and present Native people (Dunn 191). Few have explored the problematic of the inaccessibility of the spiritual realm (see chapter 3). Ortiz offers longing rather than comfort in claims about the unity of these realms; the disjuncture his speaker experiences is too immediate and intense. In *After and Before the Lightning*, he sets aside the certainty of generalized statements to explore the lived experience of striving to apprehend this unity in a secularized, often alienating world. Religious uncertainty permeates this book. Its section titles and the seasonal structure do suggest a confident hope for renewal, and the preface ends with "that's my certainty" (xvi). However, the poems (including the prose poems) focus on the speaker's difficulty in reconciling belief and experience. He finds alienation as much as integration, restlessness rather than rootedness, and longing much more than certainty. Quite unlike most other literary accounts of Native spiritual journeys, this is a book about doubt. It does not end with the religiously reassuring conclusions found in classic Native works like *Winter in the Blood*, *House Made of Dawn*, or *Love Medicine*. (It is closer in spirit to D'Arcy McNickle's *The Surrounded*.) In these novels, hope finally transcends bleak conditions as protagonists find the beginnings of healing through their geographical and religious homecoming. In contrast, Ortiz's book comes to an end while still in the in between time, after and before illumination: "We wait, spirit, mind, blood, nerves, / for the image that will catch us again moments away" (95).

Ortiz takes the risk of wrestling with this experiential religious problematic of the disjuncture between belief and experience. In a later work, *Out There Somewhere*, Ortiz writes, "Risk has to be more than personal risk. It has to concern itself with ethical, moral, political, social, historical, spiritual, material issues and questions. Personal risk is the least at stake. Life is at stake" (10). This is the risk Ortiz has taken in *After and Before the Lightning*. The epistemological nature of this risky journey is suggested by some of the poems' titles: "Meaning," "Comprehending," "What We Come to Know," and "Rivers and Winter Knowing." However, the book's opening poem, "Lightning I," contrasts with the confidence of these titles, with the words and phrases "not eager," "tenuous," "can never be measured," "takes more," "cannot even bear the total shudder," and the concluding "assumed / only. It is not affirmed fact." Epistemological uncertainty pulls at the speaker striving to find cosmic meaning in harsh material conditions that strip away reassuring clichés. The companion poem, "Lightning II," guardedly offers, "We wait . . . / hoping for miracles we've heard about." However, this is not a book about miracles, dreams, or visions, as the concluding "Lightening" poems make clear. The speaker participates in no formal religious or cultural ceremonies. Lakota or Acoma elders' wisdom is not invoked. "Story, / . . . helps" (7), Ortiz writes, but few traditional ones are told. As noted, in the preface the author acknowledges the disjuncture between stories and experience. Rather, we observe the speaker struggling through the winter to apprehend spiritual–material wholeness, with the promise of spring unfulfilled.

Section 1, "The Landscape: Prairie, Time, and Galaxy," establishes the material and spiritual setting for the journey the book presents. Although the first poem begins with an affirming title, "Mother Earth, She Cares," what follows is "ceaseless, dry prairie wind" and a sense of human powerlessness in the face of nature's bleakness (3). The speaker tries to suture the disjuncture between the poem's title and its stanzas by urging himself to pray hard and by asserting that Mother Earth *does* care. Yet the apparent contradictions in the agency of both parties, praying/powerlessness and caring/bleak inhospitality, raise dark questions. In this section the speaker strives to discover the means by which he can experientially, relationally apprehend the nature of nature. As his experiences shift, so do his apprehensions.

In the poem "Meaning" (6–7), the speaker finds that "Nothing can measure distance here." Since nature transcends the grasp of science, he then tries out the idea that there is "no need for semantic sense" because language creates an equally false sense of comprehension and thus mastery. He instead imagines unmediated experience: "the meaning / of winter is this fact of nature—." Similarly he asserts that in spite of the harshness of winter, we humans are a part of nature: snow is "[l]ike a second skin" for the horses, and for humans as well. And yet as the speaker steps back from this rumination, he confronts again the hard reality of everyday experience. The prose poem that follows calls for action, not just meditation on being: "Pray hard then, pray hard and tell stories. The stars are not so far away" (7). As the spiritual realm of prayer connects to the social sphere of storytelling, new challenges arise in the speaker's project of apprehension. "Story, / . . . helps," the following poem states, but it tells of winter's harshness nearly killing a traumatized Korean War veteran (7–8). It takes toughness to live in these natural and social conditions. The next story, a prose poem, indicts the brutal coldness of fellow humans in the face of winter devastation as well as their colonial assumptions (8–9). The dream of an unmediated experience of nature has quickly become socially mediated, and nature itself is troubling.

The conceptual leaps and juxtaposition among this section's poems can be jarring. They are part of the urgent experiential struggle to apprehend nature. For example, in "Salvation," the speaker considers the idea of survival by means of "brutal winter work," but he rejects this material answer as he finds nature more brutal than his ranching neighbor's efforts to control it (9). In contrast, the following poem, "An Insistent Gentle Animal," depicts nature, even next door to a tractor dealership, as energy and motion, a "spirit-creature" that is both outside of us and "within" (9). It gently "brushes" away the walls that separate inner and outer nature, personal experience and cosmic grandeur, in a promise of wholeness. Then the depiction of a cold house needing a fire's warmth breaks into this hopeful apprehension. And yet this too is infused with cosmic meaning as the speaker finds the stove's warmth and aliveness through imaginative transformation (10–11). The speaker troubles this apprehension by recognizing human difference and distance from nature: He is indoors while the blue jays and pheasants are outside. They are "Hearts and Hearts," separated by glass and consciousness (11). Here again Ortiz takes on a difficult question few others have engaged in their writing: what to make of human consciousness and the demands that go with it. That is, what is the nature of reciprocity as the speaker and the birds peer at each other through the window? Does that glass imply fundamental human alienation from nature? Does it deny the dream of a whole and healing relationship with nature that the speaker has imagined? In the last stanza of "Hearts and Hearts," the speaker finally rejects either/or answers as he imagines, creates, or finds a mediated but no less authentic bond in the experience of winter: "Each of us is an adjustment / to the force that nature is."

Yet in the prose poem that follows, the freedom of the bluejays contrasts with the "slavery" imposed on humans by the modern world (12). To challenge this sense of alienation, the poet offers two hopefully titled poems, "Comprehending" (12–13) and "Destiny" (13–14). But he is awed by the human capacity to comprehend mortality, our "final margin," rather than the ability to transcend it cosmically. Human difference is what he apprehends. Our destiny is to consciously experience rather than escape or transcend the materiality of nature (14).

Further perceptual and conceptual explorations ensue before section 1 concludes with the speaker's assertion of the connectedness of humans in spite of the inevitable motion of life. As the poem "Coping" asserts, in the face of this constant change, we are both unknowing and unprepared (28). Whatever light we have hurts our eyes, the final prose poem states (29). We experience this pain as an awareness of our awareness: In our consciousness we lose our orientation to the cosmos. We cannot stop the motion of life, the speaker states: "[w]e can only return" to our belief in the reciprocities of nature. This is part of the human "adjustment / to the force nature."

This opening section offers a report on the religious experience of liminality: longing but not quite belonging. The speaker's exploratory mapping exposes the complexities, contradictions, multiplicities, and, finally, mysteries at the heart of what is often expressed simply and confidently: that humans can have a relationship of balance, respect, and reciprocity with nature. Longing to experience this oneness with the cosmos, the speaker finds or creates only moments of unity. The poems follow a pattern of asserting spiritual hope only to question it. And yet there is the "grace[]" of "a winter certitude" (5). Writing about *After and Before the Lightning*, David L. Moore identifies this as "a leap of faith" (235), a term borrowed from Christian existentialist theology.[3] Ortiz explains that the struggle to apprehend spiritual reality in the material world of our immediate experience is a human problem (personal conversation, March 30, 2010). His speaker's effort to make, and not just make up, this leap is fraught with anxiety. When cosmic dilemmas are faced as honestly as Ortiz does, troubling uncertainties must be confronted. The opening section sets forth the topography of the book's experiential journey with material and spiritual coordinates.

Section 2, "Common Trials: Every Day," shifts focus to more specifically engage the structure of feeling resulting from the everyday material conditions of reservation life. The date now is December 4; nights are long and cold. Hope is hard to come by; doubt permeates inner life. The opening poem, "Barren," states the basic facts: "This land is barren, poor. / The people just as poor" (33). The speaker then confronts what he calls "a foolish question" resulting from all that has been lost through military destruction, foreign diseases, and continuing colonization: "How . . . can? Can they . . . ? / the people get back . . . / their lives?" Numbed by everyday traumas, as the ellipses suggest, he responds first that "Answers falter" (33), just as they did for the cosmic questioning of the first section.

The poems that follow chart the natural, social, and religious difficulties of winter life. The prose poem linked to "Barren" opens with "bending and breaking sometimes, and then healing." However, before the sentence ends, the speaker has come back to the problem of doubt: "and we're not always sure" (33). The rest of this section depicts time spent in prison, running out of gas on icy roads, financial desperation, marital desperation, lack of firewood, the hardness of winter ranch work, the farm debt crisis with its rage and helplessness, and more. The speaker himself is not in danger of losing a farm or needing to scavenge for food. His struggle for survival is internal, as are the answers he offers, yet he sympathizes with others' material difficulties.

And yet the work of apprehension involves more. In a nighttime medi-tation the speaker muses, "The only way we know" that there is a world "beyond . . . the headlights" is because "[w]e would be false to ourselves if we did not believe that." If "the great prairie is unfathomable[,] . . . winter[] has entered the spirit [and] . . . [t]he future is secured without the construction of certainly," then the speaker must make an existential choice to believe. He does this not as a cosmic orphan but as an Indigenous person living in an alienated world and yet having some memory of tradition on which to build. One poetic meditation makes this point by alluding to a key modernist, secular poem: "Do not go gently, Dylan Thomas whispered loudly into the dark" (39). This would be us, the speaker implies, if we did not have belief, the leap of faith that he struggles to make. This is not the conclusion of the book but rather its underlying structure of feeling, something that North American colonization of Indian land and people has not destroyed, even if it has strained it to near breaking.

Thus the effort to rightly reconceive nature continues—the need to rec-ognize, for example, that it is not merely a production machine. We must remember that it belongs to the deer (35), is amazingly crafted (37), is unfath-omable (39), and has "Beauty Unmatched" that goes beyond the material (48). Nature is not just a hardship to be endured, and it is more than material. The second section concludes with this sentence: "The vast and limitless are within the necessary knowledge we have" (56); yet the preceding prose poem shows the speaker grasping for this cosmic knowledge. He responds to "an unusual light" by surmising, "Perhaps it was a signal from a galaxy beyond" (54–55). This vague, uncertain, seemingly self-constructed hope, which concludes section 2 on December 14, is the cosmic answer to the opening poem, "Barren," with its question of how to survive the material conditions of a poor people in a poor land. Most of the winter is still ahead. Answers still falter.

Section 3's title, "Buffalo Dawn Coming," suggests relief from a winter of doubt. One might imagine a Lakota band finding relief from winter's hunger as a medicine person's vision leads them through blinding snow to a small

herd, or White Buffalo Calf Woman, who brought the people their Sacred Calf
Pipe (See Looking Horse). Yet the speaker is baffled, right from the beginning.
Vine Deloria Jr.'s comment is apropos: "Even if the sacred medicine which
called the buffalo to the tribe still worked today, there are no buffalo" (*The
World* 42). Caught in this disjuncture and numbed by the everyday traumas
of the previous section, the speaker attempts to negotiate the social world by
avoiding commitment: "So we leave things up to chance," he states, "don't
really deal with anything." (59). Because traditional structures of belief have
come to seem inadequate for making sense of the communal experiences of
crisis ordinariness, the speaker does not know how to respond responsibly.

Two linked poems from the heart of winter elaborate the speaker's disori-
entation. Dated January 31 and February 1, both are about horses, vision, and
loss. The matter-of-fact title of the first, "Horses by a Fence," suggests a reassuring quotidian certainty (81), yet the speaker reaches for larger meanings.
The horses suggest spiritual aliveness and connectedness, a wild unmediated
state of nature. However, "[l]ightning in my eyes" lasts only a moment. The
revelatory moment is abruptly interrupted without obvious cause: "But for
that, / nothing is there." In the speaker's mind, the experience (the process
of constructing meaning out of events) has not just disappeared; it seems
to have never existed. The communal structures that provided for spiritual
seeing are no longer sustainable. And so the speaker is left "recalibrating
intuitions about the intensified present (Berlant 233)."[4] Usual, reassuring ways
of responding to events break down when crises make traditional ways of
apprehending seem inadequate. This is "the theft of the sacred," the "sacredness / necessary to acknowledge / for it all to be whole" (Momaday, *The Man*
76, 62). Thus the speaker, "[f]erocious with necessity" (62), struggles to align
traditional understandings with the reality of his experiences.

"Dawn Prayer for All," the linked poem that follows on the next morning,
again reaches for hope. However, the alienation it expresses runs even deeper
(81–82). The horses have moved beyond the speaker's sight, but something in
the heart remains. Looking out at the trees along the creek, he confidently
states, "beyond that is more." A line break allows us to ponder the promise,

but then the poem continues, "yet it is not within my ken." This benumbed statement that follows the promise is "part of trauma's affective archive: the resistance to vulnerability" (Cvetkovitch 25). The trauma here is both experiential and conceptual. The speaker does not exactly doubt the existence of a spiritual realm, but he resigns himself to its seeming inaccessibility to him. And yet beneath the numbness, a leap of faith is still possible because the speaker still holds to a fundamental communal apprehension: "the memory / ancient, not lonely or unreasonable" (82). This reassures, but it is not the cosmic certainty the speaker longs for.

These two poems are the heart of this hopefully titled section. They offer material signs of spiritual realities. These realities, however, are not unmediated experience of a unified cosmos. They require human interpretation. With communal structures weakened, meanings must be self-consciously constructed. The implications of this are significant. "Becoming Human" states,

> People are not born.
> They are made when they become
> Human beings within ritual,
> Tradition, purpose, responsibility.
> (64)

After and Before the Lightning depicts few overt rituals or traditions to help the speaker become human and navigate his immediate corner of the cosmos. In part, this is because he is in a foreign land with a different Native nation and people. However, the problem is not so much the newness of the place but rather that the newness makes it difficult for the speaker to find unconscious comfort in abstract beliefs. Instead he must confront the immediacy of his particular experiences. The speaker does share communal experiences and Indigenous understandings with Lakota locals, but he feels alone in constructing cosmic meanings. In the preface, Ortiz explains his use of the pronoun "we." It is not quite an escape from individualism but rather an assertion that we all face a similar cosmic context. The "we" is an extrapolation from the "I." Ortiz further explains that as he put together this "map of where I was in the cosmos," he felt doubt not just about the outcome but about the process (xiv–xv). He is mapping "[t]ime and place and memory" as a way of making meaning that includes both "distant ranch houses and ghost buffalo" (xv). This mapping stretches space–time as it engages material reality, human processing of that reality ("memory"), and Native, specifically Lakota, spiritual understanding ("ghost buffalo").

In this disorienting time of crisis ordinariness, the speaker continually comes up against the disjuncture in his mapping between belief and experience. Not surprisingly, this section concludes with questions rather than answers. The final poem, "When Is It Enough?," shows life stripped of material and spiritual comforts.

The gas goes off.
We're cold.
It costs too much.
We have to pay.
For everything.
We're cold.
It hurts.
We work every day.
The gas goes off.
We're cold.
What has to happen?
When it is enough . . .
will it happen.
(91)

The short declarative sentences offer no explanations. The questions elaborate on the opening of this section: "We don't know what to do sometimes. . . . We don't understand, they don't understand. So we leave things up to chance, to question and bafflement, hardly forgive ourselves. . . . It's a kind of security, the ambiguity" (59). The speaker has experienced "trauma as the rupture or penetration of the psyche's protective shield" (Cvetkovitch 41). As a result of this rupture to his traditional structure of belief, numbness becomes a means of coping.

As Ann Cvetkovitch explains, trauma is a moment when abstract social systems can be felt (43). Ortiz presents the trauma of "desperation, death, and loss of hope" in this book and assigns the cause as "oppressive colonialism" (xv). Here Ortiz's writing "transform[s] the abstract and pervasive power of capitalism into something that can be felt, and shock or trauma becomes the paradigmatic sensation of everyday life under capitalism" (Cvetkovitch 41)—concepts more fully explored in his earlier works *Fight Back* and *from Sand Creek*. This capitalist colonialism affects not only material but also religious life. It insidiously imposes modern individualistic, secularized culture through a kind of spiritual allotment act that undermines communal Indigenous spirituality and instigates the speaker's struggle to reorient his intuitions in a time of crisis ordinariness. In this we see "capitalism's ability to reshape the very structure of everyday experience" (Cvetkovitch 43). Capitalism is not brought up directly in this section, but its impact is evident: "the violent repeat of murder and suicide" is not just news "but more like prophecy. These are the acts of bewildered dreamers dismayed by the American Dream" (60), Ortiz writes in a poem titled "Redemption Slipping Away." Communal confidence for many, not only Native peoples, had dissolved during this farm crisis of the 1980s.

Section 3 is a meditation on living with doubt in this time of crisis. Much of it has a personal tone and lyrical outlook. "My imagination / is a safety net," the speaker claims (71).[5] Yet he finds "planets wondering like lost children" rather than a reassuring cosmos. Not surprisingly, then, his maps are inadequate for reaching his hoped-for destination (75). Poetry here is a kind of archaeology of the present, the speaker's depicting the fragments of a contemporary wasteland (66–67). This alienation is both historically particular and commonly human. In spite of the section's hopeful title, its poems are disturbing on many levels.

Section 4, with its sacred number, suggests wholeness, and its title, "Near and Evident Signs of Spring," returns us to the prospect of hope. As with the previous sections, however, the promise leads to meager fulfillment. The section's concluding date, the spring equinox, does signal that winter will soon be transformed. The book's seasonal structure calls for a certain kind of ending, and the final poem in this section, "Our Eagerness Blooms," seems to offer it (126–27). However, it is longing, "eagerness," that blooms. The speaker recognizes the human hope for a change in inner weather, a thawing of winter's bleakness. The poem's last stanza vacillates from certainty to doubt and back again as it shifts from "sure sign" to "We trust" to "It's not" to "may disappoint" and then, somehow, to the final assertion, "and we bloom."

This last phrase, the book's most positive statement, concludes what is for me its least convincing section. There are parts that stir us—for example, Coyote spotted crossing Highway 18 and the explanation that "[i]t is real and actual, the truth of Existence within the strangely beautiful vastness of the prairie" (103). This, however, contrasts with the flatness of the section's opening prose poem. The use of the pronoun "he" rather than "we" or "I" makes the reader step back and observe an internal drama that reads more like a fable than experience. In it, Mother Earth is not particularly fascinating for the benumbed character. Absent rabbits prompt questions about life's continuities, but in response the character realizes that "he hadn't really looked much for them" (95). Rather than experiential knowledge, the story offers an abstraction: "They were there somewhere in the winter all around." The character appropriates old intuitions rather than revivifies them. Following this prose report are the final episodes of an Acoma story that begins in section 1. There the episodes are part of an actual storytelling incident. Here the episodes are not integrated, and the language feels stilted (95–96). Later references to South Africa, the Philippines, Heidegger, and Buber also seem out of place (97, 99). Many poems, although not all, feel prosaic compared to the lively everydayness of earlier ones. All this suggests that the poet is struggling to shift the tenor of the book to fulfill the requirements of its seasonal structure and the need for a reassuring ending.

More convincing is the experiential statement "Right now, simply, the tough dry husk of living / shelters us, keeps us intact" (98). Reflecting back with striking honesty and vulnerability, the speaker suggests, "Perhaps the power I expected to come forth from being in a difficult winter has not shown itself. . . . And I am only a man joined with winter turning toward spring" (115). Mother Earth is changing, the speaker knows, but the change is not religiously experiential for him. This is the demoralizing structure of feeling the speaker experiences as he strives to create a map to help him find that place where "we bloom."

The two "Lightning" poems that conclude the book present the speaker again riding into a storm. In "Lightning III," he states, "We have no choice / . . . / no assurance of safety at all." With only "exhortations and tiny prayers," he journeys through the storm of Existence with all its contingencies. "Lightning IV" concludes *After and Before Lightning* with these lines: "How completely we feel the tremoring / and shuddering pulse of the land now / as we welcome the rain-heart-lightning / into our trembling yearning selves." This is a book about longing. It is the tension between experience and desire that gives the book its power and poignancy. There is no doubt that "[o]ur eagerness blooms," but only in that quite guarded sense does the concluding "we bloom" seem convincing (126–27).

Simon Ortiz's *After and Before the Lightning* (1994) was published more than a decade after *from Sand Creek* (1981). Once again, Ortiz was living near the site of a massacre of Native peoples, teaching on the Rosebud Reservation. Sinte Gleska University was named for the Brulé Lakota chief (also called Spotted Tail) who, like Cheyenne chief Mo'ôhtavetoo'o (Black Kettle), camped along Sand Creek, had seen the devastating power of the US Army and believed that further war would only bring disaster (Ostler 34). One hundred and twenty miles west of the college—no farther than the Fort Lyon veteran's hospital is from the Sand Creek National Historic Site—the 1890 Wounded Knee Massacre had ended the so-called Indian Wars; three centuries of conquest seemed complete. Yet the massacre began a struggle "against—in some ways—an even more destructive and demoralizing enemy" (James Wilson 285). Two decades before Ortiz's South Dakota winter, at the village of Wounded Knee, hundreds of Lakotas and their supporters came under a seventy-one-day siege by the FBI and federal marshals. As Mary Crow Dog explains, "We stood on the hill where the fate of the old Sioux Nation, Sitting Bull's and Crazy Horse's nation, had been decided, and where we, ourselves, came face to face with our fate" (qtd. in James Wilson 403).

In *After and Before the Lightning*, Ortiz makes no reference to either Wounded Knee event. Given his powerful engagement in *from Sand Creek* with history's connections to present Native conditions, this absence is noteworthy. Reviewing Ortiz's work in 2004, Moore observes that his focus is "increasingly in the inner territories of the mind and heart as well" (35). Although Ortiz acknowledges the "despair, death, and loss" as a result of "oppressive colonialism" (xv), his focus is experiential as he shifts mainly between personal and cosmic concerns. Reflecting back on the book, one wonders who is the "we" the speaker speaks for. Acknowledging in the preface the ambiguity of reference, Ortiz states that he uses both the "subjective personal" and the "objective universal" in a process that meshes individual experience with "memory, speculation, fantasy, and intellectual thought" (xiv). As noted in the discussion of section 3, the communal "we" is less evident.

Does the reservation as a communal or social body bloom in the end? One would not ask this question of every Native poet, but Ortiz has given us *Fight Back* and *from Sand Creek*. He has spoken out in his poetry more than most about social injustice. However, *After and Before the Lightning* was not written in the 1970s or its aftermath, times that shaped his earlier two books. The heady language of confrontation and revolutionary hope perhaps did not seem fitting to Ortiz in the 1990s. This was a time of important but limited steps. In 1990 Congress passed the Native American Graves Protection and Repatriation Act as well as a bill providing compensation for some Native uranium miners who suffered often devastating health consequences, the struggle *Fight Back* engages. Throughout the American hemisphere, Native peoples reflected back on the five hundred–year aftermath of Columbus's arrival. Although the Mashantucket Pequots opened the Foxwood Casino in 1992, the economic outlook for South Dakota reservations remained bleak. The only industrial jobs on these reservations were at a shirt factory in Pine Ridge. The meat-packing plant that had opened a few years earlier was closed down in 1989 (Pickering 17).

Kathleen Ann Pickering's *Lakota Culture, World Economy* usefully contextualizes *After and Before the Lightning*. Her analysis of conditions on the Rosebud and Pine Ridge Reservations begins with a sixty-year-old man who could be the speaker of Ortiz's "When Is It Enough?" (91): "We had some bad winds come through here a few weeks back and just took part of the roof right off." Three adults and five children live in the too-small house, a corner of its roof patched with black plastic garbage bags and duct tape. The inside is "sparsely furnished with a hodgepodge of well-worn chairs." This man's work history, given in Lakota, includes a string of low-paying jobs. "I've tried hard to get something steady," he explains, but in the end he only has his Social Security check (xi). Yet he is not alone. "Family is the primary social unit for interaction on the reservation," a fact that is clear in Pickering's description of his world. In spite of severe disruptions to Lakota society, "of all the aspects identified as fundamental to Lakota culture, the importance of relatives and the obligations of each individual to his or her relatives is still the most pervasive" (6). The person Pickering describes has maintained a Lakota sense of identity, as evidenced by the language he uses, yet his life condition will not make sense if we do not see it connected to the larger picture that Pickering analyzes: "Each day, the Lakotas think and do things that make them distinctively Lakota, yet every day they also experience the far-flung effects of a global economic system" (xii).

After and Before the Lightning potentially works the same way, yet we must, in an act of co-creation, bring to our reading the necessary historical understandings for showing how the pain and poverty referenced in the book are enmeshed in national—both Sicangu Lakota Oyate (or Rosebud Sioux) and US—as well as global socioeconomic structures. By doing this we can co-create the book as still part of the "revolution going on [that] is very spiritual and its manifestation is economic, political, and social" (Ortiz, *from* 54). To do that we must recognize that "like many indigenous communities on the periphery of the world economy, the Lakotas confront such challenges as high unemployment, pressure to migrate for wage work, limited access to credit, and high rates of alcoholism" (Pickering xii). These circumstances, and the spiritual crisis they foster, make clear the need for the revolution Ortiz has called for. The revolution that *After and Before the Lightning* implicitly evokes through desire needs to engage the problematic of spiritual apprehension as it recognizes that religious revitalization does not take place in isolation. It must confront the disorienting, traumatizing conditions of a continuing colonial capitalism that insidiously impoverishes, both materially and spiritually, Indigenous places like the Rosebud Reservation.

5 TRAUMA RELIGIONS

GREG SARRIS'S *GRAND AVENUE* AND
WATERMELON NIGHTS

"Trauma is the suffering that does not go away. The study of trauma is the study of what remains" (Rambo, *Spirit* 15). Religions in times of trauma, or trauma religions, are part of the remnant, assertions of cosmic meaning in times of bafflement as violence and cultural dislocations cause traditional religions to lose at least some of their resonance. Trauma religions emerge from the theft of the sacred and the theft of so much more. They are shaped not only by particular traumatic material conditions but also from the structures of feeling and believing within the modern social imaginary. The changing nature yet continuing prevalence of Indigenous trauma religions is here represented in two novels by Greg Sarris, *Watermelon Nights* and *Grand Avenue*. Their reckoning with what has been stolen and what remains, the conclusion explains, has implications for Indigenous religious and cultural revitalization.

Writing about what remains within contemporary northern Ontario Cree and Anishinaabe communities, Ronald Niezen addresses the insidious destructiveness of colonialism for all aspects of Native life, including religious life. He explains, "Events that struck me as sad, compelling, and extraordinary were described by witnesses almost casually, as though they were normal occurrences. Deaths from suicide and reckless behavior . . . paralyzed the communities in mute grief" (xiv). He sees this response to trauma as part of a spiritual crisis, the "radical instability in the human relationship with the spiritual world" (xiv–xv, 4). Like all religions, trauma religions are not merely sets of propositions believed but are experiential apprehensions, individually and communally structured. Community practices and beliefs still matter, yet religions within the modern social imaginary have become increasingly individualized.

For almost all interpreters of Native experiences, understandings are mediated by texts: literature, histories, films, works of art, and other forms. In her work on intergenerational trauma, Gabriele Schwab explains that literature, and art in general, allows readers to "tap into experiences that were never fully known but have nonetheless left their traces" (43). Literary writers working as cultural pathologists (and of course much more: conservators, celebrants, aesthetic interventionists) can translate the "psychic life of violent histories" into narratives that make these histories apprehensible (Schwab 26, 3). Rather than providing an "accurate reconstruction" of historical traumas, their writing offers a "committed exchange with it" (Dominick DaCapra, qtd. in Schwab 52). These stories enact the ways characters "pass on the ineradicable legacies of violent histories through generations" and thus help readers grasp the ways that traumas unsettle, even interrupt, a range of relationships (1–2).[1] They enact the ways traumas challenge assumed ways of making sense of the cosmos as well as more immediately experienced realities. Complicating this process of reckoning with the past is the present reality of continuing physical, psychological, and cultural violence (Schwab 30).

This chapter, an explication of Sarris's fictional "committed exchange," recognizes the ways his two novels reckon with many of the challenges faced by Native revitalization projects in a time of trauma. This is one thing that makes his novels so valuable. In them various forms of trauma shape the possibilities for and nature of personal and tribal change. His characters, within a multigenerational context, suffer both historical and ongoing traumas. Yet they experience not only "the theft of the sacred" but also "what remains." These remnants allow for new but also traditionally oriented religious beliefs and practices within the context of their trauma. Literary reckonings of

trauma can open up new forms of apprehension useful for creating revitalization strategies relevant to contemporary conditions. Sarris's writing has
particular significance since his novels emerge from his experience leading
the Coast Miwok and Southern Pomo people's successful effort to gain
federal recognition as the Federated Indians of Graton Rancheria and then
his experiences as tribal chairman (*GA* ix).[2]

Following Schwab's pragmatic approach of using "theories as heuristic
tools," this chapter engages trauma theories to more fully grasp the ways historical and contemporary traumas shape Native lived religions (Schwab 33).
"Religions offer and substantiate accounts of the world that render the chaos
and pain of experience meaningful and tolerable," Robert Orsi explains
(*Between* 73). *Watermelon Nights* and *Grand Avenue* present fictional ethnographies of how the Waterplace Pomo people, a representation of the
tribe Sarris chairs, have individually and collectively constructed religious
meanings for their traumas. Their efforts to create meaningful trauma religions increasingly and more thoroughly take place within the modern social
imaginary (see chapter 1). Characters' religious experiences thus have become
less certain, less communal, more individualized, and more interior than those
created within the Pomo aboriginal or premodern social imaginary. For one
thing, tribal religious authority increasingly diminishes in Sarris's accounts.
Nevertheless, his novels narratively argue that forms of traditional healing
adapted to present conditions are possible, both for individuals and their tribes.

The types of traumas that shape characters' lived religions change over time
as their context shifts from crisis to crisis ordinariness (see chapter 4). The
tribe's historical traumas have been caused by settler demands for land, cheap
labor, wealth, and power. These resulted in the people losing their homeland
and other resources for self-sustainability. Members were economically
reduced to doing agricultural labor on land that had been their tribe's. Later,
in a nearby city, they depend on precarious low-wage work or government
checks. Isolated in "South Park, a convenient place for the town to stash its
skeletons," most characters have little hope for change (*WN* 334). This present reality with its everyday traumas impacts how characters imagine their
relationships with their families, their community, their common past, and

the cosmos. In addition, contemporary traumas are part of a "cumulative trauma." "The intersections of violent histories," Schwab explains, "generate a structure of condensed experience in which the encounter with new violent histories operates via the recall of earlier histories—not only cognitively but affectively and experientially as well" (30). This is part of a disturbing continuity between past and present.

In reckoning with cumulative trauma, this chapter first explains key concepts as tools for understanding characters' changing trauma experiences. It then turns to Sarris's two novels to analyze the cultural traumas and resulting trauma religions for three sets of characters.[3] Big Sarah and Elba, faced with fundamental cultural disruptions, create resistance narratives that work to make sense of the tribe's historical traumas. Big Sarah is the spiritual leader and Elba an ambivalent follower of the traditionally adapted, revivalistic Bole Maru religion. Iris and Faye from the next generation respond to intergenerational and cumulative traumas in ways that reflect their somewhat similar middle-class standing but different relationships to the tribe. Finally, Nellie, spanning the novel's history, embraces a trauma religion that offers a model of hope for contemporary Indigenous revitalization. This analysis considers the effective and ineffective ways these characters adapt traditional Pomo religion to changing traumas and socioreligious imaginaries. *Grand Avenue* and *Watermelon Nights* offer models for better apprehending how Indigenous lived religions created in times of trauma work in the world.

"Trauma has become a major signifier of our age," states Didier Fassin and Richard Rechtman. "It has become our way of connecting present pain to a violent history" (qtd. in Million 3). It is also a key signifier in writings about Native America (Gagné 355).[4] In connecting Native pasts to the present, Dian Million (Athabascan) defines trauma narratives dialectically as interpretations about what happened and, importantly, what still needs to happen (3, see also Alexander, *Trauma* 4). Yet, as much contemporary Indigenous literature attests, the individual and collective wounds of trauma make a new life difficult to envision (Rambo, "Spirit" 13). Toni Morrison has noted, "Certain kinds of trauma visited on peoples are so deep, so stupefyingly cruel, that . . . art alone can translate such trauma and turn sorrow into meaning" (qtd. in Kurtz 15). Indigenous literature, Sarris's novels in particular, does that work as it imaginatively confronts the particular traumas of continuing colonialism and reckons with characters and their communities' processes of making these experiences meaningful in negative and positive ways.

Using the James Bay Cree First Nation as an example, Marie-Anik Gagné argues that "colonialism is the seed of trauma because it leads to dependency, then to cultural genocide, racism, and alcoholism. These in turn lead to sexual abuse, family violence, child abuse, and accidental deaths/suicides" (358). Her historical and sociological approach, including the use of dependency theory, works to make sense of the traumas Indigenous people continue to experience. It models the importance of considering the economic and political motivations behind colonial dominance. Gagné charts a path that begins with the Hudson Bay Company establishing it first post to acquire valuable natural resources. The company did this by turning First Nations homelands into colonial peripheries, with the various forms of violence that entailed. Sarris similarly recognizes these colonial motivations as his characters use both accommodation and resistance to sustain themselves in related exploitative circumstances. The historical trajectory of cumulative trauma his novels track leads to the everyday, sometimes violent traumas suffered on Grand Avenue.

"Novels," Laurie Vickroy explains, "effectively chart the progress of characters' original and subsequent traumas, the associations that create fears, and the fixed ideas that help individuals cope" (8). As a social genre, novels can reveal the historical and structural conditions that provoke crises that require the individual and collective work of cosmic sense making. Yet at the core of trauma is "the enigma of suffering" (Rambo, *Spirit* 18). Maurice Stevens explains that as individuals and groups try to make sense of past events as traumas, this desire for meaning is unfulfilled because the events "produce enigmatic signifiers, indelible and indecipherable" (26). If religious trauma narratives are about making cosmic meaning, they also must teach how to live with these "indelible and indecipherable" earthly enigmas. These narratives are theodicies that leave traces of longing that require a leap of faith to fulfill. (On the concept of theodicy, see chapter 2.)

Cultural traumas occur when a group suffers atrocities that are inexplicable within its traditional narratives. Again, "enigma" is a key term, and bafflement is a common emotional response. As traditional narratives can no longer adequately address new material and spiritual realities, the group struggles to create new religious narratives that not only make sense of their present traumatic experiences but also provide dignity and identity within them. Trauma religions develop in response to events that disrupt long-standing, culturally agreed upon apprehensions of the cosmos. Aboriginal religions, because of their pre-contact hegemonic status, were not structured to resist but to conserve. Because they fostered acceptance of the imagined cosmic order, they had no quarrel with life (Taylor, *Dilemmas* 223). After colonial encroachment and then domination, Native religions were forced to take on the fundamentally new task of resistance.

Understanding how Indigenous peoples have taken on this task requires an understanding of the nature of trauma itself. The common understanding is that trauma lies in events. This explanation is useful but needs to be supplemented. Trauma studies tends to explain traumas as occurring when individuals and communities are unable to emotionally and cognitively assimilate disturbing events within their structures of understanding. However, atrocities can be assimilated if a community can make sense of them. It is the bafflement of inexplicable events that causes trauma. Literature has the potential to create for readers the experience of constructing meaning in the face of unprecedented events and conditions; it thereby can speak what can seem unspeakable (Alexander, "Toward" 2, 7, 13). It can reveal individual and communal processes of coming to terms, in productive and unproductive ways, with specific events and ongoing structures that baffle. The truth of trauma narratives as "cultural script[s]" lies not in their descriptive accuracy but in their "symbolic power" (4). Trauma stories are not clinical reports but, within a religious context, experiential maps that make sense and thus potentially provide healing.

Jeffrey Alexander emphasizes the communal quality of trauma as "members of a collectivity feel they have been subjected to a horrendous event that leaves indelible marks upon their group consciousness, marking their memories forever and changing their future identity in fundamental and irrevocable ways" ("Toward" 1). People's social and spiritual relations, including relations to the land and all beings, suffer a "soul wound" (Duran, Duran, and Yellow Horse Brave Heart 64). A character in Linda Hogan's *Solar Storm* similarly explains that the old people talked about "soul loss, an old sickness" (98). Trauma religions are both recognitions of new forms of wounding as well as newly adapted efforts at healing. Stevens explains that constructing trauma narratives gives their creators agency as they narratively counteract "the creeping loss of predictability as one's own compass for reality slips into unreality" (24). This is just the structure of feeling followers of the Bole Maru experience in the face of unpredictable losses from capitalist economic and cultural encroachments. Stories help create order out of the chaos of seemingly incomprehensible events. In this sense, "trauma does not describe, trauma makes" (Stevens 20). This is a key understanding. By constructing collective trauma narratives, groups and individuals take responsibility for the materially caused spiritual disjunctures they experience. One way they do this is by learning to share each other's suffering as they come to terms with their own losses. This becomes increasingly challenging for the Waterplace Pomo as social cohesion erodes under the pressure of changing socioeconomic conditions and imaginaries. One response is the Christian trauma religion practiced by Old Uncle and others at the YMCA Bible studies. From Anna's perspective, they take not only responsibility but also blame for what has happened to them. Anna's Christianity is an individualistic repudiation of this stance even as she is vulnerable to the submissive comfort of followers sharing their common suffering (41–42).

Many of Sarris's characters consciously or unconsciously struggle to imagine and embody religious meanings for the losses that have led to their present material and spiritual condition. Some adopt forms of Christianity as their means of making sense (see chapter 7 for further analysis). Others, the focus here, create trauma religions that adapt Pomo traditions to the new forms of suffering. Many characters seem oblivious to the process of meaning making and yet are inevitably enmeshed in its social operations. Others make conscious efforts to construct conceptual understandings out of their historical and present socioeconomic situations. The meanings characters make, their lived religions as theodicies, are explanations and justifications for their cosmic and local situations. Their religions shift generationally as the traumas that shape them accumulate and the tribe's material conditions deteriorate.

Big Sarah's 1930s religious reimagining, practiced in the tribe's roundhouse, takes place at an intense moment of cultural trauma. Sarris's account makes clear the importance of trauma religion as resistance while also reckoning with the damage trauma can cause immediately as well as for next generations.

Big Sarah fictionally engages Richard Taylor's intertribal, "revivalistic" Bole Maru, or dream dance. This religious adaptation, founded in the late 1800s, was related to the Ghost Dance movement. By the early 1870s, massacres, disease, and slave raiding had reduced Pomo tribes far below their pre-contact populations. Because they had also lost 99 percent of their traditional homeland, they were forced to shift from a subsistence to a wage economy as low-paid agricultural workers (Sarris, *Keeping* 65–66; Dyck, afterword to *GA* 207). In response, Taylor adapted traditional practices to create an apocalyptic trauma religion that envisioned a world emptied of white people. Although his prophecy was not fulfilled, the Bole Maru religion continued. Leaders, mainly women called Dreamers, cultivated a "an impassioned Indian nationalism," with adapted Christian or Victorian moral strictures against drinking, gambling, and adultery. These prohibitions helped sustain tribes and families "after white people had taken everything but their souls to Dream" (*Keeping* 65–67; Sarris, *Mabel McKay* 8). Sarris argues that the Bole Maru "laid the foundation for a fierce Indian resistance" that still continues (*Keeping* 67).[5]

In the middle section of *Watermelon Nights*, the Bole Maru is led by Big Sarah as she resists religious and cultural fracturing. Through her and the community's story, we see the strengths and limitations of a fundamentalist response to life-shattering events. Other roundhouses were shutting down as many turned to the comforts of the white world, including Catholicism and Pentecostalism (*WN* 151). In this time of economic desperation and cultural dislocation, traditional beliefs could no longer be taken for granted. In response, Big Sarah translates traditional Pomo beliefs into strict cultural boundaries that can hold the tribe together by strategically using guilt and fear as means of social control (168, 180). Through them she emphasizes personal responsibility to tribal rules as a bulwark against disintegration. Blurring tribal boundaries by mixing with whites was dangerous for survival. The demands of Big Sarah's preaching become increasingly stringent; Moki, the embodiment of a supernatural being, comes to judge the loyalty of her followers. He would bring back the old beliefs and ceremonies that evoked an aboriginal social imaginary to challenge the modern one. "He's testing," Big Sarah pronounced. Yet the terror he brings to the roundhouse is a mark of desperation rather than strength (152–54).

The cultural boundaries that Big Sarah imposes are negotiated by some of the novel's characters as, for example, sexual prohibitions run up against the economic necessity of sex work. While the community is still a powerful force field shaping characters' lives, Big Sarah must contend with the individualizing impulse. Characters now choose to fully participate in the roundhouse, attend meetings but reject Big Sarah's strictures, or absent themselves altogether. Elba as a child, for example, is torn between submission and the appealing example of the beautiful, daring, and defiant Chum (155–56). Old Uncle embodies another option. He has moved away from the group, seems to embody an alternative sexuality, and practices an individualized form of the Bole Maru that is nevertheless not condemned by Big Sarah (191, 202, 204). Religious beliefs and practices have become negotiations rather than cultural givens.

The Bole Maru as a trauma religion brings the group together in shared suffering and resistance, but it is not innocent. Stevens, writing out of his clinical and academic research experiences, cautions that a trauma narrative "does not always help, and it never only 'helps'" (20). Characters in *Watermelon*

Nights are healed but also damaged by Big Sarah's trauma religion. Elba's experiences with Zelda corroborate Stevens's point.

Both Elba and Zelda experience the deep personal consequences of Big Sarah's trauma religion. In one of the most heartbreaking incidents in the novel, Elba's baby Charlie dies in a house fire that is no accident. Elba's pregnant friend Zelda's hunger for a fulfilling life narrative to counter her bleak circumstances leads her to sex work and naive dreams of romantic relationships with privileged white men. When that strategy fails, she rejoins the roundhouse as the only alternative for belonging that she can imagine. She then construes Big Sarah's fundamentalist teachings to mean that she should sacrifice Elba's baby to save her own. This trauma narrative emerges from a desperate and dispossessed people. For Zelda it is a way of making sense of chaotic experiences that continually defy her dreams. She places a lantern on Charlie's blanket and starts the deadly house fire (*WN* 274). Immersed in a traumatized culture, Zelda lashes out with further traumatic violence. With this incident Sarris registers the potential destructiveness of revitalization movements. They are not innocent. We also see the ways "trauma disrupts relationality" for Zelda (Schwab 2) as she desperately and abruptly shifts her loyalty from one group to the next in a search for belonging. Further, Sarris uses this incident to depict healing within disastrous situations.

When Elba learns that the fire was not an accident, she wants to break Zelda's neck. Instead, she (retrospectively) says, "I forgive you." With this Elba comes to her great religious realization: Zelda as "a pitiful representation of all of us, Zelda just being more obvious about the fear and related wretchedness in each of our lives. . . . Wasn't we all burning some baby or other so that we'd be safe in that home?" (*WN* 286). With this stunning recognition of the consequences of historical trauma, Elba understands that individual actions and their meanings are embedded in structures, colonial as well as tribal.

Zelda, Big Sarah, and Elba all engage in constructing culturally resonant religious trauma narratives. Zelda's embodies the perversity of her condition, the hegemonic lure of the dominant society, and the oppositional reassurance of the roundhouse. Big Sarah's narrative is also found lacking. In this crisis she can only offer further repression—"*Mensi*, Hush!"—in response to the moral crisis that challenges her authority (265). It is Elba, living on the tribe's margins, who can construct a narrative of forgiveness by seeing in this crisis "our common misery" (286). Tribal members are all shot through with the misery of historical and cumulative traumas caused by a virulent form of California colonialism that undermines their traditional understanding of the cosmos. The failure of the tribe to create a collective response similar to Elba's personal one indicates the fragility and limitation of the tribe's narrative abilities at this point.

Elba experiences the rapidly engulfing shift from collective religions to ones "of personal commitment and devotion" (Taylor, *Dilemmas* 215). The givenness of the Bole Maru socioreligious orientation, while under threat, had been powerful enough to draw even characters like Chum, pregnant with a baby conceived with a white man, to the communal comfort of the roundhouse despite their religious skepticism. Elba, when living with the tribe, is also one whose marginal position lessens their commitment to a community-sustained, transcendent religious belief. Elba's choice is part of the increasingly prevalent experience of religious individualization. This emerging individualization, Charles Taylor explains, significantly contributed to "the disenchantment of the world of spirits and higher forces in which our ancestors lived" (*Dilemmas* 215).

Elba's shifting lived religion links the conclusion of her narrative to the opening of her daughter Iris's story, the third section of the novel. Between the two, Elba gives birth to Iris, and together they move from the country to the city. This geographical and cultural change has a significant impact on Elba's religious sensibility and practice. Iris reports that, away from the tribal community, Elba's city religion has become more traditional than her rural lived religion. Urban Elba "prays in the old language," approvingly recounts Old Uncle's miracles, experiences supernatural apprehensions, and makes "an offering to the trees" (291–93).[6] More or less alone in the city, Elba develops an individualized religious revitalization that she wants her daughter to join. With this parental project, Sarris addresses how the psychic damage of one's youth can go unresolved and thus create irreconcilable barriers between generations. Elba can construct a trauma narrative that offers a degree of healing for herself, but it does not resonate with her daughter. This is because individuals not uncommonly repress their violent histories, with the result that the trauma is transmitted to the next generation. "It is through the unconscious transmission of disavowed familial dynamics that one generation affects another generation's unconscious" (Schwab 46, 36). Elba can extend empathy to Zelda and the tribe, but with her daughter she has "a defensive traumatic silence" (Schwab 13). This is part of the intergenerational trauma Iris experiences.

"We got bad blood in us," Sixto explains in Tommy Orange's *There There*. "Some of these wounds get passed down" (182). This sums up Iris's experience of being raised by Elba. Much has been written about the intergenerational trauma of the Jewish Holocaust.[7] Recent research demonstrates similar intergenerational consequences of historical trauma for Native adolescents. Sociologist Les B. Whitbeck and fellow researchers investigated the long-term effects on those who grow up with a history "filled with defeat, relocation, isolation, removal of children, and broken promises," even though they did not directly experience the original triggering events.[8] Past traumas affect the next generations' beliefs about life opportunities, family dynamics, sense of safety, and all aspects of development. These researchers hypothesize that historical loss, what they call "the reminders of ethnic cleansing," may contribute to Native young people's "depression and demoralization" as well as early use of drugs and alcohol. However, they also note that Native historical contexts provide "protective factors" that include "traditional spirituality, traditional practices, and cultural identity" ("Depressed" 35). Sarris's novels include many adolescent characters defeated by inherited historical loss, particularly Justine in *Grand Avenue* and Felix in *Watermelon Nights*. Yet Justine's sister Alice, for example, embodies the protective qualities that traditional yet adapted Pomo religious practices can provide.

Bonnie Duran (Opelousas/Coushatta), Eduardo Duran, and Maria Yellow Horse Brave Heart (Hunkpapa/Oglala Lakota) emphasize the significance of intergenerationally cumulative trauma, with its "inevitable disintegration of the rationality of everyday Native American life" and the "bankrupt[ing of] many meaning structures" (62). Facing threatened structures of meaning, individuals must come to terms with their religious uncertainties (Harper and Pargament 353; see also Whitbeck et al., "Conceptualizing" 124). As other chapters in *After the Theft of the Sacred* also suggest, these uncertainties have become a central aspect of the Indigenous lived religion depicted in its literature. Shaping intergenerational religious uncertainties are shifting socioreligious imaginaries. Traditional imaginaries sustain certainty through a consensus strong enough to make alternatives unthinkable. Because the modern socioreligious imaginary reckons with a cosmos that has come to seem increasingly disenchanted, traditional Native structures of belief in times of trauma come to be experienced as increasingly fragile.

Elba and her generation apprehend their world to a considerable degree as still enchanted with supernatural beings and forces in a porously boundaried cosmos. This apprehension helps make Big Sarah's apocalyptic warnings convincing. Yet even for that generation, many Pomo characters find that material conditions make this belief difficult to sustain. For example, Chum is an unsubmissive skeptic who still longs to belong socially. Characters like her indicate that believing and belonging are becoming individually negotiated rather than communally chosen. This undermines the givenness necessary to sustain the life-encompassing practices of the roundhouse. As characters become more enmeshed in the dominant society, particularly as they move to the city, they face greater difficulties accepting a Pomo communal belief in the self as open to spirits and ancestors.

The enigmatic suffering of historically instigated communal as well as individual traumas continues cumulatively as intergenerational trauma: One generation's traumas impact later characters even though they did not directly experience the triggering events.[9] Intergenerational traumas are shaped by fractured family life, a key site of transmission. An elder character in *Solar Storm* explains this intergenerational wounding: "There are things living in humans that bruise the sweet-bodied human fruit, she said, things like what poisoned the hungry tribe of my ancestors. Rage and fear. Mortal wounding. She knew the wound and how it was passed on, the infinite nature of the wounding" (94). Iris and Faye live with the traumatic legacy of

Elba and Zelda's generation. Intergenerational trauma that intersects with a changing social imaginary gives their religious life a more fragile, less socially structured quality than that their mothers experienced, despite their mothers' more profound immediate traumas. "Spiritual practice, like culture itself, is both reproduced and transformed with every transmission, shaped inevitably by social and political contexts," explains Philip J. Deloria (Foreword xii). Iris and Faye offer case studies of this.

With them, Sarris develops fictional life stories for understanding the devastating consequences of trauma transmitted intergenerationally and experienced within shifting socioreligious and cultural contexts. A religiously indifferent community is now experiencing crisis ordinariness rather than major traumatic events. In varying degrees and permutations, this situation also arises in, for example, *Ceremony*, Louise Erdrich's reservation novels, Hogan's *Power*, and Irvin Morris's *From the Glittering World*. However, these are all rural novels. Sarris brings the problematic to the city, where most Native people now live. Both Iris and Faye are urban characters, part of the first Waterplace Pomo generation to experience the world unmediated by formal religious and cultural structures. The roundhouse has been closed; there is no spiritual leader.

Elba's generation comes to adulthood in a rural tribal community continually threatened but still clinging together. When Elba and the others move to the city and eventually develop new forms of tribal community, religious disenchantment becomes significant for many and dominant for their children. In the city, Big Sarah is not even mentioned. Religious sense making, to the extent that it continues, has become individualized. No communal ceremonies are described. These conditions shape Elba's evolving Pomo religious experience and parenting practices (292). Rather than spiritual well-being, Elba passes on to Iris a frustrating sense of religious and cultural alienation. Out of the traumas Elba has experienced, she has gained religious resilience, but at a significant psychological cost. It is a cost that her daughter continues to pay.[10] As narrator of the third section of *Watermelon Nights*, Iris registers an intergenerational wounding even though her material circumstances are much less severe than her mother's. At the end of her section, Iris's healing is limited; she gains only an individualized, disenchanted trauma religion bereft of specific traditional content. Yet it is meaningfully Pomo to her, and it depends, even though limited, on tribal connections.

In Iris's telling, differences in socioreligious imaginary permeate her conflicted mother–daughter relationship and create an intergenerational disjuncture. Iris is religiously haunted. Her narrative begins by focusing on Elba's lived religion as Other to her own. Iris defines her mother's religion as "Indian, old school," part of the family's "unusual ways." These include Old Uncle's accounts of supernatural occurrences: "His story makes that of the man who walked on water look tame" (291–92). In her mocking tone we hear both the bitterness and longing of her exclusion. Iris has a frustrating absence of tribal and family history because her mother cannot speak of her own trauma. The resulting alienation is part of Iris's intergenerational trauma. Her and Elba's generational difference is most irreconcilably experienced in their response to the rape at the now-abandoned roundhouse. Reflecting on the drunken gang rape, Iris constructs its meaning: "the girl, left like a discarded animal by the center pole, a mean and reckless offering to whatever God once dwelled there" (397–98). Linking material and religious conditions, Iris finds only horror and bafflement. Her "whatever God" comment marks a religious alienation that Elba never experienced. Andrea Smith helps clarify Iris's failed meaning making by explaining that rape is "designed not only to destroy peoples, but to destroy their sense of being a people" (33). Iris's cosmically enigmatic, intergenerational trauma surely shapes her negative attitude toward being Indian (292).

Elba's inability to pass on a usable narrative about her past is made clear in Iris's unawareness of the tribal history that led to closing the roundhouse (366). Thus Iris's reaction to the rape is fundamentally different from Elba's, even as it is shaped by her mother's past sexual traumas. When Elba confronts her daughter for not intervening at the roundhouse, she is at her most angry and least understanding (400–03). Finding at the roundhouse the same violence that she herself had experienced at about the same age, Elba desperately holds to a communal morality of looking out for each other and condemns her daughter for failing to uphold it. Iris, however, has never felt part of the Waterplace Pomo community, and Elba has never taught her how to belong. Elba is blind to the ways she herself is implicated in the traumatic intergenerational damage her daughter suffers. Elba seems so certain in her judgment grounded in a moral righteousness similar to Big Sarah's. Her stance is a desperate act of self-protection; its intensity marks Elba's repression of past traumas. She cannot recognize Iris's naivete because she at Iris's age had already had the trauma of losing her mother and then being forced to have babies as a purchased bride or concubine, a different form of rape. Another rape then followed for Elba in an ambiguously commercial situation. The roundhouse rape thus resonates with Elba's past trauma, but Iris has no way of knowing this.

"The pain from violent histories includes shame and guilt, which, in turn, mobilize powerful defense mechanisms" (Schwab 29). These inhibit Elba's parenting. She cannot help her daughter internalize Pomo communal ways of apprehending the cosmos; nor can she reflect on the causes of Iris's not understanding. There is so much in Elba's hardscrabble experience: the historical trauma of various dislocations, the continuing personal traumas of her youth and young adulthood, the everyday crisis ordinariness of the colonized world's degradations, and her ambiguous place in the roundhouse religion. These all have wounded her soul and kept her from the emotional maturity and empathy she needs as a mother.

Iris lives with the consequences of Elba's soul wound, her personally protective refusal to discuss those wounds with her daughter. Iris is ignorant of not just tribal history but also Elba's trauma and her resulting lived religion. Elba is an eager storyteller for a sympathetic outsider like Patrick but does not tell her stories to Iris, the character who needs them the most (378). Schwab notes that the second generation must "patch a history together they have never lived by using whatever props they can find." They become "avid readers of silences and memory traces" (19). Yet Iris learns little. Schwab concludes, "It is through the unconscious transmission of disavowed familial dynamics that one generation affects another generation's unconscious" (18, 36, 32). This unconscious transmission infects Iris's struggle to overcome her religious and cultural disenchantment, which is embodied in her view that most Indians are "bankrupt" and in her inability to imagine any religious possibilities for herself (292, 425).

Iris's continuing conflict with her mother and their misunderstandings are shaped by their assumptions about the way the cosmos works. Part of Iris's intergenerational loss is her inability to apprehend a spiritually charged reality. Iris as an adult reflects on her mother's spiritual ability: "the world opens itself up to my mother; stars in the night sky roll back like stones that have been guarding secret passageways." Iris imagines Elba looking down on the world as if it were a chess board, and the spirits tell her "how to win her game" (292). One senses again a mocking tone that marks Iris's resentment at being excluded from the realm of the spirits. Elba has ineptly tried to teach Iris to see more than the material order, but she lacks the necessary empathy and sympathy to do this. As a result both are emotionally and religiously wounded.

Intergenerational trauma continues into the following generation, even though Iris's son Johnny has a much closer relationship with Elba than Iris ever had. Johnny's experience is no more enchanted than is Iris's, and he finds no more spiritual guidance from Elba than Iris did. The conditions of belief within the Pomo post-roundhouse world are fundamentally secular, in Charles Taylor's sense of the term (see chapter 1). The problem is not just Iris's; her experience is emblematic. Part of the tribe's intergenerational wounding is the loss of the conditions of belief necessary to communally sustain a traditional socioreligious imaginary. Nevertheless, Sarris concludes this three-generational account with Iris able to imagine, if not yet practice, a new sense of community that will potentially overcome a key part of her intergenerationally created alienation (425). In the end Iris is sitting in her suburban garden, an echo of Elba sitting in hers on Grand Avenue. Yet their experiences are fundamentally different. Iris's story and the novel's conclusion are marked by the absence of religious experience; religious recovery from intergenerational trauma is not available to Iris. The difficulty is not just disbelief for Iris but the irrelevance of a belief in the more-than-material realm. Iris finds spirituality without spirit. She cannot (yet) see beyond. Rather than experiencing "Heaven, the far stars" as she sits in her garden, she has only "a wish" for a new earthly community (*WN* 425). At least for now, she "find[s] the mortal world enough."

The cultural emersion into the modern social imaginary and the concomitant shift to an individualized lived religion impacts Iris and Faye's intergeneration trauma quite differently even as they both have a sense of social and religious alienation. Iris, baffled by Elba's way of apprehending the cosmos, separates herself culturally and geographically from the Waterplace Pomo community. For her, an enchanted Pomo religion seems irrecoverable. In contrast, supernatural powers are a key part of Faye's fragile religious conceptualization. Unlike Iris, who is most immediately impacted by her relationship with Elba, Faye's religious insecurity is shaped most immediately by her tenuous middle-class position within a community belonging mainly to the underclass.[11] Faye creates her Bole Maru–related trauma religion out of a desperate need for personal, social, and spiritual efficacy. Yet this contrasts with the efficacy Big Sarah strove for a generation earlier. Faye's story, told in *Grand Avenue*'s "The Magic Pony," confronts the problematic of reconstructing healthy religious traditions that can meet needs within a modern fractured Native urban enclave. "Urban religions," Orsi explains, "have offered occasions for new possibilities of selfhood to be crafted, discovered, assayed, and represented" ("Introduction" 56). This is what Faye attempts.

Even as she challenges the common spiritual disenchantment by creating an individualized yet traditionally oriented lived religion, she is in the end unable to sustain her improvised belief and selfhood. Faye's fragile middle-class sense of personal agency shapes the inventive nature of her lived religion. Sharing Big Sarah's spiritual desperation, Faye constructs a modern Bole Maru–related Pomo fundamentalism as rigid and passionate as Sarah's 1930s roundhouse preaching.[12] Faye individually reimagines Pomo traditions as a cloak of protection when hostile socioeconomic and cultural circumstances become overwhelming. The consequence for her, however, is further social alienation. Jasmine speaks for the Grand Avenue community when she tells Faye's daughter Ruby, "Your mother's crazy. . . . She's a freak and so are you" (8). Faye's cosmically oriented religious beliefs do not fit in the tribe's mainly secular socioreligious imaginary. Because they threaten the tolerable, seemingly naturalized status quo, she must be disciplined. Her personally improvised religion is undermined as the community, together with governmental authorities (social workers, the juvenile detention system, and so on), disciplines her spiritual and material practices.[13] Almost all of Faye's generation (except for the fundamentalist Christians) have no place for either communal religious ceremonies or supernatural experiences. Only traces of the traditional Pomo religious imaginary remain. Supernatural forces have no place in tribal meetings (Nellie's opening prayer not withstanding), Steven Penn's storytelling, or Stella and her sisters' dream interpretations (55–61, 164–66, 149–50, 160).

Poisoning, the casting of a spell to make someone sick, had been a Pomo form of social control and cohesion since precolonial times. Traditionally, Pomo beliefs like this had provided people with "cultural unity and spiritual strength" that was necessary for individual growth (Brown and Andrews 46). Faye's use of poisoning is quite different; she uses it individualistically to explain the disorienting and disillusioning world she lives in. It is a desperate response to fracturing intergenerational trauma inherited from her mother, Zelda, and her generation. Poisoning, rather than exploitative social structures, is her explanation for tribal failings.[14] Living within a generational and geographical shift from Big Sarah, Faye can imagine only a religion decoupled from politics, an opiate to ease rather than a means to confront the pain of powerlessness. The religious emptiness of most other characters makes clear that their disenchantment is no better an alternative. Sarris leaves readers with a difficult dilemma. He recognizes the fragmentation of Pomo beliefs caused by the historical and continuing colonization. The Bole Maru was an act of recovery as Richard Taylor, in the 1870s, translated traditional beliefs to meet the community's needs at that time. In the present, however, traditional beliefs have become "a free-for-all about the self," Sarris explains (phone interview, November 29, 2006).

Faye's individualized religious commitment contrasts with Iris's concluding desire for social integration. Nevertheless, both have crafted their sense of self-in-the-world within the realities of intergenerational trauma. That Faye seems a strange character while Iris is easily recognizable speaks to their culturally secularized tribal context.

Klavdia Smola's *Reinventing Tradition*, analyzing Jewish literature set after the Holocaust, emphasizes the "postmemory" generation's culturally distinctive experiences of "performativity and autoreflection" (3, 4). Both responses are part of the religious unraveling Sarris notes. Faye's trauma religion is performative, a desperate set of rituals traditional- seeming enough to offer her some reassurance and sense of control in a personal world that is falling apart. It is Nellie, with the wisdom of an elder, who has the settled quality necessary to reflect back historically and forward into the historical present and future. Through her Sarris imaginatively assesses the Pomo past and future.

Grand Avenue opens with a story revealing the limits of individualized trauma religions. Faye's Bole Maru–oriented lived religion proves inadequate for personal protection or social healing. The novel, however, concludes with Nellie's story of guarded social hope in a time of crisis ordinariness. An important character in both of Sarris's novels, Nellie tells a story of religious rejection and belonging. The context includes the trauma of a lost rancheria and the fracturing of the Pomo community before it regroups on Grand Avenue. Nellie is an anomaly there and within contemporary Indigenous literature. Given the common praise of wise elders guiding the next generation, fewer of them show up in this literature than one might expect. Sarris's fiction itself reflects this; most other elder characters are more important for their Social Security checks than for their wisdom (*GA* 14, 114).

Both Faye and Nellie improvise their Pomo religion in the city. With many Indigenous leaders calling for a return to traditional land and place-based religions, city religions can seem suspect, even as a large majority of Native people now live away from reservations. First Nation Toronto participants in Bonita Lawrence's ethnography often experience a similar disjuncture (see particularly her chapter "Maintaining an Urban Native Community").

Alasdair MacIntyre's social explanation of this situation is applicable to Sarris's Waterplace Pomo characters: "When the working class were gathered from the countryside into the industrial cities, they were finally torn from a form of community in which it could be intelligibly and credibly claimed that the norms which govern social life had universal and cosmic significance, and were God-given." This is the world of the aboriginal or premodern social imaginary. Supernatural religion was a life-encompassing given. However, as forms of rural work and thus social organization changed, and then as individuals and groups migrated to the city, community norms shifted, as they were now seen as engaging only "partial and partisan human interests" and so lost their universal or "cosmic significance" (qtd. in Orsi, introduction 42). This is the condition of Sarris's characters. Characters like Faye and Nellie still believe in spiritual realities, but as a choice rather than a given; they have an adapted belief. As Lawrence finds, Sarris illustrates, and Orsi observes more generally, "It is often precisely the disjunctures between environment and religious idiom that occasions crises, cultural creativity, and religious innovation" (Orsi, introduction 42). Nellie and Faye's urban trauma religions typify all three.[15]

William James's broad heuristic of sick and healthy religions within the modern social imaginary offers a framework for differentiating the two characters' urban translations of traditional Pomo beliefs and practices (*Writings* vi–ix). This evaluative framework also helps clarify how Sarris works through dilemmas for Native religious revitalization in his novels, offering positive and negative lessons. He depicts the individual factors and social conditions that lead to the successes and failures of fictionalized Pomo trauma religions. Faye's religion is sick in the sense that it offers only moral condemnation, even if this does give its creator a desperately needed although only temporary sense of control over her world. It offers no strategy for healing; it can only explain and critique. Her trauma religion's moralistic center apprehends the signs of the spirits without regard for their social context. While this is reassuring for Faye herself, its individualized authority carries no weight in the community. In contrast, Nellie has improvised a healthier trauma religion that nurtures community through cultural, including religious, continuity.

The causes of this difference are multiple. Nellie has a less traumatic childhood, learns early to resist although not reject Big Sarah's authority, has success in love along with failure, and has a more secure and religiously related and thus more integrated income with her healing and basketmaking. Nevertheless, Frankie calls Nellie "a witch, a poisoner." Although the latter description does confer a certain kind of community power (4, 60), Nellie is still wounded by the community's mixed response: As a healer, she is desperately called upon by some but found threatening and self-serving by others.

Unlike Faye's trauma religion, Nellie's healing practices are not self-sanctioned. She received her healing basket years before from Old Uncle as he was doctoring her. Others then prayed for her as she was gaining spiritual power (67). The aunt and her husband who raised Nellie supported her new life as healer. And a "chorus" of other healers support her if needed as she begins her healing practice (69). In the present she is called on by tribal leadership to open meetings with a prayer and is respected at least by other elders for the authenticity of her healing songs (WN 56–57). Hers is an ambiguous religious leadership, yet it is still effective. She has self-doubts but also Pomo centeredness. Nellie's cosmic vision includes the permeable boundary between material and spiritual worlds; her traditional healing ceremonies engage this reality (GA 195–97).

Nellie's conceptual grasp of the world and the cosmos is not rigidly traditional but rather embodies the improvisational practice Neal McLeod calls for: community oriented and grounded in tribal traditions while attuned to the new social imaginary in which Pomo beliefs must be nourished (see the introduction). For example, her basketmaking is a commercial endeavor with social prestige outside of the Pomo community, yet she makes considerable effort to use traditional materials and methods. Like Faye, Nellie believes in the supernatural power of spirits, songs, and poisoning. Living in a secularized society and community, they nevertheless find the world traditionally enchanted.

Although they both believe that poisoning is corroding their community, their understanding of it is fundamentally different and marks the key contrast in their approach to religious revitalization. While Faye's understanding is centered moralistically on individual behavior, Nellie grasps the spiritual and social nature of community problems: "Poison is the handmaid of hate. It works where we are weak. It plays on the sourness in our hearts," she states. Later Nellie explains the pervasiveness of the problem within the community: "The thing is, poison hasn't gone anywhere. It's everywhere so people can't see, and what they can't see they don't believe" (85, 89). She translates a traditional rural religion into urban beliefs and practices that reckon with the effects of poverty, lack of job opportunities, loneliness because of social fragmentation, alienation from land and nature, and the community's pervasive materialist assumptions. Nellie has the perceptiveness to make sense of these social dangers, including the resulting internalized oppression with its psychic and communal fragility and silences. Her diagnosis fits with the research findings of Whitbeck on adolescent trauma. Through Nellie, Sarris offers an explanation of the internalized oppression he asserts is a root cause of individual and tribal dysfunction (*Keeping* 119–20). Seemingly speaking for the author, Nellie painfully concludes, "My grandchildren . . . are angry, full of self-loathing. They don't like who they are. Their hearts are clogged. Their eyes don't see. Most kids are that way, and at such a young age" (*GA* 197). While deeply troubled by the religious disenchantment and social alienation she sees in the Grand Avenue community, Nellie nevertheless finds spiritual hope for herself and for at least some of the younger generations, Alice in particular.

With Nellie, Sarris has constructed his most positive character and one of the most humane, admirable, spiritually attuned, and approachable figures in contemporary Indigenous literature. Nellie offers a model for how to live in a modern world and within a porous cosmos. She helps readers better see how traditional beliefs and practices can be adapted to contemporary situations not amenable to them. It is not insignificant that Sarris in *Grand Avenue* gives Nellie as narrator the final chapter.[16] She looks at tribal realities with clear vision, but this does not sicken her soul as it does Faye's. She can still believe in miracles, not for herself but for her tribe (203). This is her trauma religion and revitalization strategy for contemporary times.

Sarris's ethnographically attuned accounts reckon with the ways intergenerational trauma can intersect with the shifting social and religious imaginaries that impact Native efforts for revitalization. His novels engage the challenge of translating beliefs sustained by traditional rural cultures into new urban contexts as forms of trauma change. The credibility and relevance of these newly adapted beliefs, however, are far from assured, and their uses can be various.

Sarris sums up his two novels as "chronicles of survival, how a people survive for better and for worse. They light the dark places so we can all—all of us, Indian and non-Indian—see where we have been, where we are, and where we might go" ("Conversation" 9). *Watermelon Nights* and *Grand Avenue* engage religion in times of trauma. They astutely reckon with how characters' efforts at cosmic and worldly meaning making work to "render the chaos and pain of experience meaningful and tolerable" (Orsi, *Between* 73). Reading these novels as trauma narratives that enact characters' lived religions can remind us of the pervasive spiritual and material damage to Indigenous peoples from past and ongoing US, Canadian, and global imperialism. The religious damage registers profoundly yet differently for the five characters considered here. Their lived religions create fictional case studies for different ways of surviving in a hostile world. Their examples can do positive work in the world. Jeffery Alexander explains: "By allowing members of wider publics to participate in the pain of others, cultural traumas broaden the realm of social understanding and sympathy, and they provide powerful avenues for new formations of social incorporation" ("Toward" 24). In different ways each character's story illuminates the challenges many Native people face in sustaining such social but also religious, cultural, and political incorporation. These stories do more than inform; they bear witness. They can also help heal. Schwab references Dominick LaCapra in stating that "trauma causes disturbances in the symbolic order" but that literature can help repair the damage (58). Sarris's "chronicles of survival" as revitalization projects are part of this repair work. As author, tribal leader, and participant in the Bole Maru (*Keeping* 70–71), Sarris offers fictional ethnographies of Pomo trauma religions that are spiritual yet material, healing yet not innocent, and unevenly efficacious both personally and tribally. His characters confront challenging, changing material conditions as they struggle to create cosmic meanings that offer hope in contemporary times.

Yet more is needed to confront the intergenerational cultural trauma pervasive in Indian Country, Sarris's novels argue. The history contained in them suggests the political dimension of intergenerational cultural trauma. Gagné's research and practice with the James Bay Cree First Nations led her to emphasize the sociological nature of the "vicious cycle of continuous exposure to traumatic events."[17] She argues that colonialism creates traumas that cannot be healed without diminishing Indigenous dependency: "A change in government policies is required" (358, 366–68). This work is the responsibility of more than Indigenous individuals and nations. We are all implicated stakeholders, particularly those of us with significant social and economic capital and thus power over the historically generated policies that create the continuing injustices to which Native trauma religions bear witness.

6 CONFRONTING THE DARKNESS, CONSTRUCTING A TLINGIT NEOTRADITIONALISM

ROBERT DAVIS HOFFMANN'S *RAVEN'S ECHO*

"And so you tell stories," states the epigraph for Robert Davis Hoffmann's poetry collection *Raven's Echo*. Through the stories his poems tell, Hoffmann, a self-described "neotraditionalist artist/storyteller" ("Robert H. Davis" 48),[1] develops an experiential reconstruction strategy for after the theft of the sacred. This chapter contextualizes and analyzes the shifting discourses and imaginaries that constitute Hoffmann's key concerns: spiritual darkness and the trickiness of Raven; the disjunctures of past and present; the Alaska Native Claims Settlement Act and the burden of history; place, land, and subsistence living; and the socioeconomics of village culture groups. Struggling to create a useful model of neotraditional reconstruction within the modern social imaginary, Hoffmann depicts a Tlingit revitalization that confronts the contemporary cosmos of Raven, with its conflicted, always changing material and spiritual realities.

The "and so" in the quote from Simon Ortiz raises questions about the purpose of stories. Hoffmann's stories express what now does not, maybe never did, go without saying. Working within the modern social imaginary (see chapter 1), in his stories of the cosmos Hoffmann confronts spiritual darkness as no other Native writer has done. That is the work of Book 1 of

Raven's Echo. In Book 2, the poems more directly focus on material conditions that impact the spiritual experiences of Tlingit people in Southwest Alaska, their traditional homeland.[2] Both books consider the changing apprehensions of identity and place. The cosmic engagement of Book 1 provides the basis for the reconstruction work of Book 2, which takes place within capitalist settler colonialism.

For Hoffmann, hope rests in Tlingit neotraditional revitalization. Neotraditionalism should be distinguished from Eric Hobsbawm's concept of "the invention of tradition." Invented traditions, he asserts, are "often quite recent" symbolic practices used to "inculcate certain values and norms of behaviour" by implying that they are continuations of past traditions (1). Writing about African colonialism and resistance, in "Neo-Traditionalism and the Limits of Invention" Thomas Spear rejects Hobsbawm's conceptual construction. Instead Spear argues that "older traditions were continually reinterpreted, customs were endlessly debated. . . . All were dynamic historical processes that reconstituted the heritage of the past to meet the needs of the present" (26). This dialectical understanding accords with Hoffmann's explanations. Rather than assuming the dominance of colonial and neocolonial forces, as "the invention of tradition" does, neotraditionalism recognizes tradition as "more flexible and less subject to outside control than scholars have thought" (Spear 26). Yet Kirk Dombrowski, focused on Tlingit villages of Southwest Alaska, notes that "the invention of tradition" concept has been useful in showing "how contemporary identities have emerged within, and not simply against, modernity" (210, n. 2; see also 65). This too is a dialectical perspective. Dennis Galvan, writing within the postcolonial situation in Africa, emphasizes the resistance potential of neotraditionalism, "a complex process, not just a mixing of old and new." Part of its complexity is its use of "popular memories of 'traditional' institutions and culture" (*State* 29). These socially developed and adapted memories, which shape the past for present needs, can challenge essences or static definitions, consolidate group identity, establish legitimacy, and create new forms of solidarity (Galvan, "Neotraditionalism"). Hoffmann's poetry attends to not only personal but also popular Tlingit memory. Its stories do not attempt to resuscitate an aboriginal social imaginary as part of its resistance, but rather they reckon with the modern one while finding continuities.

Stories as popular memory are a way of knowing that is generally considered foundational to Native cultures. Because stories are central tools of continuity within traditional oral cultures, modern Native revitalization strategies also emphasize them as a key form of knowledge. However, another force shaping the modern Native emphasis on storytelling is the linguistic turn within the humanities, with its analytical emphasis on language, discourse, and structures of knowledge as mediators of experience. Two key forces have given impetus to the linguistic turn: the anthropology of Clifford Geertz, which reads cultures, including their religions, as systems of symbols; and deconstruction as a philosophy and interpretive strategy, summed up in Jacques Derrida's statement "There is nothing outside the text." However, both Geertz and Derrida have been challenged for failing to address the material realities out of which texts emerge. The New Materialism, affect and trauma theories, the emphasis on the body, and the critical focus on everyday experience in their material reckoning have all shaped my analytical approach, just as the linguistic turn has. *After the Theft of the Sacred* pragmatically brings together signs and experience (see chapter 1). Both concerns are also implicit in Hoffmann's neotraditionalism. Stories, including those in his poems, are cultural mediators, communally and individually shaped responses to particular material conditions. Stories change as cultures evolve but also at times transform because of profound material and spiritual disruptions. *Raven's Echo* is both a personal and cultural record of these disruptions. It also offers a guide for constructing the future, just as traditional Raven stories did.

The linguistic turn recognizes that reality, material and spiritual, becomes experiential through the mediation of language—cultural structures of apprehension that include systems of knowledge, structures of feeling, discourses, ways of being (in) our bodies, sense perceptions, forms of relationality, and so on. This in turn helps us understand the common cultural shift toward symbolic modes of engaging tradition. Concomitant with this turn is a shift from fundamentally communal to more individual ways of experiencing Indigenous traditions. Part of the broader transformation from the aboriginal to the modern social imaginary, this individualization of tradition is evident in the deer dance literary works discussed in chapter 3. For Native peoples, but also many others, the shift toward symbolic apprehensions includes the experience of place. Neotraditionalism creates new meanings and functions for past practices, such as subsistence living or clan songs, which can sustain groups and individuals as socioeconomic conditions make the givenness of traditional ways an unavailable yet longed-for source of reassurance. Neotraditional stories told through contemporary poetry such as Hoffmann's emerge in part out of the individualized, interiorized, choice-driven sensibility of the modern social imaginary. His poems express the need to re-create past practices and apprehensions in ways that build new forms of cosmic and cultural belonging.

Raven's Echo engages and questions traditional spiritual and material apprehensions. Its poems are an effort to imagine new reconstructions of Tlingit ways of being in the cosmos. The need for these reconstructions arises from the changing, often confusing material and spiritual conditions that cause contestations over definitions of authentic culture and historical memory. Although cultural in its focus, Hoffmann's neotraditionalism can be understood as a political strategy in a broad sense. It challenges essences or static definitions, helps consolidate group identity, establishes forms of legitimacy, and creates new bases of solidarity. Within the context of globalization, neotraditionalism is a localist resistance to external domination or cultural homogenization. It provides a language and a strategy for accomplishing these goals (Galvan, "Neotraditionalism").

Hoffmann's poetry gives us neotraditionally adapted stories that interrogate the claim that Native people can do "as we have always done."[3] In depicting pre-invasion Native religious experience (imagined within a contemporary context) as alluring but unavailable, Book 1 in particular comments on the very desire for reassuring stories, a desire that can be damaging. What makes Hoffmann's engagement with stories stand out is the restless questioning, doubting, and reconstructing his poems do as they confront, as a necessary basis for continuance, the cosmic uncertainties and spiritual absences that have always existed but are now intensified after the theft of the sacred.

Thus Hoffmann states, "My desire to create comes from a drive to connect my past to the present. . . . When I create new forms out of the old, using non-traditional materials and styles, I bridge the past and present" (qtd. in "Robert H. Davis"). Further, "Tradition and ritual are re-enactment or reproduction. . . . They are necessary because they ground us and affirm who we are in relation to where we have been. But we are more than just our pasts. We are also reactions to the immediate present; we require rituals for contemporary themes. Form and content of older ritual are modified as they accommodate newer circumstances" ("Robert H. Davis" 48–49). The stories of *Raven's Echo* experientially work out the implications of this neotraditionalism.

Raven poems open Book 1 by reckoning with an ominous desire at the heart of stories. The first one, "Raven Tells Stories," explores the desperate human need for cosmic reassurance, even at the cost of blindness (1). The poem is an ironic supplication: "call up another filthy legend, / keep us distracted from all this blackness" (2–3). Darkness here is not just the destructiveness of colonialism; it is older and deeper. Like Raven, it is part of the experience of the cosmos itself. We can choose to deny this darkness, the speaker explains, and desperately call on Raven for distracting stories that falsely reassure us that all is well in the cosmos.

> . . . . Answer us
> our terror of this place we pretend to belong,
> the groping spirits we're hopeless against
> from where this bleakness keeps arising. (4–7)

These are some of the darkest lines in contemporary Native poetry, challenging easy assumptions not only about stories but about place, another concept generally considered foundational for a Native sense of being. With iconoclastic mocking, the speaker describes the spirits themselves groping in the dark rather than offering a sense of connection or protection. Humans are reduced by an inherent terror to "parasites" clinging desperately to dangerous spirit beings (10). And the cosmic frustration and anger implicit in the poem are intensified by the material realities transforming Tlingit people and all Native Alaska, as explained in the history below.

To the north of the Tlingit homeland, aboriginal Inuit shaman Aua, referenced in the introduction, elaborates the speaker's troubled sense of place:

> We fear the weather spirit of earth, that we must fight against to wrest our food from land and sea. We fear Sila.
>
> We fear death and hunger in the cold snow huts.
>
> We fear Takanakapsaluk, the great woman down at the bottom of the sea, the rules over all the beasts of the sea.
>
> We fear sickness that we meet with daily all around us; not death, but the suffering. We fear the evil spirits of life, those of the air, of the sea and the earth, that can help wicked shamans to harm their fellow men.
>
> We fear the souls of dead human beings and of the animals we have killed.
>
> Therefore it is that our fathers have inherited from their fathers all the old rules of life which are based on the experience and wisdom of generations. We do not know how, we cannot say why, but we keep those rules in order that we may live untroubled. And so ignorant are we in spite of all our shamans, that we fear everything unfamiliar. We fear what we see about us, and we fear all the invisible things that are likewise about us, all that we have heard of in our forefathers' stories and myths. (qtd. in Merkur ix–x)

Fear and unknowingness are responses to both material conditions and spiritual mysteries. Harsh geographical experiences are linked to equally harsh spiritual ones: not just weather but weather spirits threaten. The aboriginal cosmos is fundamentally mysterious and ominous; the only safety in the face of this unknowing is in following the rules that have come to govern people's lives, even if the rules are not understood. This is not a comfortable cosmos, like the one so often evoked in modern Indigenous religious explanations.[4]

Pre-contact Tlingit people believed that everything has spirit and must be respected. Conduct was governed by taboos and rewards because many situations were considered dangerous. This world was not an easy one to live in; disrespectful behavior could cause bad luck. Individual actions impacted the cosmos: "The moral order of the universe was maintained not by a single and omnipotent god, spirit, or deity, but by a set of rules for proper thinking, speaking, and behaving, vis-á-vis its nonhuman inhabitants" (Dauenhauer 162–64; see also de Laguna 221–23). Yet "the spirits are not generically benevolent, and are probably ambiguous at best," write Nora Marks Dauenhauer and Richard Dauenhauer ("Introduction: Form and Function" 115). Witchcraft was the negative counterpart of Tligit shamanism (Dauenhauer 167).[5]

"SoulCatcher," the title of Book 1 and one of its poems, reassuringly refers to traditional medicine practitioners or shamans and the amulets they use for healing ("SoulCatcher" 9, 15). Shamans were central to "the entire Tlingit sociocultural order" (Dauenhauer 164), but they were a troubled center. Shamanism ideally offered "physical and spiritual healing." However, "in practice, the ixt' [shaman] was also a source of anxiety because of the tremendous power in his or her hands—spiritual as well as economic and socio-political power. There is little doubt that shamans could harm deliberately" (Dauenhauer and Dauenhauer, "Introduction: Form and Function" 123). Given this background of mixed-use power, one can understand Hoffmann's speaker experiencing ambivalence toward Raven and the cosmos he created. Facing severe persecution and humiliation from "missionaries and the US military" (see the history below), shamanism survived in secret for a time but then died out (Dauenhauer 170–71). Dauenhauer and Dauenhauer report that today they do not know of any practicing shamans ("Introduction: Form and Function" 124).

Re-creating this spiritually charged imaginary within the materiality of modern everyday Alaska village life challenges the speaker. Traditional apprehensions of the cosmos were givens that did not require the self-conscious explanation and belief that are central to Hoffmann's poetry. And the form of darkness evoked by Aua's cosmic fear is related to but different than that created by Hoffmann, even as his poems evoke the aboriginal figure Raven.

Although integral to the aboriginal socioreligious imagination, the spirit-haunted apprehensions that Hoffmann includes in Book 1 are seldom included in explanations of modern Indigenous religious experience. In Southwest Alaska, "the workings of Tlingit tradition become increasingly incomprehensible with each passing generation" (Dauenhauer 176). Surely, Tlingit people are not alone with this dilemma.

The poems that open *Raven's Echo* negotiate the disjuncture between aboriginal and modern imaginaries as they evoke traditional apprehensions but also express a modern form of existential darkness. There is a fundamental difference between the two. Ancestors, and sometimes elders, experienced terror in response to spiritual powers. The darkness of Hoffmann's poems is more about emptiness, alienation, even absurdity. Thus, soulcatching within the modern social imaginary that his poetry necessarily engages takes a different, neotraditional form. His speaker has an intense need to explain what is no longer a given but rather is fundamentally contested. The poems of Book 1 in particular express the internally focused, doubt-ridden drama of modern belief. In this they have an affinity with the spiritual apprehensions in Young Bear's *Black Eagle Child*, discussed in chapter 2.

Cosmic darkness is not the only theme of Hoffmann's poetry, but it is its starting point. Spiritual forces are as destructive as they are creative, as absent as present, as tricky about the high-stakes game of life as they are reassuring. The second poem, "Raven Laughs," lists the disjunctures between cosmic hopes and unsettling realities. The speaker imagines one thing but must reckon with another. Because Raven offers many gifts, "we dare to follow. Little men, middle of nowhere" (8). This desperate faith is too often met with spiritual absence represented by Raven: "you're off—no footprint to trace." Or there are only "Signs . . . we can't figure" (13–14). No communal support or reassurance from the elders is offered as the speaker includes the tribe in his searching. They wait for Raven's shadow, which promises spiritual presence, but when Raven comes it is only to "crap over everyone" (20). The mixed nature of spiritual presences is not new to the Tlingit socioreligious imaginary; the interiority is. Yet the speaker chooses to continue his spiritual pursuit.

By the fourth Raven poem, the speaker more fully recognizes what was stated in the opening poem: "we're your parasites" (10). His being emerges from and is sustained by this relational, spiritually alive cosmos represented by Raven. "Raven Movies" opens,

> If I make words, they are Raven's echo.
> If I move, it is in that rhythm, Raven's heart,
> The air pulsing and rumbling.
> It makes me restless. (1–4)

There is no escape from the material and spiritual realities of the cosmos. As the poems develop, particularly in Book 2, Hoffmann's speaker comes to learn something about how to live meaningfully in this cosmos, how to reconstruct a Tlingit life. The poems acknowledge that efforts to heal cosmic relations necessarily take place within history and thus are contingently marked by "outside forces: relentless change, government subordination, painful acculturation, and assimilation . . . feelings of being severed from a tradition, from an identity" (Hoffmann, "Robert H. Davis" 49). Healing necessarily must address both cosmic and colonial conditions.

The erratic process of healing begins in "Saginaw Bay" with the history of Hoffmann's Tsaagweidí Clan, an account that goes back to Raven recklessly creating the world. Despite the people living by the seasons, the world of the ancestors had been troubled, the poem acknowledges (section II). Strife meant dislocation and a new home, the village of Kake. Colonial destructiveness enters the story with the "black robes." Villagers internalized their spiritual oppression as they themselves cut down and burned their totem poles. Traditional culture fundamentally changed (III). The rest of the poem documents the details of the modern industrial transformation. Yet Raven continues to haunt the poem and hover over Tlingit life. His tracks are in fossils, but he is not trapped in the past: "Raven moves in the world" (VII, 5).

Even if the earlier poems warn that Raven's stories are slippery to interpret and that his listeners desire reassurance more than truth, these stories of the past still matter in the present because Raven keeps "hopping about"

(VIII, 34). With Raven always moving, the speaker neither discovers nor creates any final answers. The modern socioreligious imaginary, with its marketplace of belief, offers little room for those certainties. Yet the restless, creative energy of Raven finds a place in the speaker as he searches for an experiential connection to the past and an understanding of the cosmos that can help repair the fragmented, disordered, and alienating present world. The next two sections of Book 1 report on experiments in this process as the speaker gradually shifts his spiritual struggle from an engagement with a mythic world to an archaeological exploration of an interior one. He finds his "treasures plundered" ("Archaeology" 8). "Eviction," the last poem of section III, suggests the seeming impossibility of finding healing for the self that is haunted by darkness.

The poems of section IV retain the self-consciousness of the previous section as the speaker looks to overcome the darkness by finding healing in a sense of place. Yet re-creating an aboriginal sense of place within nature is fraught with conceptual and material difficulties. Romantic fantasies can easily be confused with Indigenous sensibilities, this section suggests. The opening poems express the speaker's longing for an unmediated experience of nature. "Fasting for Eight Days" begins with the speaker wanting to shed his clothing and "embrace" the trees as "long lost brothers (4, 5). The last stanza extends this experience as nature comes alive:

> Where you bathe in salt breeze
> And stare
> Right into the face
> Rock mountains
> Breathing blue light. (11–15)

The direct language, the staccato rhythms, and the emphatic assonance, alliteration, and rhyme all give a matter-of-fact but urgent quality to this spiritual apprehension. Yet this poem, as well as the four that follow, has an uneasy undertone or undertow pulling us into dangerous water. Shedding clothes sounds more Romantic than Tlingit. Burying compass and watch ("Change of Season" 13) seems borrowed from Faulkner's "The Bear," a story of lost connections implicit in the alienating concept of wilderness. This becoming "uncivilized" strikes one as another of the reassuring "filthy legend[s]" that tempt the speaker right from the beginning ("Change of Season" 15, 1; "Raven Tells Stories" 2).

Hoffmann then presents a jarring acknowledgment of the material–spiritual interpretive problematic that is deeper than Romantic distractions and involves more than the material destructions of colonialism. The reality of Raven returns to the story. "Raven Is Two-Faced" asserts that there is no escaping the baffling incomprehensibility of the world Raven has created and the speaker must live in.

> Raventracks lead everywhere.
> You can tell he's been busy.
> Shifty. That he's got this game
> of intrigue down, because
> he's made certain everything
> about him has two sides.
>
> There's no way out. (5–11)

Raven has always been and continues to be difficult to both apprehend and comprehend.

Ceremonies bridge the material and spiritual worlds (see chapter 3). Book 1 concludes with "Raven Dances." In the midst of "any other time," spiritual reality breaks in as the speaker witnesses a child's harrowing "performance" or transformation (10):

> Ravens flash in his eyes,
> Beat him to the ground. You hear a crunch
> Of shattered skull
> And in that instant
> Black shadows escape. (14–18)

The speaker does not explain this overwhelming ceremony. Instead, engulfed by the mystery,

You withdraw and find
Your head too is full
With raven wings beating. (21–23)

The "you" throughout the poem is unsettling; it is an odd rhetorical move used in many of the poems. By abstracting the poem from the speaker's experience and thus generalizing the experience depicted, the "you" broadens the spiritual uncertainty in the process of cosmic apprehension.

Years after creating the poems in Book 1, Hoffmann explained their personal context: "I was . . . struggling to make sense of my cultural identity, attempting to piece together the bits and pieces I thought would give me clearer vision. Because of the disconnect to so many vital parts of those 'bits and pieces,' such as my father, history, place among my people, and so on, I wrote mainly from a place of anger and blame." He continued, "Eventually, the angry years took quite a toll on me. My epiphany came when I went back to Kake [the island village in Southeast Alaska where Hoffmann was born] and lived with my tribal uncle with whom I explained my perceptions, my struggles. He helped me arrive at clearer perceptions, and corrected many of my misunderstandings—about my father, about traditional ways of being" (Personal email, n.d.).[6]

Hoffmann here refocuses the poems by historicizing them within his own experience. In doing this, he makes the "you" a personal projection as it focuses on the speaker's response to the particular personal and collective traumas that created his sense of cosmic and cultural alienation. Now we hear the poems as imaginative re-creations that make up a lived religion. The poems have become an accusation that is a plea.

The plea of Book 1 for meaningful experiential engagement with cosmic realities emerges from the modern social imaginary. The speaker is skeptical of final answers and, focused on inner reality, self-consciously constructs personal meanings out of communal perceptions. The plea is to experience an enchanted, Raven-filled cosmos that does more than frustrate and confuse the speaker's attempts to live responsibly within it. Book 1 is a reading project, an attempt to decipher the signs of the spirits to grasp the relationships among inner, earthly, and cosmic geographies. The resulting lived religion is as restless as Raven himself. It is a poetry of hard questioning with no comforting clichés.

In response to the spiritual crisis of Book 1, Hoffmann states, "I believe there comes a point where one must name and own who and what he is, in order to take responsibility for where his actions and attitudes are coming from" ("Robert H. Davis" 48). These actions and attitudes, as expressed in *Raven's Echo*, come from within a social imagination embedded in traditional Tlingit understandings but are now mediated by historically conditioned cultural, socioeconomic, and political conditions. These conditions are more directly taken up in Book 2, where Hoffmann develops a new poetic language for creating a Tlingit neotraditionalism, situated in the historical present, that can satisfy the longings of Book 1.

The history of the Tlingit present is part of global imperialism. Although Russia was the first outside power to make a claim on Tlingit territory, major sociocultural changes for Tlingit people came when Russia in 1867 sold Alaska to the United States.[7] For US settlers and government, the rich natural resources of Southeast Alaska seemed irresistible. In response Tlingit clans, the traditional centers of social and political power, began to unite in resistance. Yet settler intrusions increased as cultural imperialism reinforced economic control. With the support of the government, Protestant missionaries carried out their "civilization" project. The extension of the federal Allotment Act of 1887 to Alaska in 1906 further undermined Tlingit society, including its economic structures.

The Alaska Native Brotherhood, honored in Hoffmann's poem "Warriors," was established in 1912 to confront racial discrimination as well as to find ways to accommodate new intractable conditions (Worl, "History" 225–26). At this time many Tlingit people were of necessity shifting away from subsistence living to wage work in canneries and commercial fishing. Those who continued trapping and fishing did so individually or as families rather than clans (Thornton 162). The nature of Tlingit cultural cohesion changed when clan social organizations could not effectively respond to changing material and spiritual conditions. Part of the impetus for cultural change was Tlingit people's newly increased but still limited incorporation into the US political and economic systems. Traditional culture lost strength as the federal government came to dominate social life.

The same year that Alaska became a state, 1959, the US Court of Claims ruled that Tlingit and Haida Natives were "the original owners of Southeast Alaska." Previously Native Alaskans had had no legal basis for claiming title to their land. In 1971 the Alaska Native Claims Settlement Act (ANCSA) became federal law. The act was a compromise between varying interests. Alaska Natives needed to settle long-standing land claims, and corporations wanted to build the Prudhoe Bay pipeline. Federal and state governments wanted to assimilate Native groups into capitalist economic development, thereby reducing welfare and trusteeship obligations. With ANCSA, 13 Native regional and 205 village corporations received 44 million acres of land, only about one-tenth of Alaska's territory, and approximately $1 billion, about $3 per acre for the nine-tenths that were lost (Berger 24).[8]

ANCSA shaped the social and cultural conditions inherent in *Raven's Echo*. It created new Native leadership based on skills in business, economics, law, and politics rather than traditional wisdom (Dauenhauer and Dauenhauer, introduction, *Haa Ḵusteeyí* 100). It "significantly expanded" Native participation in the Alaskan and global economies. Among its other consequences were "extinguishing aboriginal title to land, creating Native capitalist elites, and forcing short-sighted, profit-motivated decisions about resource management" (Clifford 14). However, the act also prompted many, as they enrolled in the Native corporations, to reengage their Indigenous identity (Clifford 7). The corporations helped "engender new Tlingit senses of place through their own investments, employment, heritage programs, architecture, symbols, and other activities" (Thornton 194). In the midst of these changes, Tlingit people renewed efforts for cultural revitalization.

Raven's Echo emerges out of this historical trajectory. As the speaker of "Saginaw Bay" explains, "I keep trying to see my life / against all this history" and so concludes,

... I might write a book
In it I would tell how we are pulled
In so many directions,
How our lives are fragmented
With so many gaps. (VIII, 31–32, 7–11)

Book 2 is that book, a reconstruction project to mend these gaps. It begins with a village boy having moved to the city, a relatively new geographical reality for Tlingit people. This first poem and the ones that follow narrate everyday struggles to live responsibly. The speaker's spiritual search, much more than in Book 1, is shaped by his struggle to find a cultural identity that fits. The poems have a presentness as the speaker strives to overcome the traumas of Book 1. This is the work of Book 2. Its poems are less about spiritual bafflement and more about living in the modern alienated social and disenchanted spiritual imaginary brought to Southeast Alaska by an increasingly dominant colonialism. They reveal that developing a sense of one's proper place in the cosmos depends more insistently on responding to conditions in the material world. Out of these circumstances emerges the neotraditional reconstruction project of Book 2.

The historical changes described above weakened the traditional Tlingit clan structure, within which members had had their sense of being. This structure came to seem "increasingly alien" to many. Life had centered on subsistence living; however, over time this traditional mode of production and sensibility became unworkable for most, so new cultural forms were developed. This "resocialization" or "fundamental reorientation" created a new meaning of tradition (Dauenhauer and Dauenhauer, "Evolving" 263, 276, 253). Book 2 particularizes this process in the experience of its speaker. The book opens with a Tlingit boy having moved to a culturally alienating city. Although mocked as a village boy, he builds a traditional bentwood box in shop class. Even in this nontraditional context far from his homeland, "his designs swim!" (218).

"Village Boy" and the other poems of Book 2 engage the problematic of sustaining Tlingit identity and culture when its social location and imaginary have changed. These poems form, to use Dombrowski's phrase, an "ethnography of a problem" (4) as they reconstruct useful meanings of Tlingit identity. The speaker feels alienated from subsistence culture, the essence of Tlingit traditional life, even as he struggles to make connections to that experience.[9] Ways of being Tlingit have become a matter of choice rather than a birthright and must be personally and socially negotiated (Dauenhauer and Dauenhauer, "Evolving" 262). In the concluding poem, "Reconstruction," the speaker similarly faces these choices, which are contingent upon the material conditions created by corporate and governmental (non-Native but also Native) structures geared toward capitalist accumulation.[10] The shift from a pre-contact aboriginal social imaginary to a modern one is registered, for example, in new uses for totem poles, ceremonial blankets, drums, songs, and other traditional special objects (*at.óow*),[11] including the dance staff the speaker is carving.

In their essay "Evolving Concepts of Tlingit Identity and Clan," Dauenhauer and Dauenhauer address this shift in social imaginary: "While many symbols and emblems remain the same or similar, their perception, function and patterns of use have changed, and we are witnessing a fundamental reorientation in the thinking and social organization of most Tlingit people" (253). The meanings of special objects are no longer maintained within "the traditional system of clan ownership, reciprocity, and ritual ceremonial display." The clan system for many is too restrictive and so not "personal and charismatic enough"; nor is it inclusive enough of community members. While traditional regalia has become more public, as it is used not just for ceremonies but also for celebrations, "the catharsis becomes more private and individualized" (270). While government organizations, corporations, and communities now often commission Tlingit at.óow as art objects for display, these special objects also continue to function spiritually and emotionally (269). James Clifford, discussing the construction of a hand-sewn kayak for a museum exhibition, explains,

One might be inclined to interpret this kayak as a 'traditional' object belonging to a nostalgic, postmodern culture—a thing with meaning only as a specimen and a work of art, artificially separated from the currents of historical change. . . . But this would privilege the authenticity of objects over the social processes of transmitting and transforming knowledges and relationships. It would miss the multi-accented, intergenerational work of articulation, performance, and translation that goes into the kayak's production and interpretation. (16)

In "Reconstruction," Hoffmann carefully negotiates this interpretive maze, the conceptual conflict between authenticity and translation, and comes to a similar conclusion. His poetry rejects nostalgia as either a strategy or a comfort. Similarly, Dauenhauer and Dauenhauer observe that the new special objects, with their translated significations, have gained wide acceptance "because they are congruent with the new Euro-American social structure in which they actually live and operate." The implication is that traditional clan-based practices no longer meet the needs for many in the community ("Evolving" 270; see also Clifford), even as clan identification remains an important identity marker.

The speaker of "Reconstruction" explicitly evokes his Tsaagweidí Clan as he begins to design a dance staff as a ceremonial object. His goal is to help make the past present, "for Topsy's memories to be my memories" (71, 79). The need to research old photographs suggests the gap between Uncle Topsy and the speaker's tribal experiences, yet the photos do come alive as they "dance and sway" (82, 91). The staff's design evokes the clan but does not emerge out of a functioning clan structure; it reflects an individually interpreted, community-engaged use of tradition. Just as language is now used mainly for display (Dauenhauer and Dauenhauer, "Evolving" 264), clan identification has come to be translated into a marker of "authentic" identity" (see introduction).[12]

Two geographical changes have affected this shift away from clans as dominant social organizations. These changes also created a need for new ways of apprehending Tlingit identity and imagining a sense of place. Traditionally, settlements were geographically made up of a winter village and various seasonal camps for fishing and gathering. Now villagers' experience of place has narrowed as fewer depend on a subsistence economy and villages have become year-long residences, Thomas F. Thornton reports in *Being and Place Among the Tlingit* (37). Place is thus less tied to seasonal changes and the procuring of necessities for many. Further, urban migration along with industrialization and wage labor increasingly determine social geography. When clan members disperse, their connection to place weakens as they become "alienated from their homelands" (Thornton 37–38). The economic development model of ANCSA as well as the earlier Allotment Act have been key instigators of this transformation.

Thornton summarizes a fundamental cultural consequence: "The loss of connection to place through *dwelling* has made it more incumbent on people to continue their identification with lands through *symbolic* means" (38, emphasis added). This is a fundamental change. Thornton nevertheless makes a commonplace assertion: "One cannot deny the special relationships that indigenous peoples maintain with the landscapes they have inhabited for hundreds, if not thousands, of years." These relationships assume "a cosmos that is alive, sentient, empowered, and moral" and that is "inhabited by a community of spiritual beings constantly in communication and exchange with human beings" (4). Within this conceptualization, the discontinuities between dwelling and symbolic identification are unremarked because the explanation is embedded within the conceptualizations of the aboriginal socioreligious imaginary without reckoning with the modern one the speaker in *Raven's Echo* must live in.

Linda Tuhiwai Smith's seminal *Decolonizing Methodologies* cautions against common assertions about place but from a different perspective. She explains that a practical, material relationship with the land is what has always sustained Indigenous people. From her grandmother, Tuhiwai Smith explains, she did gain "the spiritual relationships to the land," but she also taught her a sense of "groundedness" and "reality." These made her "skeptical or cautious about the mystical, misty-eyed discourse. . . . I believe that our survival as peoples has come from our knowledge of our contexts, our environment, not from some active beneficence of our Earth

Mother. We had to know to survive" (12–13). This dialectical relation that is both spiritual and material allows for considerations of new conditions and thus new relationships to land and place. For example, in Hoffman's poem "Kake Township Survey 3851," the "misnamed silence" of a now surveyed, colonized, "no longer simple woods" is alienating rather than comforting to the speaker (26, 22, 25).

Glen Sean Coulthard's (Yellowknives Dene) *Red Skin, White Masks* also confronts the changed economic constraints and political conditions that now shape Indigenous people's experience of place. He himself has participated in the Dene people's ongoing conflicts over land claims, which have similarities with those that resulted in and from ANCSA. Central to both Canadian and US settler colonialism is an "extractivist capitalism" that is "territorially acquisitive in perpetuity" (152, 55). To challenge this, Coulthard calls on "Indigenous peoples [to empower] themselves through cultural practices of individual and collective self fashioning." His reconstruction project also calls for "direct action" that "seek[s] to prefigure radical alternatives to the structural and subjective dimensions of colonial power" (18). This self-fashioning and prefiguring symbolic experiences of place, like Hoffmann's narrator going fishing, are cultural activities that can become positive politically as new and renewed connections to place and people develop. Coulthard argues that only through political and cultural activism that focuses on a tribal self, rather than through federal recognition, can Indigenous peoples create proper connections to their land and traditions.[13]

Raven's Echo grasps this modern problematic of self-fashioning. Writing out of a similarly conflicted political situation of land claims and cultural negotiations that Coulthard addresses, Hoffmann engages the problematic of place experientially but also structurally. Poems like "He Was a Dancer," "Rock of Ages," and "Leveling Grave Island" make this clear. Although none of Hoffmann's poems directly address the political–cultural project Coulthard addresses, many do suggest political critiques. "Saginaw Bay," for example depicts the consequences of capitalist forms of production and the resulting socioeconomic situation, as do poems such as "At the Door of the Native

Studies Director," "Global Warming," and "Division." If Coulthard's strength
as a political scientist is his attention to changing economic, political, and
social conditions, Hoffmann brings spiritual acuity, courageous honesty,
and experiential intensity to his modern apprehensions of place.

People's sense of place is continually being reconstructed as material
and religious conditions change. Increased mobility and migration have
had a significant impact. Changes to the land brought by modern industrial
production—clear-cut logging, commercial fishing, and other extractive
industries, for example—continue to impact Tlingit experiences. Changes in
political organization similarly mediate their relationship to the land. Tribal
apprehensions of the spiritual–material world do have historical continuities,
but they have been inexorably and indelibly changed as federal and corporate
colonization have become more intrusive and destructive.

This political, social, and religious shift is the deep structure of the darkness
in Book 2, the problematic it experientially works to resolve. It is not the
haunting cosmic–interior darkness of Book 1 but rather the crisis ordinariness
(see chapter 4) resulting from cultural, economic, and political loss. Yet in
the end the speaker is able to reconstruct useful forms of cultural belonging
that depend on symbolic meanings rather than renewed dwelling.

Stanzas 2 and 3 of "Reconstruction" take up the central issue of place in
this context. The clichéd, ironically toned phrase "feed us like mother with
milk" (9) challenges simple understandings. Instead, Hoffmann depicts
alienation layered with longing: "I never hunted, could not speak the language
of the forest" (10; see also "Blind Man" 26–31). The speaker here addresses
the now common dilemma of Native urbanization, even within villages.[14]
His efforts to "liv[e] right by the land" fail to "come to life" (7, 15). We see the
speaker's attenuated sense of place by the way he lists randomly observed,
vague geographical details: "mudflats here, cliffs there, clouds above" (12).
His cursory list suggests the speaker's distance from traditional lifeways
as it contrasts with the explanation given by Kake elder Fred Friday half a
century earlier: "The Native people know all the points and rocks and every

little area by name. . . . These areas were used so much that we were familiar with every little place" (qtd. in Thornton 116).[15] Friday's form of attention is essential for subsistence production.

Since the passage of ANCSA, with its devastating consequences for subsistence economies, neotraditional revitalization has given renewed attention to the sense of place that subsistence living has embodied.[16] Subsistence fishing, hunting, and gathering continue, albeit within changed circumstances, for only about one-third of village households. For others, subsistence practices are used symbolically for identity reconstruction (Dombrowski 91–92). The speaker's efforts to make the land come alive use this symbolic strategy. Thornton acknowledges that new roads, technologies, and other material changes have affected the ways Tlingit conceptualize places, yet he asserts that "many of the cognitive and symbolic principles that inform the Tlingit views of place and the environment have been maintained and even enhanced despite . . . pressures to assimilate and develop" (9). Hoffmann's speaker is much less sure of the efficacy of these efforts. He enthusiastically participates in a subsistence experience, fishing with his uncle: "We pulled in fat halibut. There was so much! / We thought we fished good!" (28–29). The exclamation marks suggest ironic surprise and identify these fishermen as outsiders to traditional subsistence living. This venture is symbolically rather than materially sustaining and thus is tenuous and fragile in a different way.

The tension between those who experience subsistence symbolically and those who depend on it for a living is shaped by present socioeconomic structures. Native corporations created through ANCSA have made subsistence work increasingly difficult, dangerous, and unproductive because their land management practices are aimed at capital accumulation. Corporations by definition must make a profit, and clear-cutting forests and large-scale commercial fishing offer significant sources of revenue. As a result of Native and non-Native corporate practices, people making their living through subsistence are often forced for financial reasons to be the first to leave their villages (Dombrowski 109). ANCSA extinguished aboriginal rights to subsistence use of lands now managed by the state of Alaska and the federal government. Genevieve Norris, from the northern Iñiupiat village of Shungnak, reflected on the consequences for subsistence work:

> Our lifestyle since 1971 has changed, even our way of life. It is not the same as how it used to be when we were growing up. We weren't told to get so many caribou for our family. Our dads, they would just go out hunting and get however much our families need. But today, you know, we are limited. They tell us we can get caribou . . . tell us how many to get. So, this has changed. Same way with fishing. Nowadays, they even give us a calendar of how many fish you are catching to keep track. (qtd. in Berger 60)

Similar consequences for Tlingit people in Southwest Alaska, including increased difficulty in sustaining economic viability, have meant that villagers practicing subsistence living are the ones who "pay a disproportionate share of the cost for an identity that does little to protect them" (Dombrowski 109, 111).[17] Similarly, potlaches, traditionally central to Tlingit life and now being revived, no longer help rectify village inequalities through gift giving (see Dauenhauer 174–75). Within this context, the fishing as symbolic subsistence that Hoffmann's speaker practices becomes a matter of privilege within inequitable village social structures.[18] Culturally symbolic projects, like the village dance groups discussed below, inevitably have uneven economic participation. These projects do not necessarily bring "economic and social justice" (Clifford 8). The cultural politics of neotraditionalism can substitute for the political activism needed to enhance the marginal lives of those practicing subsistence living. Hoffmann's speaker does not reckon with this.

In contrast to symbolic cultural engagements, subsistence living has come to mean poverty and marginalization. Those who depend on economic subsistence are drawn more to Pentecostal churches than to neotraditional Tlingit culture groups as a way of making sense of their world. Churches in villages most affected by economic collapse during the 1960s and 1970s were the ones to gain the most members (Dombrowski 120, 167, 146). Dauenhauer also observes that Pentecostal and other fundamentalist churches have had

"the greatest recent impact on Tlingit religion." He found that the popularity of Pentecostalism fits with the shift away from traditional clan-oriented
cultural identity toward identification with "the wider culture of American individualism." Further, new religious formations "seem to . . . address
growing spiritual needs such as drug and alcohol abuse, AIDS, teen suicide,
family violence, and other contemporary problems at the most personal and
individual level." The new religious organizations create bitter divisions
within communities. Pentecostal churches are generally opposed to reviving
traditional practices. They create oppositional "local, tight-knit, and logically closed systems of meaning" integral to sustaining their sense of group
identity (176, 172, 123). As one revival preacher explained, "You won't find any
Chilkat [a Tlingit village] dancers dancing in heaven" (Dombrowski 2).[19]

Tlingit villagers who depend on subsistence practices for their livelihood
tend to embrace Pentecostalism, while those like Hoffmann's speaker practice
subsistence and other aspects of Tlingit tradition symbolically. This presents
challenges for understanding contemporary Indigenous meanings of place.
Economic and cultural realities within the present neoliberal regime need to
be confronted in the search for a meaningful sense of place within land that
has been transformed by colonial capitalism. *Raven's Echo* offers a partial
and yet important poetic map for traversing territory and reconstructing
Indigenous life on a proper foundation.

As "Reconstruction" concludes Book 2 and *Raven's Echo* as a whole, Raven
dances in mythic time while the Kake dancers rearticulate his dance in
the present (40, 75). The speaker, Village Boy, now an experienced artist,
at first wants to re-create the past with his carving, but then he finds the
right design (78, 91). He creates his own synthesis of past and present as he
"design[s] a dance staff / to tell our story," a special object that is "connected,
not disjointed" (69–70, 91). Old photographs and tapes of traditional music
now become part of his reconstruction experience. The speaker apparently
creates the ceremonial staff for one of the new dance groups, which are often
supported by Native corporations as a means of sustaining Tlingit culture
(Dombrowski 7, ch. 3). The point is not re-creating an authentic object but

rather "transmitting and transforming knowledges and relationships." The staff rearticulates traditions "without merging past and present into a seamless 'culture'" (Clifford 16–17). Hoffmann similarly notes, "But we are more than our pasts" ("Robert H. Davis" 49).

The Keex' (Kake) Kwáan dancers performed at the 2012 Kake centennial celebration, which commemorated the first Alaskan village to be federally recognized as a municipality. At that time villagers became US citizens. The decision to reorganize in 1912, the year the Alaska Native Brotherhood was established, was controversial. It marked for this predominantly but not exclusively Tlingit community a shift toward Western laws and language. The same year a new cannery opened, offering economic opportunities and liabilities not equally shared by all villagers. That year was a turning point for Kake. As Magistrate Mike Jackson explained at the celebration, becoming a municipality had meant that traditional ways would need to be changed so that children would be prepared for new forms of work and social organization. He commented on the 1912 leaders: "I can't put myself in their shoes. They had to make the best decision for their people." Then he added, "We're still here. . . . People in this community choose to stay to put a face to the land." Land has come to evoke conflicting meanings as today's Kake leaders focus on "economic development, culture and language" (Nu). These goals do not easily fit together. For Kake is both a village and a Native corporation, and place can mean something quite different within the two structures.

Contemporary dance groups are an important part of reconstructing Tlingit traditions; every village has at least one (Dombrowski 63). Groups like Keex' Kwáan reflect a shift in material and spiritual authority within villages. Although songs and dances are still clan property and permission must be granted for a dance group to perform them, the dance groups themselves are community based, with members from various clans and even non-Natives participating. Elders, in a clash of socioreligious imaginaries, have expressed concern "lest the spirits evoked by the young people wander aimlessly, floating in space unanswered, unattended" (Dauenhauer and Dauenhauer, "Introduction: The Form and Function" 111–12). The elders' religious beliefs take them beyond immediate, everyday realities of contemporary dance and song practices as material and spiritual realms merge. The dance staff Hoffmann's speaker wants to carve is detached from the real presence of the spirits traditionally evoked by the dance. Instead he is creating a symbolic adaptation of the meanings invested in past religious objects. And yet, as is mentioned in previous chapters, religious expressions may have become symbolic in their adaptations, but that does not necessarily mean they still cannot engage a belief in actual spirits (112–13). The level of continuity depends on the particular participants' religious beliefs.

Most Tlingit culture group members and most villagers are Christian, although not necessarily exclusively so. They have found a satisfactory intersection between adaptations of Tlingit tradition and contemporary Christianity. Dauenhauer and Dauenhauer report, "What seems to be evolving on the spiritual level is a blend of generic worldviews: generic pan-Christianity and generic Native American, with important features from both sources" (272). Kake, with less than a thousand people, has six Christian churches. Some are supportive of Tlingit cultural revitalization. Dombrowski describes the home of a prayer group leader: "wall hangings depicting romantic images of Native Americans," some that include Jesus; dream catchers; and "a crucified Jesus figure with accompanying American eagle carved from wood" (Dombrowski 115–16). Dombrowski shows that this position of sustaining Tlingit traditions through contemporary translation, like Indigenous Pentecostal belief, is complexly economic, social, and political as well as religious.

Tlingit people, including Robert Davis Hoffmann, are not alone in struggling to find both material and spiritual meaning within their changing culture and world. "No one, or at most few people, anywhere," Dombrowski importantly observes, "can live easily with his or her culture. This is true for Alaska Natives as well" (3). This is a point worth reflecting on as we read Hoffmann's poetry. The common uneasiness has its specific manifestation within Tlingit and Alaska Native political and economic complexities: the challenge of Kake being among the most industrialized Native Alaskan villages (Dombrowski 59), resulting village inequalities, the range of meanings for subsistence activities, conflicting interpretations and evaluations of recent and mythical pasts, the variety of religious practices, and other material and spiritual conditions. These all shape the continuing effort to reconstruct a Tlingit "way of being human" ("Reconstruction" 46), the project of *Raven's Echo*. Hoffmann's poems offer an "ethnography of a problem," but more than that they present a poetic lived religion that addresses this problematic in material and more-than-material ways.

7 IMPROVISATIONAL BELIEVING IN A TIME OF OPTIONS

LOUISE ERDRICH'S *LOVE MEDICINE* AND GREG SARRIS'S *GRAND AVENUE*

Many Indigenous characters long for a sense of personal and communal fullness.[1] Through ceremonies and amid everyday life, they strive to live out traditionally inflected Native ways of being. As these characters variously experience their religious and cultural commitments within the modern social imaginary, their religious practices tend to be more individual and interior than communal. More specifically, a post-secular ethos (defined below) shapes their experiences as they improvise on inherited religious traditions.

Religious life in Louise Erdrich's *Love Medicine* and Greg Sarris's *Grand Avenue* is similarly shaped by the modern socioreligious imaginary. Many of their characters live secular lives fully within the material world. For them, traditional beliefs and practices no longer are sustaining or even particularly relevant. Those who do live religiously face the shift to more individualistic beliefs and practices, a shift experienced quite differently by the four characters analyzed here. For Fleur and Lipsha from *Love Medicine* and Faye and Anna from *Grand Avenue*, religion remains a significant although not necessarily or exclusively positive part of their lives. Their religious experiences develop within tribal contexts, but they are also shaped by dominant cultural norms. The four characters' differing interactions with these two social force fields, tribal and dominant, shape the nature of their experiential beliefs. All are engaged in individualized religious improvising within the context of their particular family and tribal histories, present class positions, material ambitions, and status positions in their communities. Fleur and Faye represent the surviving remnants of an adapted premodern or aboriginal religious imaginary. They experience personal, often uneasy relationships with supernatural powers or spirit beings. In contrast, Lipsha and Anna embody post-secular believing as they reshape religious traditions to fit their particular circumstances. Their beliefs are individualistic and interior; they maintain religious authority as they choose and adapt practices rather than submit to systems of belief. These practices are not grounded in transcendental realities but rather in an immanence that is more closed than open (see chapter 1).

Love Medicine, by depicting Fleur as an anachronistic remnant of the aboriginal socioreligious imaginary, valorizes Lipsha's humanistic religious belief and practice. His form of healing is efficacious but with significant limitations and losses. *Grand Avenue* presents Faye's and Anna's quite different religious improvisations as markers of loss within the Pomo community's troubled socioreligious condition. They offer much more overtly troubling case studies as their improvisations transgress community norms. The two characters' different class positions and social standings profoundly impact the practice of their inherited but improvised beliefs, Pomo and Christian, respectively. Faye's religious experience, like Fleur's, centers on the relationship between supernatural spirits and humans, a relationship no longer at the heart of their communities. Unlike Lipsha's Anishinaabe improvisations, Anna's rebellious form of Christianity, the Protestant gospel of aspiration if not wealth, fails to sustain her and thus leaves her even more frustrated with her present socioeconomic situation. Like Lipsha, her improvising is focused on humans rather than spirits.

The variance and complexity of these four characters' religious experiences alerts us to the range of meanings "Native spirituality" or religion has today. Their experiences model possibilities and challenges for Indigenous cultural revitalization. Analyzing them can clarify the social implications of their choices and situations. Their various attempts to engage Native traditional and Christian beliefs and practices within the modern socioreligious imaginary call for consideration of their efficacy. This necessarily involves establishing, explicitly or implicitly, standards of religious evaluation.

In response to Indigenous religious improvisations, particularly within an urban context, Bonita Lawrence asks, "How much change can traditions accommodate and still be maintained as valid cultural practices?" (168). This question provokes consideration of a range of complexities. One of Lawrence's Toronto study participants addresses this problematic of religious validity as he explains his own experience: "The traditional Métis spirituality is fairly orthodox Catholicism. But I'm not living that tradition. I go to sweats. I guess I'm pursuing . . . Aboriginal spirituality." This is an unusual acknowledgement of a not uncommon Indigenous reality: Christianity as a hegemonic Indigenous religion and aboriginal spirituality as a form of conversion alternative. Lawrence's participant further complicates the religious situation by stating that "tradition was rural, and I'm urban. . . . in Native traditions, I see myself as a visitor." The tension between traditions as Native or Christian and rural or urban troubles this person's religious experience (163). Another urban participant presents a related tension. While he joins sweats and tries to learn about Native traditions, he concludes, "I think, especially for modern people, *being traditional is an internal state*, more than anything. . . . there are obviously traditional economies and traditional ways of living—and those are disappearing for a lot of people. But the *values*, I think, are still there" (162–63, emphasis added). This valorization of internal realities rather than communal practices as the now essential Indigenous religious quality situates this participant's experience and conceptualizations within the modern rather than aboriginal socioreligious imaginary.

Similarly, in Erdrich's account, no tribal authority disciplines religious practice as it did in the past. This is evident in Lipsha's comment on love medicine healing: "the real actual power" was not in the goose heart but in his "faith in the cure" (246). The individual carries the burden of belief and its efficacy. He does not look to traditional practice as the criterion for evaluating present religious validity; rather it offers a framework to start from. His substituting supermarket turkey hearts is an incisive moment in

Erdrich's ongoing fictional religious history. The humor of the incident is uneasy as Lipsha's experiences help clarify the underlying shift in socioreligious authority that Lawrence and her participants struggle with. Lipsha is part of a "slide toward expressive individualism and an ethic of authenticity" (Taylor, *Dilemmas* 246). This conceptualization of authenticity, being true to oneself, undermines the social uses of it as a communal evaluative criterion. Lipsha's improvisations are focused not on re-creating traditions but on creating "an analogue of the original sensibility" (Taylor, afterword 302). This distinction is significant, similar to the difference between dwelling on the land and experiencing it symbolically (see chapter 5). The analogue is close enough to be meaningful for many, like Lipsha, living within the fundamentally different socioreligious context. And it may be their only option.

This shift in authority seems to resolve the rural–urban dilemma: "The differences between urban traditionalism and the practices in land-based communities should not be seen as evidence that urban traditions are not valid—provided that the urban traditions are *filling the needs of the individuals* who live by them," Lawrence asserts (169, emphasis added). Erdrich's fictional account substantiates this. Yet Lawrence acknowledges an unresolved tension with this evaluative stance when she cautions that "the strength of Indigenous spirituality lies precisely in its rootedness to the physical world we live in. For urban Native people, an index of their alienation from the land might well be expressed in the extent to which a spirituality of abstract ritual becomes their mode of traditional cultural activity" (166). Symbolic relations to the land have replaced dwelling for many characters. Can urban religious experiences meet individual and community needs? Through his character Nellie, discussed in chapter 5, Sarris models an affirmative answer. And Lawrence recognizes the strength urban religious experience gains through its "range of practices" (166). However, the characters discussed here suggest the difficulties of practicing traditional religions within new social, cultural, political, and economic—that is, material—circumstances.

Lawrence wonders about the validity of focusing on individual needs and ceding religious authority to individual inner experience. Lipsha's spiritual analogue fits Lawrence's criteria of filling needs, yet this pragmatic evaluation sidesteps her question of cultural validity. In the neoliberal religious cultural-ism of *Love Medicine* and many other contemporary novels, tribal religious leaders and traditional societies have little or no role to play. An exception occurs in a novel that is in many ways religiously exceptional, as has been noted in earlier chapters. In Leslie Marmon Silko's *Ceremony*, Tayo does report to the tribal elders and receives the necessary tribal validation for his religious experiences (238).

Glen Coulthard works through the related problematic of developing the most useful and valid political theory for "Indigenous resurgence." The parallels with Lawrence are instructive. He rejects essentialism in relation to Native political tradition just as he deplores the compromises required by the liberal politics of recognition (155). Coulthard positively references the resistance strategies of Taiaiake Alfred (Mohawk) and Leanne Simpson. With Alfred, Coulthard focuses on values rather than specific practices within Native traditions. He uses Alfred's phrase "self-conscious traditionalism" in calling for "culturally grounded" strategies (155). In *Wasase: Indigenous Pathways of Action and Freedom* Alfred states, "I am searching for an under-standing, a way to articulate and then to think about replicating not the surface aspects of the lifestyle and manners of our people in past times, but the quality of an indigenous existence, the connective material that bound Onkwehonwe [original people] together when 'interests' and 'rights' were not a part of our peoples' vocabularies" (19, 254). Alfred's minimizing use of "lifestyle and manners" to describe traditional ways of living, say subsistence means of production, seems a religiously liberal gesture of abstraction and an act of improvisation. Coulthard commends Simpson's call for "significantly reinvesting in our own ways of being," which include political, intellectual, and legal traditions. This means "reclaim[ing] the very best practices of our traditional cultures" (155), a similar gesture of evaluative winnowing. These three political theorists, like Lawrence focused on religious experience, call for a nonfoundational traditionalism that is directive without being determinative. For them revitalization or resurgence focuses on an ethos (a way of being or a set of values) rather than specific practices. They call for situational thinking in deciding which practices are best for meeting present needs. Within this paradigm, there are no specific criteria for judging the validity of religious, cultural, or political practices. There is no set definition of "usefulness"; it presumably must be determined situationally within a dialectic of individual and communal evaluation as particular values are argued for. This is the pragmatic strategy advocated by Alfred, Simpson, and Coulthard. It is significant that, unlike Lawrence, their focus does not include specifically religious beliefs and practices. One might respond that they reject religion as a distinct category within Indigenous understandings, but I do not think their writings reckon with the more-than-material experiences traditionally included in aboriginal apprehensions of the cosmos. Nor do they reckon with the political issue of power in making evaluative decisions.

Only Lawrence raises the question of how much improvisation can be accommodated and still have religious practices and beliefs remain legitimately traditional. Scott Richard Lyons's *X-Marks*, in a related discussion on nationalism that engages Alfred's works, raises an opposite concern, external authority that limits the range of valid Indigenous experiences. Rejecting the paradigm of peoplehood as demanding conformity to its model of Native beliefs and practices, Lyons calls for "a nationalism that starts from, rather than denies, the actually existing diversity of Native communities" (139–40). Within the "nation-people," he finds legitimacy for "other cultural beliefs and practices," including forms of Christianity that do not reject Native origin stories. Lyons argues for an inclusiveness that "acknowledges constitutive myths and stories as the privileged *milieu*." Yet these are embraced "not as religious dogma but as explanations of ethnic origins" (141, emphasis in original). Emphasizing the need for diversity rather than questioning the validity of diverse beliefs and practices, Lyons, like Lawrence, resolves the dilemma by calling for a pragmatic understanding of usefulness.

The analysis that follows considers the ways four characters negotiate the problematic of religious validity. It considers the extent to which and the ways they engage or ignore supernatural realities as they search for useful ways of finding fullness. The point of this analysis is not evaluation or prescription but rather clarification of these characters' structures of belief and practice as well as the force fields that shape them. It considers the healing that results from characters' religious experiences: by whom and for whom and with what means and results. *Love Medicine* provides a fictional study of a reservation community's experiential transition from an aboriginal to a modern socioreligious imaginary as Lipsha's therapeutic healing supersedes Fleur's cosmically engaged beliefs and practices. This religious shift in imaginary has already been made by the community Sarris has created out of his experience leading the Federated Indians of Graton Rancheria. This shift took place as they migrated from their traditional homeland to urban Santa Rosa. Through Faye and Anna, *Grand Avenue* reckons with the individualizing impulse within the modern socioreligious imaginary as they engage Pomo traditionalism and Christian Protestantism respectively.

This analysis develops out of the differentiation Charles Taylor makes between the premodern or aboriginal and the modern socioreligious imaginaries discussed in chapter 1. New conditions and practices of belief within the modern imaginary impact all four characters' religious improvisations. Taylor's three definitions of secularity within the modern imaginary, together with his differentiation of these definitions from common understandings of modern secularism, are particularly important for understanding the characters' tribal situations (see chapter 1). This framework is extended by engaging John A. McClure's explanation of post-secular religious improvisations in contemporary literature.[2] Recognizing the four characters' individualized efforts at sustaining what had been communally grounded religions helps clarify some of the challenges Native revitalization efforts face.

In *A Secular Age*, Taylor delineates the fundamental shift from the aboriginal socioreligious imaginary, in which religious believing was accepted more or less without question, to the modern imaginary, in which religious belief (as well as unbelief) is "one option among others, and frequently not the easiest to embrace" (3). In the modern world of both *Love Medicine* and *Grand Avenue*, characters individually assume religious authority through the choices they make. While a religious marketplace may be an overly simple metaphor for describing the dominant religious ethos today, it does alert us to the central role individual choice plays in present Indigenous religious experiences.[3]

If contemporary Indigenous literature is an indication, many have chosen not to engage with Indigenous religions even if they are committed to their Native cultures. They are basically secular. However, Taylor explains that secularity is not the opposite of religious belief.[4] Rather, secularity shapes both believing and nonbelieving. He describes three forms of secularity, each relevant to modern Native experience. First is the separation of the public or political and private spheres, with religion absent from the public sphere and only experienced as private (1). One does not see traditional ceremonies having a role in the work of tribal governments—for example, in the running of the tomahawk factory in *Love Medicine* or regaining federal recognition in *Grand Avenue*.[5] Taylor's second definition has to do with "the falling off of religious belief and practice" (*Secular* 2). Being religious is no longer the community norm. Nector, Lyman, and most other characters have no apparent connection to the religious beliefs and practices that previously permeated all of society, although some change in their old age. Their Anishinaabe identity is experienced secularly.[6] One could easily create a similar list of characters for *Grand Avenue*.

Taylor's third definition of secularity, most relevant here, concerns "the conditions of belief"—that is, the change "from a society in which it was virtually impossible not to believe in gods and supernatural beings to one in which faith, even for the staunchest believer, is one human possibility among others." Secularity in this sense is the condition of belief for believers and nonbelievers alike (*Secular* 18). Erdrich's fictional tribal community exists within a mix of Catholic, Anishinabek, and nonreligious (non-supernatural yet cultural) beliefs and practices. In *Grand Avenue* Protestantism attracts many, although historically other religions, including Catholicism and Mormonism, have been part of the Pomo religious marketplace. Yet the tribes in both novels must live within the ambit of a US society in which "the presumption of unbelief" has become more and more pervasive (*Secular* 13). Traditional religious practice is a choice that goes against the cultural grain. This has become part of tribal culture within *Love Medicine* and *Grand Avenue*.[7]

Taylor differentiates these three definitions of secularity from the definition of secularism, an Enlightenment belief that rejects any claims of transcendence and interprets them solely as false human constructs. Seeing traditional supernatural religions as superstition, Enlightenment thinkers asserted human reason as the basis for social morality (*Dilemmas* 304–07). Secularism has often been taken as a central tenet of modernism; however, it does not account for the significant role religious experience has continued to play for many, particularly in the United States, where the Enlightenment was not antireligious as it was in Europe (Beck 20).

The term "social imaginary" is a useful tool in explaining secularity as a cultural shift. For the present analysis, I have engaged the term "socioreligious imaginary." Individuals and their communities intersect dialectically within imaginaries. They are mutually constitutive (*Secular* 20), but the intersections take particular forms within specific situations. Fleur and Lipsha experience different individual–community dynamics because of their positions within competing imaginaries as the reservation community experiences the end of a cultural transition. On the other hand, even though Faye's and Anna's religious experiences are shaped by different traditions, they fundamentally share the modern socioreligious imaginary that invests authority in individuals and thus enables their improvisational believing. Sarris's *Watermelon Nights*, with its broader historical reach than *Grand Avenue*, tracks the transition away from the waning aboriginal socioreligious imaginary as the fictional Waterplace Pomo community moves to the city and more thoroughly becomes enmeshed in the modern imaginary (see chapter 5).

While Taylor provides a basic framework for understanding this cultural shift, John A. McClure helps clarify the nature of the new religious practices that result. His *Partial Faiths: Postsecular Fiction in the Age of Pynchon and Morrison* uses contemporary US literature, including a chapter on Native fiction, to delineate the "religiously inflected disruption of secular constructions of the real" (3).[8] In the special issue of *American Literature* "After the Postsecular," editors Peter Coviello and Jared Hickman open their introduction by proclaiming, "The secularization thesis is dead. There is no doubt whatever about that." After a "sustained and multidimensional assault," its story of progress from a religious to a secular worldview is no longer convincing. The effort to "unwrite secularist presumption," however, "is just getting underway" (645, 647). Post-secularism challenges the utopian claims of secularism: "When the secular discourse of reason, science, and democracy sought to discredit religion, they did so both by challenging its 'truthfulness' and by claiming to more effectively address, by purely natural and rational means, the terrors it sought to assuage." McClure explains, and many Native characters realize, that these claims failed to deliver the personal or social utopia they promised (88). We see this conflict of worldviews, secular versus post-secular, in novels like *House Made of Dawn*, *Ceremony*, and *Winter in the Blood*.

More contemporary Native novels, on the other hand, no longer tend to focus on the conflict between secular and post-secular apprehensions. More often they engage what sociologist Ulrich Beck in *A God of One's Own* calls "the re-mystification of reality by religion," a twenty-first-century "return of the religions" (2, 19). This significant cultural reversal is part of a broader cultural shift: "Individuals now experience social and psychic life as one of unceasing experimentation and transience" because old institutional stabilities have been undermined. They have become "deregulated and privatized" (Speck 299). This socioreligious imaginary shapes much of the Indian Country cultural landscape. The return of the gods is evident, for example, in Angeline Boulley's YA novel *Fire Keeper's Daughter* and Elissa Washuta's (Cowlitz) essay "White Magic," with its celebration of occult beliefs, as well as the two novels considered in this chapter. Many contemporary novels include an ambiguous supernaturalism that was not a part of Native American Renaissance fiction. Recent examples include Cherie Demaline's *Empire of the Wild*, Brandon Hobson's *The Removed*, and Stephen Graham Jones's *Ledfeather*.

While critiquing the failed claims of secularism, post-secularism also challenges traditional religious authority, including the authority of Indigenous traditions. *Partial Faiths*, for example, analyzes Lipsha and his community's embrace of an improvisational form of Anishinabek religious practice cobbled together out of traditional materials, both Native and Christian. McClure presents a specifically Indigenous context for these post-secular practices while recognizing that the religious experiences within *Love Medicine* are also profoundly shaped by the dominant society's modern socioreligious imaginary.

Beck addresses a "paradox of secularization" that is similar to Taylor's secularity and McClure's post-secular understanding. Secularization "emancipates" religion, he argues, from its burden of scientifically explaining the cosmos as well as its connection to the state, both of which are causes of alienation from religion. (Native critiques of Christianity often make the same assessment and assert Indigenous beliefs as an alternative. However, this elides the institutional or tribal quality of aboriginal religions.) After this emancipation, religion is then purportedly free to engage its true purpose, "spirituality" (Beck 24–26). Similarly, post-secular fiction "aims at once to reaffirm and to weaken the religious, to represent it as a resource for personal and collective empowerment that must itself be weakened in order to be responsibly deployed." This weakened religion "avoids absolute assertions and totalizing schemes." It also aims to limit institutional tendencies to gain power and position (McClure 12). This means that post-secular religion now is centered in the private sphere and focused on individual experience (Beck 20, 26). Does this offer a solid enough basis for sustaining more than individual religious renewals? Can Indigenous ways of knowing be collectively revitalized within "the renaissance of a new kind of subjective anarchy of belief" (Beck 85)? *Love Medicine* and *Grand Avenue* depict the possibilities and limits of the individualizing tendency for sustaining communities.

The shift in cultural ethos thus does not entail a full return to the religious experiences of the past, particularly communal authorization. The post-secular religious orientation is not grounded in institutional or cultural authority but is a self-authorizing, nontranscendent believing focused on life right now. Beck explains that the "authority principle" of this new religious sensibility is "the sovereign self." Yet self-authorizing beliefs and practices do not provide the experience of ontological certainty that either secularism or the aboriginal socioreligious imaginary offered. A significant implication is that this "individualism is a *contingent* process, and for that reason is *highly ambivalent* in its consequences" (Beck 29, 16; emphasis in original).

Post-secular religion is this-worldly, claiming to offer the possibility of a fuller present life to those who are "religiously unhoused but spiritually hungry." Individuals choose selectively and tentatively from a range of options, even as traditional impulses toward religious experience continue; "ancient fears, hopes and recipes for survival long associated with the religious" still survive (McClure 64, 3–10). This skeptical hunger, with its strengths and limitations, is evident in contemporary Indigenous literature; Lipsha, Faye and Anna are clear examples. Relevant to their examples, Beck reports that sociological research indicates that participants in the new religious but non-church revitalization movements tend to have "highly modernized backgrounds" and are young, educated adults (28). Compared with their communities, these three characters stand apart because of their relative modernization and higher social status.

McClure sums up the improvisational form of religious believing with the term "partial conversions," a useful concept for understanding the religious choices made by characters in *Love Medicine* and *Grand Avenue*. McClure makes clear that conversion or belief within the post-secular turn takes different forms within different cultural contexts (133). Not surprisingly, Erdrich and Sarris's characters and communities experience considerably different forms of spiritual striving and practices of belief within their specific histories and tribal situations. Yet they share an individualization of belief that is experienced as a choice but is part of a common imaginary. Within it the characters discussed respond to the breakdown of tribal religious authority by renewing and revising traditional tribal religions. Gains and losses, the novels make clear, accrue in this "subjective anarchy of belief" (Beck 85).

Love Medicine provides a rich contextual understanding of this shift in socio-religious imaginary. McClure calls *Love Medicine*, together with Thomas Pynchon's *Vineland* and Don DeLillo's *While Noise*, "spiritual comedy," a "ludic avowal" that tends to enervate characters' traditional religious beliefs (126). We see this as Lipsha Morrisey, with a humorously improvisational ceremony, tries to heal the marital rift between Marie and Nector Kashpaw. Lipsha has established a comfortable place within the new imaginary, in which gods have lost their bodies and become immanent influences within a modern, considerably colonized, somewhat resistant tribal world. Erdrich depicts his religious innovations as the intuitive choices he makes in response to circumstances—for example, his poor hunting skills. Yet his individualization of tribal religious practice is part of a common imaginary that offers what traditional religion for many no longer can: "the promise of subjective certainty" (Beck 91).

Lipsha seems a character of hope, the bumbling, good-hearted underdog who confidently translates Anishinabek traditions into the present. He explains his healing power this way: "I know the tricks of the mind and body inside out without ever having trained for it, because I got the touch. It's a thing you got to be born with" (230–31). What Lipsha understands as innate and somehow miraculous can also be understood as his intuitive reading of the reservation's present structure of religious feeling. He has what Pierre Bourdieu, writing about cultural systems, calls a "feel for the game" (66) or a talent for engaging in acceptable innovation within continuously changing circumstances (Verter 153).[9] For Lipsha and the community, his love medicine, a new hybrid adaptation of traditional Anishinaabe and Catholic practices, fits within their habitus or sense of the world. And so it *makes* sense. With irony, Erdrich brings the reader into sympathy with this religious "game" while gently showing us the absurdity of his "miraculous" touch from an outsider's perspective.

However, Lipsha is not the only healer on the reservation. Although Fleur Pillager is acknowledged as a traditional healer and has displayed great power unlike anything Lipsha performs, the present community has turned away from her. She has lost the feel for the reservations' present religious game.[10] Some instead look to Lipsha for help. They are looking for consolation rather than cosmological healing. Fleur's supernatural power scares them, and it seems out of place in their world. Religion is no longer about terror at the unknown. Within the novel, it is unremarkable that tribal members now make choices about healers and forms of healing. Authority rests not with elders but with individuals choosing an exceptional leader who has charisma (in Weber's sense, as opposed to a traditional or rational–legal sense; see

Love Medicine 127). And Lipsha's healing ceremonies do meet real needs as he improvises on traditions.

Lipsha at one point evaluatively contrasts the Anishinaabe gods to Christian ones (236). Humans have become the judge of the gods. Lipsha chooses among available religious options as he filters the traditional love medicine ceremony through his sense of the social world and the cosmos. Lipsha is part of a fundamental shift: "We say that we have moments of transcendent experience . . . rather than moments when we experience the transcendent character of reality" (Warner, VanAntwerpen, and Calhoun 11). In contrast, Fleur is the community's last direct connection to the interventionist power of the Anishinaabe gods. She had been ravaged by a water monster, the last god to appear (236). She lives close to nature and the spirits and participates only minimally in the dominant economic, social, and religious culture of the reservation. She can "put[] the twisted mouth on people, seizing up their hearts," among other powers, and is a specialist in love medicines. Fleur traditionally experiences a porous cosmos in which supernatural powers intersect with material realities. As a result, she is now something of an outcast because her religious practices are no longer communally sanctioned. In this sense Fleur participates in the transition away from the aboriginal socioreligious imaginary even as she shares its cosmic apprehension. Individually sustaining what had been a communally maintained traditional relation to the cosmos, Fleur still has traditional powers strong enough to induce Lipsha and the others in the community to "steer clear" (241). It is not that characters no longer believe in the powers Fleur can marshal but that those powers do not seem useful. Momaday's phrase "the theft of the sacred" captures their loss of the traditional, tribally sanctioned way of experiencing the cosmos. It is the theft of an imaginary. In the old dispensation, tribes recognized that the gods' powers were not always used to enhance human well-being; their cosmic outlook was not anthropocentric. Book 1 of Robert Davis Hoffmann's *Raven's Echo*, discussed in chapter 6, certainly understands Raven that way. This religious conceptualization no longer is appealing to Erdrich's fictional reservation community; actually, it is hardly imaginable. For them the sacred has been so thoroughly transformed that they are unaware of the loss.

Lipsha and other post-secular characters have a "distrust of permanent structures and fixed locations"—that is, the previous timeless-seeming tribal apprehensions of the sacred. Traditions are used selectively rather than submissively (McClure 5). After rejecting the idea of consulting Fleur for traditional guidance, Lipsha spends days "trying to think up something that would work" based on what others had gossiped about (241–42). These are the religious resources available to him on the reservation. There is a humorous, gentle, and yet unsettling quality to Lipsha's improvisational traditionalism, since "choices must be made but individuals' resources for doing so have been undermined" (Speck 299, 300). From Fleur's point of view, Lipsha has only half the cosmos to work with. Yet if his religious practice weakens traditional religion, it also reaffirms the fact that religion still matters, even if beliefs have become "fragilized" (Warner, VanAntwerpen, and Calhoun 23), as religious practice becomes historically contingent rather than transcendentally outside of time. Lipsha even wonders if "maybe we got nothing but ourselves" (236–37); experientially that seems true for many, him included.

Fleur's believing, still mostly within the aboriginal socioreligious imaginary, is not privatized or focused on interiority. Although supernatural powers directly experienced by her require interpretation, the level of abstraction is much lower, and the powers feel more real because interpretations have been communally developed over time. Although she feels embattled, she experiences social rather than religious alienation as her retreat from modern tribal society sustains her in the community of the past. For Lipsha, believing is a satisfying self-efficacious engagement. His belief is grounded in his commitment to believing rather than to cosmic forces that confirm belief. Lipsha fosters the fractured and fragilized believing that his community now maintains. The structure of feeling this fictionalized version of the Turtle Mountain Reservation maintains includes spiritual skepticism, cultural fragmentation, and a low level of religious intensity within Native and Catholic traditions. The community experiences little religious desperation, Marie's early life notwithstanding.

Because their individualized beliefs operate only in the private sphere, those beliefs have no direct relationship to the reservation's political structure.

In contrast, living in the enchanted, pre-contact world meant communal believing with public consequences. Those who did not participate in ceremonies risked harm, and not only to themselves. They put "the efficacy of these rites in danger and thus pose a menace to everyone" (Taylor, *Secular* 41). Religious experience thus needed to be disciplined by the community. In *Love Medicine* religion has been quarantined. Lipsha's reflection on his own spiritual journey wonderfully indicates its fragile interiority: "Your life feels different on you, once you greet death and understand your heart's position. You wear your life like a garment from the mission bundle sale every after—lightly because you realize you never paid nothing for it, cherishing because you know you won't come by such a bargain again" (256). This imaginatively individualized, privatized understanding provides little room for imagining a revitalized communal and cosmic belief and practice.

Within this context of shifting imaginaries and experiences of believing, Lawrence's question about how much traditions can be changed and remain valid is an important one (168). Have Lipsha's improvisations strayed too far from the remnants of aboriginal religion that Fleur embodies? Is *Love Medicine* a model or a warning? A pragmatic evaluation of validity that focuses on usefulness suggests that one should reckon with both gains and losses. Post-secular characters like him are "transformed and steadied" by their sense of a hopeful world "seamed in mystery and benignity" (McClure 20, 6). Healing but also alienation result from Lipsha's abstracted, supermarket connection to the land. Similarly, he gains "subjective agency" but lacks societal engagement with political consequences. Thus Lipsha is baffled when trying to explain the social world of self-destructive characters like King, Gordie, and his mother June (236). Characters like them need more than Lipsha's love medicine, and he has nothing more to offer.

Grand Avenue depicts the fictional urban Waterplace Pomo community, which is also engaged in a religious marketplace offering various forms of Native and Christian experiential beliefs as well as religious nonbelief. However, Sarris offers more troubled accounts of individualized, improvisational religious practices. His fictional ethnography presents a community that has largely left behind the religious structures and imaginary of its rural past for various forms of post-secular believing. While class stratification troubles reservation life in *Love Medicine* (see Dyck, "When"), class status in the urban setting of *Grand Avenue* plays a more conspicuous role in shaping religious experience. Also, the religious improvisations of Faye and Anna, unlike Lipsha's, isolate rather than integrate them into the community. This is both wounding and sustaining. Engaging an urban context closer to the Toronto one Lawrence studied, *Grand Avenue* offers another opportunity to consider her criterion for evaluating religious improvisations: meeting the needs of practitioners (169).

Key to Faye's and Anna's religious experiences is their socioeconomic status and striving. Their class positions must be understood relationally.[11] People commonly assume that Native people are "homogeneously . . . underclass" (Howard-Bobiwash 569) and so see "Native" and "poverty" as synonymous (Lawrence 124). In her research, however, Heather Howard-Bobiwash found a "diversity and complexity in the socioeconomic life of Native urban migrants" (569, 567). Within that diversity was "a Native 'aristocracy' or 'affluent' group, which is defined not strictly by wealth, but by such factors as living in stable families and comfortable, well-located homes with infrequent address changes. They also tend to have job stability, which is essentially defined as an 'absence of dependence on public welfare'" (Howard-Bobiwash 570–71). This is the social position Faye and Anna aspire to. They have achieved at least a tentative and partial grasp of this social position but aspire to a more stable and solid place in it. Their relational or community-dependent status is also fundamentally shaped by larger socioeconomic forces.

Although both of their situations are precarious, their economic and cultural capital place them above most others in the community, as represented by Faye's welfare-dependent sisters. Faye and Anna are recognized for their middle-class ideals, ambitions, and sense of agency. Their personal appearance is different, as are their more orderly homes and engaged childrearing practices. Another middle-class marker is their interactions with the non-Indian world. For Faye this takes place through work. She is one of the few able to find a job that is more than temporary. We see Anna's interactions with the dominant society as she negotiates with authority figures—for example, with the doctor about her daughter's medical treatment and with the police on behalf of community members in trouble (25–26, 122–23). Faye and Anna's class status provides them with a limited, often frustrated sense of efficacy, which then instigates their religious improvisations. However, the tenuousness of their class status limits their ability to feel religiously (or socially) settled. They are only partly able "to see themselves as independent actors, free to choose their possible selves and to create their future paths" (Stephens, Fryberg, and Markus 87). As their material distinction slips away, so does their sense of agency. This gives a tenuous, sometimes desperate, and ultimately frustrating quality to their religious improvisations.

While their class aspirations are shaped by capitalist social structures, they also have their roots in the 1870s Bole Maru revitalization movement, which remains part of contemporary Pomo culture (Sarris, *Keeping* 68–69). Bole Maru, as explained in chapter 5, was a response to economic and consequent spiritual devastation resulting from US occupation of Pomo lands. Emerging from the aboriginal Pomo socioreligious imaginary, the Bole Maru adapted "the Protestant work ethic and the Puritan [or Victorian] principles" of cleanliness, abstinence, and women's modesty to traditional Pomo structures of belief (*Keeping* 66–67). While this has been interpreted as a capitulation to dominant cultural norms, Sarris reads the Bole Maru movement as a powerful nationalist effort of continuance, enabled by strict rules of behavior necessary for the people's survival. Yet he recognizes that resistance can also be counterproductive; this is significant for understanding Faye's experience. Sarris explains that Bole Maru founder Richard Taylor imagined the return of a past uncorrupted by colonialism. When this did not happen, some members became further alienated. Their isolation could actually "weaken their resistance, and hasten their demise" ("Living" 34, 39). However, Sarris also concludes that the movement "enhanced the resurgence and fortification of many pre-contact structures integral to Pomo life and ideology" (*Keeping* 67). This interpretive ambivalence also inheres in Faye and Anna's postsecular improvisations, but with a difference. The isolation that prompts and enables their improvisational religious strategies saves them from at least some of their community's social pathologies, but it also leads to their soul-wounding loneliness.

Faye and Anna experience what one of Lawrence's study participants describes: "The loneliness is so deep, and I think it's been in my generation, and my mother's generation, and my grandmother's generation and further back" (162). The different religious improvisations Faye and Anna make, Pomo and Christian, can in part be explained by their family histories. Both involve poisoning, a traditional religiously inflected practice used to maintain social order and sustain particular power relations (See Dyck, afterword, *Grand Avenue* 224). Poisoning was integrated in the traditional Pomo socioreligious imaginary in which the natural and supernatural were inextricably woven together.[12] Traditionally Pomo beliefs "gave the people a feeling of cultural unity and spiritual strength" (Brown and Andrews 46). However, as material conditions changed, religious practices also changed and weakened. No *Grand Avenue* characters are poisoners, and fear of poisoning is almost lost on the younger generation. However, as a teenager Faye had used the community's lingering fear of poisoners to attack Anna to her own social advantage in gaining a stronger sense of community belonging (19). As an adult Faye is still an insecure Pomo community member, striving for a higher socioeconomic status than the others while continuing to need their acceptance. The world is a dangerous place for Faye because her status is precarious. She attempts to protect herself, her daughter Ruby, and her niece Jasmine by improvisationally mapping the cosmos onto her kitchen wall as a means of gaining some sense of control over her world (21). Faye's is an individualized form of the Bole Maru, with its rigid, judgmental morality.[13]

Her religious improvisation follows the failure of her first strategy for safety, her class striving. When her ambitions are blocked by entrenched socioeconomic structures, she turns to religion to understand and counter her economic failure. Thus Faye's experiential religion emerges from her material conditions as she engages her fragile middle-class sense of agency to improvise a post-secular Pomo fundamentalism for one that can explain, at least for her, the alienation and frustration she experiences in the workplace and on Grand Avenue.[14] For a short while she can create a sense of relative spiritual and material safety. Her kitchen becomes an orderly if fragile outpost of middle-class desire transposed into spiritual practice. Yet her practices further alienate her because they do not have the community sanction that poisoning had earlier. By the end of the story, Faye's religious improvising, like her middle-class striving, is not secure enough to help her resolve a family crisis or maintain a sense of dignity through difference. Faye's individualized traditionalism fails to meet her material or spiritual needs. Her experience alerts us to the complex personal motivations and social contexts that shape religious revitalization projects that might otherwise seem incontrovertible when abstracted to the level of principle.

With *Grand Avenue* Sarris reckons not only with changing Pomo traditions but also with changing Christian ones. He offers a more complex depiction than the common literary caricatures of Christian believers, particularly women characters—for example, Paula in *Tracks* and the mother in both *Ceremony* and *Winter in the Blood*—as he constructs intersections between the two traditions. Anna's religious experience follows a pattern somewhat similar to Faye's. With her mother, Ida, she as a child had to escape the rural Pomo community when Ida's brother was accused of poisoning (20). Exiled physically and religiously, Ida turns to Christianity and its middle-class mores as a means of differentiating and sustaining herself and her daughter Anna. Their behavior follows the moral expectations of Bole Maru—hard work, determination, cleanliness, orderliness—while their Christian identity creates a sense of difference from present Pomo poverty and communal dysfunction. The lessons remain with Anna as she improvises a form of Christianity strategic for her social and economic ambitions. Her story reminds readers of the significant role Christianity plays in present-day Native religious experiences. Anna has learned her mother's strategy of differentiation. Understanding the necessary social codes, she accepts the dominant culture's hierarchy of Christianity over Indigenous beliefs, claiming, "I'm no Indian from the bush. . . . I'm a Christian and don't believe in any of that old stuff" (27–28). By escaping "the bush," Anna, like her mother, did improve herself materially but at the cost of isolation from the Pomo community. Moving to the Grand Avenue neighborhood, Anna resists the defeated older generation's colonial Christianity centered on self-blame and passivity (46). Anna offers an almost Nietzschean critique of this Christianity as a slave religion as she improvises out of the materials available within her habitus a personalized post-secular Christianity.

Anna asserts her religious agency as she strives to follow a set of moral guidelines for middle-class success. She states, "I take what's good in the Bible and use it in my life" (45). Her improvised Protestant gospel of success does give Anna a less tenuous sense of social efficacy than what Faye gains through her improvised Pomo beliefs. Those beliefs cannot offer the same cultural capital that Christianity does. Anna embraces what she knows is a sin within her uncle's Bible study circle, her "blinding drive against hard luck, against the curse" (47). The curse she attacks is not poisoning but poverty. In identifying the problem as "bad luck," Anna seems blind to the structures that determine her socioeconomic condition.[15] As a result she experiences both cognitive and spiritual dissonance as her religious beliefs, class position, racial identity, and community commitment all clash in her struggle for social dignity and economic stability. Her personal drive cannot overcome the dominant social structures that trap nearly the whole community. This positions her as useful to the community but alienated from it.

Faye and Anna, like the fictional Bole Maru leader Big Sarah before them, improvise religiously in disciplined ways. Unlike Big Sarah, their religious efforts are not aimed at sustaining the community. On Grand Avenue both Faye and Anna challenge what Foucault calls "a coherent series of gestures of separation" that sustain community boundaries. Their improvisations, Pomo and Christian, fall within the community's "system of the transgressive" that is neither "illegal" nor "revolutionary" nor "monstrous" (50). Their religious engagements are permissible yet transgressive adaptations within the community's informal cultural disciplinary systems (unlike Big Sarah's more formal system of discipline). Neither is banished or even quite ostracized, as transgressive as their religious improvisations are. Intersecting with their religious improvisations are their challenges to community norms against individual self-improvement, which are part the group's internalized oppression (see Sarris, *Keeping* 134–35). Faye and Anna hold on to their liminal position for as long as they have the strength to sustain themselves, but both have a reckoning that breaks their strength and at least temporarily reunites them with their community: Faye when Ruby is arrested and Anna when she asks for prayer for herself and her terminally ill daughter (*GA* 23–24, 42).

These two characters' post-secular religious improvisations reveal that when social conditions changed, new community boundaries were established, and they proved effective. After the Pomo community moves to the city in *Watermelon Nights*, traditional religion loses the unifying force it had with Big Sarah's Bole Maru. For example, Elba's newly improvised urban experiential religion, which emerges from her traditional roundhouse experiences, is not a transgressive holding on to the past because it is quietly individualistic and self-contained. In contrast, Faye, from the next generation, creates improvisations on Pomo traditions that are both religiously and socially provocative within their present context and so must be disciplined. Since religion has lost its formal community character, disciplining is interpersonal rather than tribal. Similarly, Anna's defiant Christianity must be contained for the success of the submissive YMCA Bible study Christianity, but this does not lessen her tribal role as mediator with the outside sociopolitical world. Both characters' individual rather than communal religious innovations suggest the limits and challenges of the post-secular individualistic efforts at religious revitalization that are most common in contemporary Indigenous literature.

Intersecting religious and social structures shape characters' and communities' religious experiences in both *Love Medicine* and *Grand Avenue*. Erdrich depicts Lipsha's ceremonial improvisations as offering healing that is effective for individuals, but it also is quietist socially. In contrast, Fleur envisions her supernatural power rescuing tribal society. However, in *Tracks*, set a generation or so earlier, Erdrich already depicts traditional supernatural powers as no longer available to save the tribe against the encroachments of dominant economic forces. For example, when hunger strikes, commodity wagons rather than Fleur's dream guidance for hunting save the tribe (*Tracks* 171). As old Nanapush comes to recognize, traditional forms of resistance are ineffectual, and bureaucratic strategies are needed to stop the lumbering of their land (209).

The tribe's present inability to collectively engage traditional spiritual powers, part of a larger cultural ethos, has led to the conditions that foster Lipsha's individualized post-secular religious sensibility. Similarly, Faye and Anna's individualistic religions leave them spiritually unmoored as their improvisations fail to provide a satisfactory sanctuary within the troubled world of Grand Avenue and beyond. In playing out the dilemmas of these two characters, Sarris more decisively than Erdrich enmeshes religious aspirations within socioeconomic conditions. He also shows that individualized religious self-empowerment is not useful enough, to use the criteria Lawrence suggests.

Although Lawrence raises questions about the validity of improvised religious traditions, she does not make judgments but rather offers cautions. She explains that because urban Indians more directly engage the dominant culture, they will more thoroughly need to adapt their religious traditions to these circumstances. Usefulness is the fundamental consideration, yet it can only be evaluated with a set of values. Neal McLeod's "Cree Poetic Discourse," discussed in the introduction, similarly addresses the need for improvisational revitalization strategies although within a rural tribal context rather than the urban intertribal one that Lawrence's participants experience. His theoretical insights into religious improvisation, or riffs on tradition, raise questions about the usefulness of Erdrich's and Sarris's characters' improvisations.

The improvising McLeod advocates takes place within rather than apart from the community. This communal orientation goes against the grain of the individualizing impulse of post-secularist religious belief and practice. This impulse creates challenges for Native revitalization movements, yet their success may depend on encouraging individual initiatives toward their intermediate goals. For McLeod, kinship relations are central, and the goal of improvised traditions is community spiritual well-being. As noted, all four characters considered in this chapter have strained relations with their tribal communities. Fleur is the most isolated because she is the most traditional. This irony can complicate the benefits of returning to tradition. In an opposite irony, Lipsha is least isolated because his individually improvised healing does not threaten his community's present decentered structure of religious feeling. He helps some members better cope with the world but cannot offer communal religious revitalization. He cannot even imagine it. Faye's individualized Pomo religion provides her with a map of the cosmos, but it does not integrate her into the community. Anna's improvised Protestantism makes her useful materially to the community, but it offers little hope or sense of direction for her or them. Thus these four characters provide cautions and warnings more than models of success.

Anna's improvisational religious experience raises the question of whether Christianity (and by implication the Native American Church) has a role to play in tribal revitalization. James Clifford observes "a pervasive dichotomy: absorption by the other or resistance to the other" (qtd. in Lassiter, Ellis, and Kotay 117). Christianity's impact on Indian communities is usually seen through the former conception.[16] However, Luke Eric Lassiter, Clyde Ellis, and Ralph Kotay (Kiowa) in *The Jesus Road: Kiowas, Christianity, and Indian Hymns* question this dichotomy, implicit if not explicit in much Native studies scholarship. They note that it "ignore[s] the deeper experiential complexities that have emerged from this multidimensional encounter" between Christianity and Native religious traditions (115). Their afterword concludes with Vincent Pointy's (Kiowa) surprising comment, "We lost our Christianity because we turned towards the white man's ways" (119). This insight and potential guidance has been expressed historically at least back to Samson Occom, a Mohegan and pan-tribal leader who spent his adult working life as a Christian minister and missionary. Both Occom and Vincent Pointy strategically distinguish between Christian beliefs and the social practices often associated with them. For Occom, these practices, particularly economic ones, were fundamentally unchristian. He experienced their harms personally and pushed against their destructive consequences for his tribe and region. Occom's economic critique of capitalism and endorsement of Indigenous economics offers an important model for addressing the present

complexities Native nations and communities now face religiously and economically (see Dyck, "Economic Education").

"Tapping into the Great Mystery" McLeod explains, involves reckoning with history and kinship (109). This tapping that connects humans to a
greater reality can be understood quite differently within historically situated contexts that involve changing socioreligious imaginaries. And yet
continuities remain. Engaging both history and kinship, disjuncture and
continuity, Linda Hogan's *Solar Storms*, with its five-generation family of
women characters, offers a fictional study that can help clarify McLeod's
improvisational poetics (see introduction). Reflecting on God Island, Dora-
Rouge, the eldest, states, "It's an appropriate name. The people there feared
no evil and wanted not." Angela, the youngest, is also drawn to the island and
reflects on its name: "perhaps it was the word 'God' that was inviting to me,
a word I thought I knew too much about." Uneasy with spiritual immediacy
within an aboriginal porous cosmos, Angela offers a modern, post-secular
commentary: "I know now that the name does not refer to any deity, but
means simply to call out and pray, to summon." She continues her rumination: "Something lived there, something I didn't understand. . . . I would call
it God. . . . God was everything beneath my feet . . . and there was no such
thing as empty space" (169–70). Is the Great Mystery in McLeod's essay
the same god of God Island as the eldest understands it? Or is it as Angela
apprehends god as an immanent, defuse object of belief. Or do McLeod's
suggested improvisations address something or someone else? Like Angela's,
McLeod's descriptions are vague: "the belief that reality is more than what
we understand on the surface" and "the force of life beyond our conscious
reality" (112). The Great Mystery is of course a mystery, but the name is
also a framework of understanding with particular assumptions. This is
true for all religious apprehensions. Religious language and symbols, with
strategic ambiguity, can bring together communities. They work that way
for the five women of *Solar Storms* in part because the words remain the
same, or nearly so, but each creates her own meanings out of her particular
cultural milieu and needs. In considering these adaptations, it is useful to
think about, even evaluate, what has been lost, what saved, and what gained

in the interpretive shifts at the heart of changing socioreligious imaginaries. Both novels considered here and McLeod's essay do not provide specific or authoritative answers but rather offer pragmatic guidance for reckoning with Lawrence's question: At what point do traditions change so much that they lose their cultural validity? (168).

Erdrich's and Sarris's fictional ethnographies offer opportunities for practicing this reckoning. The interpretations developed here suggest the importance of considering not just religious practices but the socioreligious imaginaries that shape their meaning. Sarris's novel in particular makes clear the importance of class positioning and aspiration in shaping characters' religious improvisations. Christianity in these novels is a colonizing force, but it is not only that. For some characters it offers something missing in present practices of aboriginal traditions; its appeal needs to be considered as both a positive and negative force field within Native communities but one that is inextricably present in one form or another. The same is true for aboriginal traditions. These novels show them to be equally complex in their adaptations and not only or necessarily enhancing for the individual or the community. And yet they too must be reckoned with.

CONCLUSION: BELIEVING IN BELIEF

TOMMY ORANGE'S *THERE THERE*

Once one starts looking for depictions of religious experiences in recent Indigenous literature, one finds them almost everywhere, including in urban settings. These experiences bear out Charles Taylor's observation that "we are beginning a new age of religious searching, whose outcome no one can foresee" (*Secular* 535). The range of experiences is considerable, some hardly recognizable as being religious. Tommy Orange's *There There*, read from this perspective, offers a compendium of contemporary Native religious experiences in an urban setting far from characters' homelands. The novel is a counterpart to the other major Native literary religious compendium, Greg Sarris's more historically oriented, tribally centered, interrelated novels, discussed in chapter 5 and 7. Two decades before *There There* Sarris published *Grand Avenue*, set in a Pomo enclave on the edge of Santa Rosa, California. Displaced from their rural rancheria, his characters have maintained communal connections of remembered history and social proximity. *Grand Avenue* explores a community rather than a collection of individuals as in *There There*. It shows how this community sustains itself in the face of dispossession. Published two years later, *Watermelon Nights* deepens the account of this urban community, in part by depicting its rural history and urban transition. Sarris's and Orange's works engage different but related forms of urban Indigenous religious experience. They are the only fiction writers to extensively address this problematic with a perspective that goes beyond theft, loss, and exile.

Characters in *There There* provide considerable religious theorizing. Edwin Black's first section begins by constructing a reading of his life. Almost immediately he explains the unsettled foundation of his experiential religion. "The trouble with believing," he states, "is you have to believe that believing will work, you have to believe in belief." Later, when he experiences what seems like a miracle, he gives thanks but "to no one in particular" (78). These comments suggest how deeply and self-consciously he is enmeshed in the modern socioreligious imaginary. While religious belief is no longer a given for Orange's characters, their choice to believe or not believe is not merely individual. It is a negotiation between the individual and their community.

Not only has the nature of religious belief changed; the content of belief within city religions has also changed. Providing context for this change, Laura Furlan in *Indigenous Cities* observes that "urban Indian writing articulates a radical shift in the often-discussed relationship between people and place, a shift in Indian identity—in the way people think about themselves as Indians" (8). She goes on to explain that while Indians bring to the city their connections to homeland and traditions as well as their kinship relations, they also create new urban communities that "offer a kind of tribal cosmopolitanism as a replacement for a more rooted tribal subjectivity" (9). *There There* offers a powerful vision of what that replacement looks like.

The most widely recognized and radically new contemporary Native novel, *There There* in its urban engagement has challenged many common assumptions about Native place, identity, and experience. Religious experiences in *There There* take place within a decidedly urban social and cultural environment. This geography is addressed in the novel's prologue, where Orange seems intent on challenging many accepted premises about urban Indian life:

"Plenty of us came by choice."

"But what we are is what our ancestors did."

"We found one another."

"The city made us new."

"and we made it ours."

"We didn't get lost." (8–10)

Rather than apologizing for this situation, Orange engages the present realities for a large majority of Indians: They know the city landscape better than the sacred places of their traditional homelands (11). He asserts that the Native present, like its past, is about adaptation. "We did not move to the cities to die," he states with troubling irony, given the deadly gunfight that concludes the novel (9).

There There in my reading is the culmination of the previous chapters' concerns, as it addresses the problematic of interpretation, the possibilities for ceremonies within the modern socioreligious imaginary, religious life within crisis ordinariness, the effects of trauma on Native religious experience, darkness and recovery, and religious improvisation as reconstruction. N. Scott Momaday's trenchant phrase "the theft of the sacred" has been a leitmotif for this book. Much contemporary Indigenous literature, including *There There*, can be read as excavating, explicating, interrogating, qualifying, and extending Momaday's claim. Statistics on suicide, alcoholism, and various forms of violence suggest the profound spiritual and material consequences of this theft of the sacred.[1] Yet the phrase does not summarize the whole story, as the previous chapters have made clear. Native religious experiences in many different forms have sustained individuals and communities, often by pushing back against continuing colonialism and the internalized oppression that it fosters. "We survived" is a common contemporary Native meme. For many, their beliefs and practices are part of what has survived in reconstructed form, what helped give them the strength to survive.

There There offers us news from the present that is distinctly urban. It is more about individualized rather than tribal religious experiences. They fit uneasily in the novel, breaking through in unusual moments. Uncertainty is as fundamental as improvisation. Native drumming is the most impactful religious experience in the novel. Christianity offers hope to a few. Many characters have no apparent religion experience and use drugs or alcohol as a substitute heightened inner experience. In the novel, religious experience and its absence take place within a marketplace of options that are urban and individualistic.

For Momaday's *House Made of Dawn*, Los Angeles is the "ultimate exile" (Miller 37). The same is true in Silko's *Ceremony*, where the city is a form of banishment. In Erdrich's *Love Medicine*, urban dweller Beverly "Hat" Lamertine is nearly completely deracinated, and King has become thoroughly alienated living in the city, even as his urbanization in turn alienates him from the reservation. As Renya Ramirez (Winnebago) notes, urban Indians are often seen as "problems to be fixed" (22). A corollary to the claim that the city has no "there there" is the idea that there can be no Native community there either. Yet the above list of quotations from *There There* focus on "we." The opening chapter, narrated by Tony Loneman, gives his name an ironic twist. His urban community is not centered on place but rather freely includes a friend, his grandmother, an Indian Center counselor, the Cheyenne people as an abstraction, Native literature, and Native drug connections. Rather than a collection of *isolatoes*, the city for Tony and most other characters is a complex human network within which they make a life.

"All our relations" takes on considerably different meanings in the city, including religious ones. For Opal and for the novel as a whole, the problem of belief has not been resolved, and yet belief in various forms continues in the city. Opal must look within, but she also recognizes "that there is power in saying the prayer out loud" (284). In a city hospital waiting room, she rediscovers religious belief as an individual and community dialectic. Rather than being anomic or atomistic, cities can be understood as complex networks (Orsi, "Introduction" 49).

Orange joins a group of scholars who challenge the assumption that Native religious experience and urban living are contradictory concepts.[2] More generally, Robert A. Orsi observes that until recently many religious scholars saw "city religion" as an oxymoron. For example, Mircea Eliade, who had been a leading authority on the history of religions, argued that "religions in contemporary Western urban settings were degraded and impotent 'survivals' of real religiosity, which necessarily existed in intimate and ongoing connection to the rhythms and revelations of the sacred in nature" (qtd. in Orsi, "Introduction" 41–42). Many in Native studies have taken a similar position. Kathryn Shanley (Fort Peck Assiniboine/Nakoda) states that "nothing defines indigenous peoples more than belonging to a place, a homeland" (3). Robert K. Thomas (Cherokee) presses the point more emphatically: "I'm not so sure in my mind if Indians can exist as city people. The city really cuts one off from the 'natural' world. Can the Indian's sacred world continue in a world of concrete and automobiles?" (qtd. in Straus and Valentino 85). The general absence of urban religious reckonings within Indigenous studies suggests that this is a common assumption.[3]

The common understanding is that cities provoke an alienation that results from the secularization of the city. Yet Orsi argues, "It is often precisely the disjuncture between environment and religious idiom that occasions crises, cultural creativity, and religious innovation" ("Introduction" 42). This adaptive position challenges the ideology of authenticity (see introduction). Brendan Hokowhitu's (Māori/Ngāti Pūkenga descent) essay in the anthology *Critical Indigenous Studies*, significantly subtitled "Post-Indigenous Studies," questions whether the "strategically essentialized cultural pillars, including land, language and culture" are still "useful" (85, 87). Bonita Lawrence similarly questions common assumptions as she reckons with the implications of "over six-hundred tiny, almost landless individual entities known as First Nations" as well as "an ever-growing body of urban, disposed individuals with no land base at all, whose ties to their communities of origin have been weakened and in some cases obscured." She thus calls for "transforming" concepts of identity related to those cultural pillars in a search for "interim processes," pragmatic experiments, and "a diversity of forms of affiliation—and of nation-rebuilding" that would address the seemingly disparate realities Indigenous peoples now experience. For Lawrence, there are no absolute answers (245–46). The implications of all this for the ways urban Indigenous people and communities experience their religions are significant.

In his prologue, Orange engages this problematic by stating that "nothing is original, everything comes from something that came before" (11). The process of adaptation has always been continuous. His novel challenges assumptions about a necessary relationship between rural homelands and Native religions when he asserts, "Being Indian has never been about returning to the land. The land is everywhere or nowhere" (11). That characters in *There There* do not share their author's awareness of the controversies over land or place suggests more than the depth of their alienation. It indicates that they are living within a different reality. None of Orange's characters connect to the land in a traditional sense. (See chapter 6 on concepts of land and place.) Even when Octavio and his grandmother Josefina drive into the countryside to get necessary materials for a medicine box, they do not experience a sense of connectedness. When the grandmother has snared a badger, she unceremoniously yells at Octavio, "Rip its fucking fur with your hands!" (184). Only at the novel's end, in incongruous circumstances, is an autochthonous moment described. On the last bullet-ridden page, Tony Loneman finds his wounds anchoring him to the earth (of a baseball stadium infield) as he hears birds singing inside his bullet wounds. It takes a semiconscious dream state to sustain this topological grounding. It is a religious experience of an imagined place that occurs in the city (290). The there there is interior. Mind has become a substitute .

The modern social imaginary shifts the sanctioning authority of religious beliefs and practices from the tribe or community to the individual, even if the options are socially imagined. The change in imaginary at its heart is a shift in a sense of religious fullness (see chapter 7, note 1). Fullness is what many Native peoples must have felt as they participated in tribal ceremonies and other religious experiences before European outsiders undermined their aboriginal imaginary. Fullness came from outside oneself; it resulted from participating in a community and cosmos sanctioned by tribal tradition. For the modern social imaginary, fullness comes from within rather than without

(*Secular* 15). Thomas Frank experiences this with drumming: "Singing and drumming had done that thing, that all-the-way-there thing he needs to feel that full, that complete feeling like you're right where you're supposed to be right now—in the song and about what the song's about" (262).

Following the trauma of material and spiritual invasion, fullness came to be an internally generated and focused condition. The focus has shifted from transcendence as a quality of the cosmos to it as an individual inner experience. As contemporary Indigenous literature shows, characters experience whatever fullness they can find largely from within themselves. This individualization of religious experience creates a precarious situation for sustaining Native traditions.

In *The Care of the Self*, Michel Foucault distinguished three closely related categories of individualism. This differentiation is useful for clarifying the Native transition from an aboriginal to the modern social imaginary and the resulting sense of fullness. Each category provides a conceptual standpoint for understanding both the ways the modern imaginary fundamentally shapes the experience of being Indigenous and the remnants of traditional experience that remain.

The first category Foucault calls "the individualistic attitude," which values the "singularity" of the individual and thus "the degree of independence conceded to him vis-à-vis the group to which he belongs and the institutions to which he is answerable" (42). Along with powwows, sweat lodge ceremonies are the most common rituals referenced in contemporary Native literature. Both register the tension between "singularity" and communal or institutional engagement. When Opal's mother choses sweats as her form of cancer treatment and calls the medicine man helping her "the real deal," she assumes a religious authority usually tribally held. For clear-eyed Opal, this supernatural healing strategy is a costly nostalgia, "like all those sacred and beautiful and forever-lost things" (59).

The powwow in *There There* similarly engages the tension of "singularity" within traditionally communal forms of experience. The dance still has a certain communal disciplinary power as the young men are guided by an older dancer. Orvil, participating in his first public powwow dance, feels the sense of pan-tribal belonging. This sense is ironically reinforced by his feeling like an outsider as he struggles to see himself as authentic, a concept dependent on communal sanction. Yet he is the judge of his own authenticity even as he judges himself comparatively. Also, the "singularity" inherent in the competition individualizes the dance "ceremony," if that is still the appropriate term for this ironic situation. "To perform and win you have to dance true," Orvil explains to himself in a description that almost seems enchanted: "your feathers a flutter of echoes centuries old, your whole being a kind of flight." He strives to imagine himself as a part of the "one dance" even as he also strives to win the prize money (231–33). Orvil's introspection is a form of inspection of the self as Native object; it marks an inescapable tension for Native revitalization within the context of the modern social imaginary. Unable to ground his being within tribal structures since they are unavailable, he experiences "an intensification of the relation to oneself by which one constituted oneself as the subject of one's acts" (Taylor, *Secular* 41).

And yet he and others want to resist this intensification of self while preparing for the dance. As an older dancer speaks to the younger men, one can imagine similarities to, say, Yellow Kidney in *Fools Crow* instructing young warriors as they prepare for battle (Welch 23–24). And the doubts that Fast Horse experiences within the collapsing Blackfoot tribal world are precursors to Orvil's modern and more thorough disenchantment. "That dance is your prayer," the leader exhorts the men as he works to give the dance a more-than-material meaning by connecting it "all the way back there." It is a healing process, he wants to make clear, yet Orvil registers its modern fragility as he recognizes that "[t]hey all needed to dress up to look like Indians" (231–32). Taylor explains that imaginaries provide a moral order that "carries not only a definition of what is right but also gives the context in which it makes sense to strive for." It offers a "hermeneutics of legitimation" (*Secular* 162). Within the modern social imaginary, the powwow dance provides a structure for the individual to bring his life into the larger cosmic dance of existence. To do that, however, Orvil thinks you must "trick yourself out of thinking altogether. Out of acting. Out of everything. To dance as if time only mattered insofar as you could keep a beat to it, in such a

way that time itself discontinued, disappeared, ran out, or into the feeling of nothingness under your feet" (232–33). The "trick" and "as if" of this
enchantment show his longing for the old order while feeling immersed
in the modern one. The mind has become the substitute for enchantment,
Taylor explains, and we now live in "uniform, univocal time." This shift can
be summed up as a shift from experiencing a cosmos to living within a universe (*Secular* 59). And yet that shift is unevenly experienced and can take
on various in between forms. Taylor misses the possibility of continuities
within the extensive disjunctures.

The tension inherent in this shift of imaginaries is evident in Leanne
Betasamosake Simpson's *As We Have Always Done,* her manifesto for "radical
resistance." The incessant use of "I" marks the modern individualization of
Simpson's cultural-religious strategies even as she asserts the centrality
of tribal relationships (139). Discussing particular controversies over ceremonial practices, she writes, "Sometimes I can . . . and be open spiritually, and
sometimes I cannot. . . . Sometimes I . . . because that's what I'm comfortable
doing. . . . I explain . . . practices to people new to our ceremony, and let them
know that they will be supported however they choose to interpret these
practices." The language marks an uneasy dance with more individual than
communal religious authority. Touching on a key individualizing quality
of the modern socioreligious imaginary, Simpson explains, "Ceremony is
about what is inside" (142). Similarly, Joy Harjo concludes her poem "A
Map to the Next World" by stating, "You must make your own map." That
is not what Native peoples have always done but rather is an adaptation
that acknowledges the shift away from the aboriginal imaginary even as
important traces remain.

Foucault's second category of individualism, "the positive valuation of
private life," situates family, domestic life, and other relational structures
contra the public life central to traditional societies. This valuation permeates *There There.* For Oakland, public Indian life has been centered in the
Intertribal Friendship House, "the heart of a vibrant tribal community." Its
website identifies it as an "Urban Reservation and Homeland" and "one of
the few places that keeps them connected to their culture and traditions"

(Intertribal Friendship House). Within *There There*, however, the Indian Center is important only to those characters who work there. None of the other characters even mention it. One employee, Thomas Frank, joins the drum group, but as noted above, for him the experience is personal rather than tribal or intertribal (208–10). Family in its various forms provides some characters with a structure beyond the self. The narrative force of the novel is in part about families finding themselves. Lawrence observes that the Toronto First Nation community "is not so much a community as a series of circles" (156). Similarly in *There There*, "All my relations" has become mainly limited to the private sphere.

The third related yet distinct category is "the intensity of the relations to the self" or the ways "one is called upon to take oneself as an object of knowledge and a field of action" (Foucault 42). Orvil's experience as a dancer has this self-focused quality. The fragility of the social structures sustaining the dance (the adapted intertribal traditions, the dancers' need to reinforce their identity as authentic Indians, and so on) does not provide a "hermeneutics of legitimation" or way of making sense that is robust enough for Orvil to move beyond the self so as to participate in communal forms of being. Earlier, when he was dancing alone, he "felt like it was all his ancestors who made it so he could be there dancing." With cosmic connections depending on his inner feelings, he remains caught within the modern social imaginary's individualizing centripetal force (126).

Edwin Black struggles somewhat differently with the problematic of legitimation and its relation to the self. Not knowing his father, he does not know his tribal identity. Yet it is not a social or tribal connection he desires but a way of relating to himself as a legitimate Indian. For urban Indians, Lawrence explains, tribal membership is "highly symbolic," particularly for those like Edwin who did not grow up around Native people (169). When he finds out his tribal identity, it is not the specific tribe that matters, as it does for his father, but the fact that he has one. As an undergraduate Native American studies major and then as a graduate student focusing on Native American literature, he has been searching for an Indian self to belong to, not a tribe. That is beyond what he can imagine (71). For both

Orvil and Edwin, their key relationship is with their internal rather than public self even as they long for that self to be Indian. Along with many (although not all) other characters who have also internalized an intertribal sense of being Indian, these two challenge readers to consider the extent to which intertribal Indianness is a relationship mainly with the self as a form of identity or a relationship to a social entity as relationally experiential.[4]

Heightening the novel's fundamental conceptual context of the individualized self is the way traditionally oriented religious beliefs fail characters who trust them. Particularly in the first sections of *There There*, this creates doubt about the efficacy of the modern uses of tradition. Eleven-year-old Opal embodies this with her teddy bear Two Shoes's imagined "sacred bear medicine" (50–51). She projects onto him her need for protection, understanding, and sympathy as well as her Indigenous sense of identity. Material reality shocks her with her sister's rape on Alcatraz Island. Not long after, her mother, Victoria, rejects modern cancer treatments for traditional medicine. Looking back after her mother's death, Opal she sees her "receding into the past" of "forever-lost things" that cannot heal her, and so she dies (59). It is hard to imagine that Orange does not mean this as a caution if not a warning about modern uses of aboriginal traditions. Victoria's having had to make a choice for traditional medical treatment indicates its uncertainty, the lack of givenness that was part of pre-contact religious life. Her individual belief lacks the reassurances of social sanction and community support. Not surprisingly Opal, when raising three boys, warns them against learning about their heritage. In another one of the novel's striking statements, she says it is a luxury and a risk they cannot afford (118–19). This perspective is seldom so directly stated.

Traditions may make sense when separated from everyday life. Chrystal (subsequently named Blue) at one point explains that in weekly ceremonies "[w]e prayed for the whole world to get better and felt it could every morning when we came out of the tipi." Yet physical abuse by her sweat lodge partner and husband destroys the ceremonies' efficacy. She reflects ruefully, "But it all made perfect sense for a while. In there" (198–99).

The one apparently supernatural incident in the novel offers not religious confirmation but rather bafflement. The spider legs found in Orvil's leg remain incomprehensible within any cosmic map his mother or aunt have available to them (125, 154; see also chapter 1). Opal herself had had the same experience, but rather than finding meaning for it she experienced shame at this "grotesque yet magical" occurrence (165). The struggle to remain grounded in tradition while being "a present-tense people, modern and relevant" (141) leaves characters in this and many Native literary works feeling uncertain and tentative, sometimes longing for but often rejecting traditional religious experience. With no tribal structures to reassure these urban characters of spiritual realities, they find the burden of belief a strain and a bafflement.

For the curandero Josefina, the most traditionally engaged character, the enchanted world with its supernatural powers and inherited curses still exists. Yet she can only use these powers as an individual remnant of a tribal past. For her religiously estranged grandson Octavio Gomez, who receives her healing intervention, traditional belief in curses is now "some old dark leftover thing that stayed with our family" (181). Even Josefina asserts a modernist doubt at the heart of healing ceremonies. She explains that the "setup" is predicated upon uncertainty: "You're not ever supposed to know. Not all the way. That's what makes the whole thing work the way it does. We can't know. That's what makes us keep going" (186). This cosmic "setup" is also expressed in "Deer Dancer," Joy Harjo's great poem of contemporary Native religious experience: "We all take risks stepping into thin air. Our ceremonies didn't predict this. Or we expected more" (8, see chapter 3). A Native leap of faith has become central to many characters' lived religions. Doubt about the nature and accessibility of the spiritual world permeates *There There* right from the title, in part a reference to Radiohead's song of the same name. Its chorus states,

> We are accidents waiting
> Waiting to happen
> We are accidents waiting
> Waiting to happen

Doubt about cosmic meaning and purpose haunts characters. With the spiritual world apprehended individually as a choice, doubt and unbelief become central to literary depictions of modern Indigenous efforts to engage traditional religious resources.

In the concluding crisis, however, Opal's trauma prompts a new religious possibility to emerge: "Opal knows that this was the time, if ever there was one, to believe, to pray, to ask for help, even though she had abandoned all hope for outside help on a prison island back when she was eleven" (284). Yet praying here is not a community-sanctioned ceremony to bridge the material and spiritual realms. She must sustain her religious experience herself, and yet "[t]he voice is hers and not hers. But hers, finally. It can't come from anywhere else." Through the narrator's voice she echoes Edwin by stating, "Before she can even think to pray, she has to believe she can believe. She's making it come but also letting it come" (285).

This is immanent rather than transcendent religion, the loose translation of tradition into a personal idiom of the modern social imaginary (see chapter 1). Taylor states, "The great invention of the West was that of an immanent order in Nature, whose working could be systematically understood and explained on its own terms, leaving open the question whether this whole order has a deeper significance." As a result, "humanism" has become a common option (*Secular* 15, 21). Within this inescapable although not necessarily predominating condition of the modern socioreligious imaginary, characters in *There There* and other contemporary Native fiction must find their religious way. Call their experiences spiritual, but that does not erase the socially and culturally constructed ways that experience is shaped. Rather than offering a culturally given grasp of the cosmos, the modern imaginary, variously experienced and to various degrees, draws characters to look inside themselves to find meanings for more-than-material experiences of gods and ancestors. This is one answer to the fraught questions raised in the introduction: Does Native revitalization necessarily require Native reenchantment, and if so, in what ways?

"There's gotta be some reason for all this," Harvey tells Jacquie Red Feather about their reunion as he clings to a hope for cosmic meaning in an act of personal belief (115). Yet its opposite, spiritual unbelief, has become a viable choice many characters wrestle with or accept without reflection. As Taylor notes, we live in a time when not believing seems more plausible to many than believing (*Secular* 12). Contemporary Indigenous literature reflects this religious situation. This cultural structure of feeling challenges even those characters striving to believe: "We cannot help looking over our shoulder from time to time, looking sideways, living our faith also in a condition of doubt and uncertainty" (Taylor, *Secular* 11).

Many of this novel's characters live with an emptiness not uncommon for urban Indigenous characters. One of the tropes of this literature, borrowed from Blaise Pascal, is the hole in the heart. Charles Taylor notes that "God-forsakenness is an experience of those whose ancestral culture has been transformed and repressed by a relentless process of disenchantment" (*Secular* 553). In *There There* Thomas Frank reflects on his own experience of emptiness: "Your parents maybe burned a too-deep God hole through you. The hole was unfillable." This burning came from the fire of his mother's Pentecostal Christianity and the "one thousand percent" Indian intensity of his father. Both beliefs have failed the family (217, 210, 215). Opal's sense of emptiness is more vague, coming from a lifetime of troubled experiences that include the Alcatraz events that culminate in her mother's death (58–59): "So she bore those years, their weight, and the years bored a hole through the middle of her" (162). For Opal, working three jobs to provide for her nephews while struggling to protect the three from a hostile world leaves her no room to look for Native religious sustenance that might help heal her traumatic wound, the hole she experiences alone.[5]

Melanie Benson Taylor extends this condition to all the characters in *There There*. They "bear little in common beyond a tandem circling around an existential void they are taught to fetishize and internalize" (593). Emptiness rather than fullness marks their sense of self. It is experienced as a feeling of loss or flatness or as something missing when transcendence becomes unimaginable even if it is still longed for (Taylor, *Secular* 307–09). Orange's character Octavio Gomez speaks for others in expressing this disenchantment: "We've got this old thing that hurts real fucking bad, makes you mean," and "Some of us got this feeling stuck inside, all the time, like we've done something wrong. Like we ourselves are something wrong" (181, 184).

Imagining religious revitalization within this pervasive condition of belief becomes a challenge for many Native literary writers as they create marginally hopeful, often quite limited, and not completely convincing or satisfying conclusions for their protagonists. One thinks of Betty Louise Bell's *Faces in the Moon*, Linda Hogan's *Power*, James Welch's *Winter in the Blood*, Craig Womack's *Drowning in Fire*, and others as examples. Existential emptiness marks the extent to which characters find a secularized world unsatisfying, but it also indicates the difficulty they experience in finding a contemporary remedy. Characters in *There There* experience "mutual fragilization" (*Secular* 303) as various beliefs and unbeliefs comingle within the loosely and variously associated Oakland Native community. They are the options in a Native religious marketplace.

Lawrence's ethnographic research leads her to this concerned conclusion: "urban spirituality" tends to be "highly individualistic, enabling individuals to adopt the trappings that can help them create an Indian identity for themselves, while ignoring the much more daunting (but necessary) task of attempting to learn about the cultural world-view encoded in their language—which is vital to any deeper understanding of what it means to be a member of an Indigenous culture, rather than simply an Indian" (167). This perspective complicates Orange's positive claims in quotations above. Lawrence sympathetically addresses the tension between authenticity and creativity, recognizing that criteria are established individually rather than tribally. Because the majority of her "off-territory participants" grew up not knowing their community of origin or no longer having family connections to reserves, they necessarily had "a somewhat abstract identity as 'a member of a specific nation'" (205–06). As with characters in *There There*, Lawrence's participants experience Indigenous identity and religious connections as "pragmatic," having "strategic flexibility," and being culturally oriented. Not surprisingly, their experiences are heterogeneous (206, 229, 231, 232).

There There depicts distinctly urban forms of religious experience within an imagined continuum of authenticity and creativity. Characters are not directly constrained by tribal rules or expectations even as their experiences are shaped by the discourses of Indianness and Indian religion available to them. Orange depicts the religious "free-for-all" that Sarris observed (interview with author, November 29, 2006). Within this cultural situation, Lawrence imagines positive possibilities that Orange only hints at. Under the heading "Reconceptualizing Indigenous Nationhood," Lawrence sees the need for "urban Native communities [to] affiliate *as* urban communities" (242). This affiliation, she urges, needs to be cultural as well as political. In *There There* the powwow could potentially do this religiously as well. Powwow committee meetings, informal mentoring among strangers in the powwow locker room, and Dene Oxendene's documentary project (in contrast to his uncle's) are efforts to counteract a corrosive individualism and to reconceptualize and begin constructing meaningful urban affiliation.

In the second section of the novel, Orange brings in Radiohead's song "There There," with its hook "Just 'cause you feel it doesn't mean it's there" (29). This suggests a key caution for urban religious experience and projects of affiliation. Feelings are not enough; structures of various sorts must be constructed within what the song suggests could be a perilous project.

Urban religious creativity is no more innocent than Native traditionalism or any other religious experience. This creativity is experienced in response to particular historical and immediate circumstances. The Oakland of *There There* is marked by violence; poverty for most characters along with a lack of work opportunities; drugs as an escape from as well as an alternative to religious experience (39); personal, family, and internet translators of Indigenous knowledge and practice rather than communities or tribes; identity anxiety (237); strained childrearing practices; recurring traumas; minimal tribal connections; religious possibilities haunted by both Christianity and Native traditions; individualized religious improvisation (50); and, as a consequence of all these, religious fragility and instability rather than rootedness.

Orange's characters "know the downtown Oakland skyline better than . . . any sacred mountain range" (11), just as Sarris's contemporary characters know the humiliation of welfare checks and demeaning seasonal work better than traditional healing ceremonies. Yet implicit in these seemingly spiritually barren social situations is the reality that the religious uncertainty inherent in them intensifies rather than inhibits at least some characters' longing for a religious fullness that will transport them beyond everyday crisis ordinariness. Rather than certainty or transcendence, inner fullness is their goal. Nonreligious experiences often work as substitutes that are more readily available if less nurturing. In *There There* drugs, charismatic Christianity, and drumming are all options for gaining a sense of fullness. Philosophically inclined Thomas Frank, musing on the range of possibilities, asserts, "Maybe we've all been speaking the broken tongue of angels and demons too long to know that that's what we are, who we are, what we're speaking" (224). Longing for fullness here speaks to the "shifting boundaries of what we call religion" as well as changing definitions of transcendence that do not fit into traditional categories of "the sacred, the holy, and the supernatural" (Vásquez 10). This situation challenges efforts to revitalize tribal traditions with their aboriginal structures of being.

Thomas's sister's drug experience showed him that "you didn't need religion to be slain." Drugs, according to their mother, mean "sneaking into the kingdom of heaven under the gates (223–24), but this can nevertheless be a religious experience for some. Yet Thomas is also skeptical of his mother's experience of "the magical over- and underworld of your Oakland-spun Christian evangelical end-of-the-world spirituality," which overwhelms her (222), even as he sees the power of these personal experiences and recognizes the inescapability of spiritual desire. Drumming for Thomas is a prayer, even if it is "to no one in particular about nothing in particular" (225). Instead, one loses oneself in the drum: "You want to drum but also to be heard drumming. Not as yourself but just as the drum" (225).

Indians gather for the Big Oakland Powwow, investing it with their hopes, identity, longing for community, and more. This event of creative religious urbanism, Orange makes abundantly clear, is not innocent but immersed in troubling contemporary experience (134–36). Out of its violent failure, new tentative lived religions emerge for Orvil, Opal, Thomas, and Tony. They find Indigenous trauma religions, individually improvised and saturated with the modern socioreligious imaginary. Yet they translate "there there" to "they're there" (289).

Recently I visited the *Stories of Resistance* exhibit at the Contemporary Art Museum St. Louis, which included works by Wendy Red Star (Apsáalooke). In the Denver Art Museum archives, she had found twenty thousand water-color illustrations from the 1930s and 1940s used to catalog the museum's collection of Apsáalooke, or Crow, ceremonial objects and clothing. Red Star's work brings together reproductions of these paintings with photographs of recent Crow Fair parade participants wearing items that are similar and sometimes identical to ones in the illustrations. The exhibit curators explain that Red Star "eliminated background details" of both representations in order to "emphasize[] the continuity of traditions."[6]

This visual rhetorical strategy, the erasure of contexts in order to construct a purer sense of continuity, creates powerful and reassuring images, yet at a cost. This strategy elides the necessary adaptations that have shaped, one might say transformed, Crow traditions into the contemporary cultural language spoken today. *After the Theft of the Sacred* uses a different strategy for apprehending Native cultural, particularly religious, depictions of con-tinuity. Using Native literary accounts, it reckons most fundamentally with the shift in socioreligious imaginary that inevitably permeates most modern Native religious experiences. Characters' lived religions are a shifting mix of adaptations, disjunctures, and continuities. They are improvisations on traditional religious beliefs and practices, translations shaped by particular material conditions and spiritual apprehensions. These beliefs, unbeliefs, and practices are, as the Bertolt Brecht epigram to the prologue states, singing in the dark times that is "singing. / About the dark times" (3).[7]

NOTES

INTRODUCTION

1. Following the lead of others, I use the term "revitalization" to include the wide range of efforts by tribal nations, intertribal organizations, communities, and individuals to sustain and advance Native cultures, including religious cultures, as well as Indigenous national sovereignties. "Neotraditionalism" is a related term, as are "decolonization" and "retribalization." Leanne Betasamosake Simpson uses the term "radical resistance," Glen Coulthard uses "resurgent practices," and others use different terms, all with their particular nuances. Following common practice, I use the terms "Indigenous" and "Native" interchangeably.

2. However, in "Religio-Spiritual Participation," Eva Marie Garroutte (Cherokee) and colleagues introduce their research by stating that "most American Indians reported belief in God (87 percent) and most described themselves as either 'religious' or 'somewhat religious' (77 percent)." For the Southwest and Northern Plains tribes in the study, she reports high levels of not only belief but also participation, whether the members associated with "aboriginal spirituality," Christianity, or the Native American Church (18, 24). Although their statistical assessment has a different purpose and scope than the work of the above writers, her conclusions need to be considered.

3. In his later essay "The Ragged Edges of Literary Nationalism," Justice emphatically includes spiritual realities in his list of responsibilities Indigenous peoples have in relation to sovereignty: "our responsibilities: to one another, to the earth and the web of kinship that binds us to the human and other-than-human world, *to the ancestors and the spirits*, to rational thought that is tempered with respect and an appreciation for *mystery* and the *unknowable*, to the cause of truth and the purpose of balance and growth, to our selves and our communities, and our mutually-constituting intellectual, *spiritual*, and moral integrity" (27, emphasis added).

Anthropologist Kirk Dombrowski, important to chapter 6, also addresses this disjuncture from a research perspective. He has gone to Native Alaskan villages in summer to participate in and investigate their political economy. Only when he came in winter and attended a Pentecostal revival service did he become aware of the spiritual experiences of the people he had been working with. "Church is a winter event throughout the region," and he almost missed the key role churches play in many Tlingit people's lives (xiii–xv). Misperceiving interpretive contexts is one more way in which Indigenous religious experiences can be missed or misread.

4. Aua's explaining his position to an outsider marks the beginning of a shift in imaginaries. The givenness of Iglulik beliefs was already being threatened. Rasmussen quotes Aua as stating, "In our ordinary everyday life we do not think much about all these things,

and it is only now you ask that so many thoughts arise in my head of long-known things; old thoughts but as it were becoming altogether new when one has to put them into words" (qtd. in Petrone 125). Further, Rasmussen encountered Aua when his expedition took him to the shaman's region and beyond. On his return trip, Rasmussen learned that "this last traditional shaman of Iglulik" had accepted Christianity (Huhndorf 96–97).

Two recent films depict the Inuit world before its aboriginal socioreligious imaginary with its givenness was threatened and then at the beginning of colonial material and spiritual incursions. The first, *Atanarjuat* (The Fast Runner, 2001) re-creates a traditional Inuit story of social and spiritual conflict, supernatural actions, and social interventions. *The Journals of Knud Rasmussen* (2006) reckons with the beginnings of the colonizing process, particularly the incursions of Christianity, with its acceptance enabled by cultural disruptions and threats of starvation.

5. With a different focus but related recognition, economist Thomas Piketty's *Capital and Ideology*, as well as his earlier *Capitalism in the Twenty-First Century*, commends literature as "one of our best sources when it comes to understanding how representations of inequality change," praising novelists for having "intimate knowledge of property hierarchies" and the "deep structure of inequality—how it was justified, how it impinged on the lives of individuals" (*Capital* 15). That is, literary writers offer experiential representations of material conditions.

6. I generally follow Charles Taylor's use of the term "cosmos" to refer to the enchanted world that includes what we might call supernatural beings, powers, and "moral forces" that interact with humans. This contrasts with the present dominant understanding of a disenchanted "modern neutral universe" (*Secular* 29). The term is complicated by Taylor's discussion of an open immanence that engages more-than-material apprehensions in contrast to closed immanence, which is exclusively material (*Secular* 550–51). However, I also use the term "cosmos" when making a more general reference to all that can be apprehended.

7. Much valuable work has been done on tribally specific religious beliefs and practices. However, many and maybe most characters and communities in contemporary Native literature have limited experience of these specifics. And even where they do, say in Silko's *Ceremony* (see chapter 2) or Momaday's *House Made of Dawn*, the experiences have been filtered through the modern social imaginary and pan-Indian (sometimes intertribal) sensibility in ways that make them different from although still connected to those of pre-contact generations.

8. See chapter 1, note 5, for an explanation of term "secular." The explanation is further developed in chapter 7.

9. Throughout the book, parenthetical numbers cite this play's sections rather than pages.

10. Sean Teuton, in his introduction to Native literature, usefully contrasts Paula Gunn Allen's emphasis on "the stability of indigenous life as intact and thriving" with Momaday's focus on "the 'process' of Native American becoming" (*Native* 79).

11. In this book Vine Deloria Jr. avoids using the term "supernatural" and instead uses "spiritual powers." Other Native scholars, for example Robert Warrior, do use the term

("Native Critics" 203). I use the two terms interchangeably. I recognize that the term "supernatural" implies a rationalistic division between the natural and the supernatural that is not part of the aboriginal socioreligious imaginary. However, the term "spiritual," as discussed in the next section, has taken on a range of meanings and does not necessarily carry Deloria's sense of more-than-material power.

Deloria's emphasis on spiritual power is different from Basil Johnston's (Anishinaabe) focus on cultural power: "Stories about the manitous allow native people to understand their cultural and spiritual heritage and enable them to see the worth and relevance of their ideas, institutions, perceptions and values" (xiii). The distinction is important.

12. This indirect depiction of present spiritual absence while also asserting the necessary continuity between past and present spiritual experience marks a new perspective for Deloria. In his earlier essays he insists on not reifying Native spiritual traditions. In "Religion and Revolution" (1974), he emphasizes "the historical nature" of Native beliefs: "Truth is in the ever changing experiences of the community." To be meaningful, he at that time argued that beliefs must be adapted to a changing community living within a constantly changing world (42).

13. David Morgan's introduction to *Religion and Material Culture* addresses this problematic from the perspective of belief as a culturally specific rather than universal practice. William Arnal provides a useful explanation of the debate.

14. Edward P. Antonio finds that scholars of African Indigenous religions make a similar claim that for Africans "everything is sacred." He rejects this position, as does the analysis here, as "logically incoherent, not to say, empirically false" (150).

15. While capitalizing the Christian God and using lowercase for all others has certainly been an imperialist gesture, the capitalization also signifies the otherness of the Christian God. Within the Indigenous conceptualization of a unified cosmos, this emphasis on otherness seems inappropriate. Thus I do not use capitalization when referring to Indigenous supernatural beings.

On the other hand, the terms "Wakan Tanka" and "Wakanta" and are capitalized, as this recognizes, to use Tinker's phrase, a sense of "The Otherness[;] this is the Sacred Mystery" (McLeod, "Cree Poetic Discourse," 109, 11; Tinker, "Spirituality" 122, 1).

16. This is not to say that evaluation and exclusion do not have a proper place in Native discourses but that this is not appropriate for the project at hand. Characters, communities, and texts may overtly or covertly judge experiences of these realities; literary critics can illuminate these judgments as part of lived Indigenous experience without participating in the judgment.

17. Orsi's editorship of *The Cambridge Companion to Religious Studies* (2012) is one indication; David D. Hall's edited volume *Lived Religion in America* is another. Hall's introduction offers a clear explanation of lived religion as an analytical approach. However, the topic's absence from *Religion, Theory, Critique: Classical and Contemporary Approaches and Methodologies* (2017), edited by Richard King, suggests that this approach has not received complete acceptance within religious studies.

18. In the introduction to the second edition of *The Madonna of 115th Street*, Orsi further explains this approach (xxxvii–xlii).

Orsi's writing comes out of his experience and research with a particular form of Catholicism, the peasant Catholicism of southern Italy transported and transformed by immigrants in an urban New York City neighborhood. Challenging the dominant critical approaches to religion within the social sciences and humanities, he offers an everyday experiential approach to people's apprehensions of the cosmos that engages rather than brackets more-than-material experiences. While reckoning with the experience of sacred presences or spiritual experiences, he insists on placing them within particular material, historical contexts without letting those contexts subsume the actual experience. The religion he describes in his seminal *The Madonna of 115th Street* and elsewhere is a popular rather than official religion that emerged out of a "the troubled, poor, constantly changing, culturally isolated and neglected community" (*Madonna* lvii).

Orsi does not idealize this Italian community expression as an outsider religion or as more authentic than more legitimized forms of Catholicism. Rather he takes seriously the spiritual experiences occurring within it, even though it has been demeaned, disregarded, and dismissed in cultural-evolutionary terms, just as Native religions have often enough been in both academic and popular culture.

19. My understanding of dialectical reading comes from Bertell Ollman's *Dialectical Investigations*, Part 1.

20. See Bucko on the history and present experiences of sweat lodge ceremonies. A relevant question about sweats and powwows is why these two ceremonies have become central aspects of modern Indigenous religious experience, regularly referenced in modern Indigenous literature although seldom in earlier works.

21. I engage this concept of improvisation in chapter 7, where I differentiate between McLeod's tribal improvisations and the individualistic ones Erdrich imagines for her character Lipsha.

Sam McKegney notes that McLeod is "well-positioned" to develop a tribally specific criticism as "a Cree speaker whose direct familial antecedents include several knowledge-keepers." That is clear from the stories of the past included in McLeod's *Cree Narrative Memory*. Commenting on the book, McKegney also asserts that the book uses "broad and abstract cultural concepts" rather than tribal specificities (418). This is part of McLeod's method for connecting past to present. In abstracting Cree people's religious experiences, he emphasizes the need for contemporary reinterpretation of rather than direct access to past religious experiences. In encountering past family histories, McLeod does not always find tribal religious distinctiveness. For some in his family's past, the difference between Christianity and "Indian philosophy" did not seem large, and so the transition was not particularly troubling (*Cree* 62).

22. The issue of transcendence and immanence is addressed in chapter 1.

Robert Davis Hoffmann, discussed in chapter 6, expresses an immanent spiritual understanding similar to McLeod's. In an email exchange (now undated), he offered a useful explanation: "My gist was that (in my opinion) our Tlingit experience of spirituality was/ is immersive; not transcendental. We become. We enter and experience."

23. Because these experiences are more than "power . . . socially conferred," they require more than a sociology of religion to fully apprehend them (Womack, "Theorizing" 364). Craig Womack makes clear his own belief in supernatural spiritual transformations. Referring to the Creek Green Corn Ceremony, he states that through ceremonial activities, "ordinary reality is transformed and spirits become participants alongside humans." Together they create changes "that can be gauged by visual observation of one's immediate environment," including a deer appearing for a hunter and cures for the sick ("Theorizing" 365–66). In explaining his position, Womack acknowledges, in a way that Deloria does not, the conceptual challenges in asserting a literal understanding of spiritual powers. Thus he acknowledges the need for "a leap of faith" ("Theorizing" 371). Greg Sarris, writing about Mabel McKay, describes the miracles he himself has witnessed (117–21). I do not know of any other Native writers who have offered similarly explicit, personal statements about witnessing supernatural transformations. The issue of critics' beliefs in spiritual realities is again raised in chapter 2, notes 7 and 18.

24. The historical referent for this journey is the early 1970s Hydro-Quebec huge hydroelectric project. Shari H. Huhndorf explains, "The dams flooded traditional territories of Cree and Inuit communities, violating treaty rights, displacing entire communities, and destroying sacred sites. As rising waters submerged thousands of square miles of Native land, they drowned the animals on which the communities depended." Indigenous groups fought back against the Canadian government for decades. *Solar Storms* connects this project to a long history of encroachments going back to the fur trades (Huhndorf 75). Part of the consequences of this rapid devastation has been "deaths from suicide and reckless behavior . . . [that] paralyzed the communities in mute grief" (Niezen xiv).

25. To my mind, McLeod's essay stumbles a bit in calling for "radically rethinking Christianity" in relation to Cree religious experience. This is not an uncommon call within nationalist approaches to religious apprehensions. His essay convincingly explains that traditional pre-contact stories should be interpreted through a Cree rather than a Christian frame of reference. For example, the snake in a traditional Cree story carries a much different meaning than the snake in Genesis does, and the former needs to be the basis of interpretation. Yet in various ways and to various degrees, Christianity has been influencing Indigenous cultures since European contact, as McLeod acknowledges. The process of dialectically interpreting Indigenous religious experience should recognize this mediation along with the others. Within this interpretive approach, stories have meaning only contextually, so one can imagine a competing Christian interpretation of the Cree snake story arising in particular situations.

As Ghanaian, now US philosopher Kwame Anthony Appiah (Asante) notes in the conclusion to his chapter "Topologies of Nativism," about European cultural influences, "since it is too late for us to escape each other, we might instead seek to turn to our advantage the mutual interdependencies history has thrust upon us" (72). The tentativeness of "might" and the vagueness of what the advantage is suggest the challenges of even acknowledging the possibilities of this project.

CHAPTER 1

1. Vine Deloria Jr.'s *The World We Used to Live In* argues that reassuring abstractions are not enough to renew Native peoples' religious life. Experience matters. Miracles are presented as evidence that the spiritual realm is real and spiritual powers are accessible. With this book Deloria hopes that stories of past supernatural interventions will inspire Native people today to make use of "the powers available" (214). As noted in the introduction, however, the absence of modern examples inadvertently suggests that this form of cosmic connection is only part of the past. History here haunts rather than helps. For present Indigenous people, Deloria only has critical exhortations (xvii, 214).

Simon Ortiz (Acoma Pueblo) recognizes this problem of apprehending spiritual realities as a human dilemma (personal interview). See the introductory discussion in chapter 4.

2. Beiger, Saldivar, and Voelz suggest that fiction in particular embodies present social apprehensions of the world, but it also is "a productive force" as "a forerunner in creating, articulating, and shaping these worlds." Fiction can register shifts in social structuring before they have developed into adjustments of social imaginaries (Beiger, Saldivar, and Voelz xi, x).

3. When referring specifically to this aspect of a social imaginary, I use the term "socio-religious imaginary," which emphasizes the social-structural quality of belief. I also use the term "structure of feeling." Using various terms helps to avoid reifying any of them.

4. Knud Rasmussen's *Intellectual Culture of the Iglulik Eskimos*, although shaped by Western biases, offers a detailed experiential and conceptual account of this group's aboriginal socioreligious imaginary. Rasmussen included extensive quotations and summaries of his conversations as well as detailed observations about their everyday lives saturated with spiritual realities impinging on material experience. He first encountered these Inuits in 1921, when no outside settlement or trading post had been established in their area.

5. Useful as a model for analysis, *Preserving the Sacred* also has limitations, as it does not directly reckon with the changing nature of belief—that is, the shift, broadly speaking, from religious belief as a given to one that is made by choice.

6. Taylor gives three definitions of secularity. The first refers to public spaces now being "emptied of God"—that is, no longer controlled by religion practices or institutions. The second refers to the absence of religion in shaping social practices. In the past, religion was "interwoven with everything else." The third definition, the one relevant here, concerns "the conditions of belief" (1–3). These definitions are further developed in chapter 7.

German sociologist Ulrich Beck, in *A God of One's Own*, notes that secularization as an Enlightenment phenomenon worked differently in the United States, where it had "no anti-religious strand." This exceptionalism certainly had an impact on Indigenous experiences of missionary colonialism. Nevertheless, religious experience even in the United States did change as it became "a private concern" within the dominant culture. This too has had its

Indigenous impact, as has "the return of the religions at the beginning of the twenty-first century" (20, 19).

7. This non-transcendent immanence seems to be the vague sensibility of the common contemporary comment "I'm spiritual but not religious."

Just as definitions of "transcendence" and "immanence" lose some of their duality in contemporary understandings, "materialism" understood dualistically has in some Western quarters come to seem inadequate. In *New Materialisms*, Diana Coole and Samantha Frost note, "Everywhere we look, it seems to us, we are witnessing scattered but insistent demands for more materialist modes of analysis and for new ways of thinking about matter and processes of materialization." Classic definitions of matter no longer make sense within the new physics and biology. "Matter has become more elusive, more immaterial" (2, 5).

8. Fagan's critique parallels the one McLeod makes (see the introduction), particularly of Canadian Indigenous studies departments: "The epistemological straightjacket and the colonial box" these departments create do "narrative violence" as they "sanitize" traditional stories in ways that strip them of the "vitality" that makes them useful for today (McLeod 109).

9. Part of the play is the novel's use of the gothic. Annette Trefzer's essay "The Indigenous Uncanny" explains the way Howe's novel uses the southern gothic to address the experience of trauma. *Shell Shaker* also "reformulate[s]" the genre by "revising and adapting the literary strategies of the gothic genre." Within this formulation, the more-than-material is reduced to Freud's uncanny (200–201).

CHAPTER 2

1. Young Bear uses the tribal name Meskwaki, which is sometimes spelled Mesquakie. It is translated as Red Earth People. In Iowa T[he] Meskwakis were given the federal name Sac and Fox Tribe of the Mississippi.

2. The Western theological terms "transcendent" and "supernatural," with their limitations and yet usefulness, are discussed in chapter 1 in relation to the term "immanence." The spiritual encounters that Tayo experiences are transcendent in the particular sense that they take place outside of the material world. Tayo's experiences with Ts'eh are of the same order as, for example, James Welch's protagonist Fools Crow when he enters the supernatural realm of Feather Woman. Yet key differences suggest the radical innocence of this modern encounter. For Tayo, "sex is ceremony," as David Treuer wryly notes ("Reservation" 358). This suggests an intimate, unboundaried and not just porously bounded relationship between the material and spiritual realms. In contrast, Feather Woman never loses her otherness for Fools Crow; there are no intimacies between them. Also, he must enter the otherworldly realm through a special portal that separates the two realms (325–26). Tayo simply walks between them (164).

3. This structure of feeling affected more than just Indian Country. *Black Eagle Child*'s characters' and readers' sense of confusion is similar to what viewers experienced with Richard Linklater's contemporaneous *Slacker*, although the title of his next film, *Dazed and Confused*, better captures the sensibility of Young Bear's novel.

4. A 1920 survey found that 30 percent of Meskwakis, then known as the Sac and Fox, were peyotists (Maroukis 109–10).

5. Taylor makes clear that he is writing within a Western framework and recognizes that secularity, and by implication enchantment and disenchantment, will have different meanings in different civilizations (*Secular* 21).

6. Betonie acknowledges contemporary social reality by stating, "In the old days it was simple. A medicine person could get by without all these things. But nowadays . . ." (111). The ellipses are in the text and mark another failure of moral engagement. Silko does not have Betonie explain the social significance of phone books from around the country. Social and historical insight into the changes that have created the need for a specifically modern healing is missing. And nothing contemporary is included in the ceremony—no phone books or Coke bottles from the hogan.

7. However, most of the novel's readers at the time (most of whom were non-Native) apparently did not feel that way, for a range of reasons. See Roemer 224–26.

8. The phrase is Leslie Rabine's. She reads romance novels as appealing social fantasies that contrast to and thus psychically compensate for the frustrations and limitations of romance readers' actual lives (981).

9. In this chapter Teuton writes movingly about his and his family's social experiences, which adds power to the interpretations he develops (125–27). His "metaphysical" interpretation of *Ceremony* would be similarly strengthened if Teuton had added personal experience to his interpretative assertions. However, very few Indigenous critics do this.

CHAPTER 3

1. See, for example, Ofelia Zepedia's "Deer Dance Exhibition" in *Ocean Power* and Leslie Marmon Silko's "Deer Dance / For Your Return" and other poems in *Storyteller*. In Marilou Awiakta's *Abiding Appalachia: Where Mountain and Atom Meet*, Awi Ude Little Deer and the material–spiritual problematic is central (2, 5, 27, 39, 54). Carolyn Dunn (Mvskogee/Seminole/Cherokee/Choctaw) links her story "Salmon Creek Road Kill" to Harjo's "Deer Dancer" (xv–xvi). Two novels, Susan Power's *The Grass Dancer* and Louise Erdrich's *The Antelope Wife*," focus on deer women. Feliciano Sanchez Chan's (Yucatec Maya) short play "Deer," like Glancy's play, addresses spiritual as well as material realities and responsibilities.

Laura Furlan's chapter analyzing Louise Erdrich's *The Antelope Wife* ("Roots and Routes of the Hub") references other works and tribal traditions related to deer woman stories. See pages 131 and 254–55, note 1.

2. The writers add that these worlds "are visible only in the private eye of dream and vision, and they are made public only when they are put into words in stories individuals tell of their own experiences and those of others" (45). Illustrating spiritual apprehension within contemporary circumstances, they tell the story of two men, Francisco Onamea and José Sanava, who went deer hunting together. Three times they made a deadly shot. Each time, after the same deer made its last dying movements, it stood up again and looked at the men. Following the third time, it ran away. Francisco realized only later that the

deer was from another world and "wanted to offer them some powers. Unknowingly, they had refused" (45–46). Their experience suggests some of the challenges of apprehending Indigenous spiritual experiences.

3. The contemporary Lakota experience is not so different from other Indians' lives. See, for example, Dean Chavers's (Lumbee) chapter "Border Towns."

4. Simon Ortiz uses the term "gentle" in his comments on the back cover: "Light. Love. Life. Linda Hogan's gentle and clear poetry in *Rounding the Human Corners* reminds me that, too often, I long and ask for more than I need." This positive assessment strikes a considerably more positive and accepting tone than his own collection written a decade and a half earlier, *After and Before Lightning*, discussed in the next chapter.

Hogan's memoir published a few years earlier, *The Woman Who Watches Over the World*, similarly engages a calmly troubled spiritual apprehension. In the introduction she mentions that difficult circumstances "turned me to the spirit in a search for healing, wherever it can be found" (14, 16). This might suggest spiritual complacency, but it also could be that Hogan wants us to see that her speakers' spiritual experiences do meet their needs. Simon Ortiz's positive comment about the book's spiritual helpfulness suggests the latter interpretation.

5. Given the commentary that has been written on the relationship between Glancy's Indigenous and Christian beliefs (e.g., Dawes 303–12, Mackay 3) as well as Glancy's own writing on this relationship (e.g., *Claiming Breath* 93–102, "Two Dresses"), one might expect this complex and conflicted relationship to be at the heart of the play's problematic. However, the Girl herself expresses no particular interest or belief in Christianity, even if she wears a jean jacket with a sequined picture of Jesus on the cross (8) and references Bible stories she has heard at work (9). The play's concluding sections show that her newly developing spiritual identity is anchored in the understanding of Cherokee beliefs that she gained from her Grandmother. Rather than a tension between her Christian and Indigenous beliefs, I think it is the liminality of Glancy's cultural and religious position within the Indigenous literary interpretive community that has sharpened her sensitivity to the spiritual–material problematic inherent in all religious belief.

6. James Mackay observes that all Glancy's work offers "a questioning, uncertain idea of healing" (6). Similarly, Daniel Heath Justice explains that "Glancy is distrustful of firm pronouncements." Further, "There's a vulnerability in her work, an insecurity of self that reflects the scattered experiences of many contemporary Cherokees who live far from the lands and cultural centers of their respective communities." He affirms the importance of her perspective by stating that she is part of the "vitality of contemporary Cherokee literature" (196–97).

7. Glancy here echoes Gerald Visenor when he states, "Familiar simulations"—that is, "paracolonial discoveries and representations of tribal literature"—that are modern Western constructions, "have more in common with the philosophies of grammar and translations than with *shadows and the silence* of heard stories in the unbearable simulations of tribal consciousness" (77, emphasis added). Earlier Visenor stated, "The shadows are the silence in heard stories, the silence that bears a referent of tribal memories and experience." Both

Glancy and Visenor want to express more than representations, which are absences. They, together with many of the Native authors discussed in this book, strive to use language, a materiality, to engage in other than conceptual ways a more-than-material reality.

CHAPTER 4

1. The introduction discusses my use of "religion" and "spirituality." I generally use the latter to refer to the more-than-material world. I use "religion" more generally: "the totality of their ultimate values, their most deeply held ethical convictions, their efforts to order their reality, their cosmology" (Orsi, *Madonna* lxi). The focus is on individuals and characters' experiences while recognizing that the experience of the more-than-material is shaped by social and cultural structures and discourses.

2. Because *After and Before the Lightning* intertwines prose poems and poetry, citations refer to page rather than line numbers.

3. Craig Womack uses the same term when he describes supernatural transformations in Cherokee Green Corn Ceremonies ("Theorizing" 365).

4. For Berlant, "Intuition is the subject's habituated affective activity, the sensorium trained to *apperceive the historical in the present* by a whole range of encounters and knowledges" (242, n. 4, emphasis added).

5. Kristina Fagan similarly calls for using "empathetic imagination" to apprehend "spiritual realities" (99; see chapter 1). However, chapter 3 notes that imagination is a "fragile epistemology" haunted by doubt. The chapter engages also Momaday's more confident deployment of interpretive imagination.

CHAPTER 5

1. Schwab notes that Freud thought "artistic representations and theories that insist on remembering the work of mourning perform important work against cultural melancholia" (22). I see Sarris and other Native literary writers doing this work.

2. Where the reference may not be clear, *Grand Avenue* is abbreviated within parentheses as *GA* and *Watermelon Nights* as *WN*.

3. One could imagine the three sections of *Watermelon Nights* as well as some of the first-person chapters of *Grand Avenue* as therapy sessions in which each narrator gains some healing through constructing meaning for their and their tribe's traumas.

4. Gagné summarizes definitions from the third edition of the *Diagnostic and Statistical Manual of Mental Disorders*. It defines trauma as "a shock that is deemed emotional and substantially damages, over a long time period, the psychological development of the victim, often leading to neurosis." It defines a traumatic event as "a nonordinary human experience that may lead to PTSD, and which would be distressing to most people, such as serious harm or threat to self, spouse, children, close relatives; witnessing a serious accident or violence against another person, who, as a result, is either killed or seriously injured; or having one's home or community suddenly destroyed" (356).

5. Yet Sarris also recognizes a complexity within the Bole Maru resistance: "Subjugated people may not see the ways their resistance may further their alienation from the dominant culture and so weaken their resistance to it and even hasten their demise as a result" (*Keeping* 68).

6. This is similar to Marie's new form of believing at the end of *Love Medicine*. As a young person she is skeptical of Indian identity because of her class exclusions, yet as an older woman in the senior center, she speaks the "old language" and is "holding onto the old strengths Rushes Bear had taught her" (263).

7. See, for example, Kellerman, *Holocaust Trauma*, chapters 4 and 5. Although this research is relevant, Whitbeck et al. note significant differences between the Jewish and American Indian genocides. First, Indigenous people had no place they could return to but instead were forced onto reservations that at least in the beginning were "very much like large concentration camps or penal colonies." This meant that old ways of survival no longer were viable, and new "culturally distasteful or impossible" means were forced on them. Further, military defeat and occupation did not stop what is a continuing genocide. American Indians live with the daily reminders of this ("Conceptualizing" 121).

8. In an earlier article, Whitbeck et al. explain the challenges involved in researching intergenerational historical trauma, including "challenges to disentangling the interrelated components of the concepts and understanding what specific mechanisms are at work." Nevertheless, their detailed findings lead them to clearly conclude that Native individuals' sense of "historical loss was significantly associated with the symptom constructs"—for example, the sadness, anger, anxiety, shame, sense of isolation, and "fear or distrust [of] the intentions of white people" ("Conceptualizing" 119, 126).

9. Schwab explains cumulative trauma: "The intersections of violent histories generate a structure of condensed experience in which the encounter with new violent histories operates via the recall of earlier histories—not only cognitively but affectively and experientially as well" (30).

10. We can imagine Iris agreeing with David Gev when he states within the context of the Jewish Holocaust, "I did not witness the most important events of my life. They happened before I was born" (qtd. in Alford 12).

11. Class needs to be understood relationally rather than as an objective social location. See chapter 7, note 14.

12. Sarris notes "the continuous reinvention" of the Bole Maru. Joining the genealogy himself, he explains, "Obviously, we no longer don Victorian clothing; times have changed." He adds, "New or revived ceremonies must come only with a new Dreamer *recognized by the entire tribe*. This practice . . . allows for a continuous reinvention of the tradition in those communities, always adapting the tradition and Indian identity to changing historical circumstances" (*Keeping* 70, emphasis added). In contrast, Faye's reinvention is individually authorized.

13. The improvisational quality of Faye's lived religion theology is also explored in chapter 7. It is the more socially "settled" middle-class families on Grand Avenue who create

resistance against that status quo through the campaign for federal recognition. In contrast, those who resist Faye's religious challenge in favor of the social status quo are part of "hard living" families. "Settled families" like Steven Penn's are headed by characters who have regular, steady, nonmenial jobs and are dedicated to "the disciplined self." The "specter of 'hard living'" or unsettled families like Faye's sisters motivate the political and religious as well as social strategies of the settled. Faye and her daughter fall dangerously between the two. Her religion is unacceptable, even threatening, to both groups but most directly to her hard-living sisters and others like them in the Grand Avenue community. The quotations and concepts are from Joan Williams (40–43). See Dyck (Afterword 215–23) for analysis of the Penn family's efforts to distinguish themselves from hard-living families.

14. Faye's explanation of poisoning is similar to the understanding of witchery in Leslie Marmon Silko's *Ceremony*, as both use cosmic rather than social explanations for the problems within the material world (see chapter 2). However, Silko gives witchery the givenness of belief within the aboriginal social imaginary while Fay's belief in poisoning, even if it has traditional roots, must make its way within the modern social imaginary.

15. Erdrich does not imagine such religious creativity and innovation for Fleur, a character in *Love Medicine* who holds supernatural beliefs. Thus she is more isolated from the community than either Nellie or Faye. Faye flexibly moves in and out of her belief.

16. Nor is it insignificant that Sarris gives Nellie traits similar to those of Mabel McKay, a traditional healer or doctor and "the last 'traditional weaver,' that is, a weaver whose work is associated with power and prophecy" (*Keeping* 51).

17. Sue Grand and Jill Salber also emphasize the link between social justice and mental health. They find an "ethical/social/historical turn" in psychoanalytic work on trauma (3).

CHAPTER 6

1. Robert Davis Hoffmann has also used the name Robert Davis and Robert H. Davis. "Hoffmann" is misspelled in some publications as "Hoffman."

2. The poems in Book 1 of *Raven's Echo* were first published in *SoulCatcher* (1986) by Raven's Bones Press. The poems from Book 2 were published as a special feature in *Alaska Quarterly Review* (2009). The order of the poems has been somewhat rearranged.

3. This is the title of Leanne Betasamosake Simpson's book. Hoffmann's poetry reckons with the impossibility of reclaiming an aboriginal social imaginary while still building connections between the past and present within the inextricable yet varied context of the modern social imaginary.

4. Aua turns the tables on Rasmussen by asking him to explain the coming of storms that make hunting so difficult; he receives no answer. Aua further explains: "We fear the spirits of the earth and air. And therefore our fathers, taught by their fathers before them, guarded themselves about with all these old rules and customs, which are built upon the experience and knowledge of generations. We know not how nor why but we obey them that we may be suffered to live in peace. And for all our angakoqs and their knowledge of hidden things, we

yet know so little that we fear everything else" (Rasmussen, *Across* 129, 131). Yet Rasmussen also transcribes a song by a woman who was one of the greatest *angakoqs*:

The arch of sky and mightiness of storms
Have moved the spirit within me,
Till I am carried away
Trembling with joy.

Listening to her, people were "hushed and overwhelmed by the glimpses of a spirit world revealed by one of its priests" (Rasmussen, *Across* 34–35).

5. This understanding parallels Sarris's explanation of traditional poisoning. See chapter 5.

6. The uncle here is Uncle Topsy, to whom "Reconstruction" is dedicated.

Coulthard's chapter "Seeing Red" in *Red Skin, White Masks* works to recuperate for political purposes the type of anger Hoffmann here expresses. Within certain circumstances, Coulthard states, "a disciplined maintenance of resentment in the wake of historical injustices" can be a moral protest (108). However, without the support of a movement (like Idle No More, which Coulthard has been active in; see 159–65), there is no positive use for anger, Hoffmann in his emails and poems suggests. In "Blind Man" the men's anger "curling like smoke that has to come from somewhere" smolders "just below the surface." Because this is a place the speaker is not used to navigating, his anger becomes associated with "cruelty" rather than resistance (19–23).

7. For a fuller account, see Dyck, afterword to Hoffmann's *Raven's Echo*, section III. See also Rosita Worl (Tlingit) and Frederica de Laguna's essays in *The Handbook of North American Indians*, Vol. 7, and Dauenhauer and Dauenhauer's introduction to *Haa Ḵusteeyí, Our Culture: Tlingit Life Stories*.

8. To participate, individuals had to have one-quarter Native blood quantum and been born before the date of the legislation (Clifford 6, n. 6). See Dombrowski, chapter 3; Dauenhauer and Dauenhauer, introduction, *Haa Ḵusteeyí* 98–103; and Sullivan for fuller descriptions of ANCSA.

9. Former member of the British Columbia Supreme Court Thomas R. Berger's official review of ANCSA, reported in his *Village Journey: The Report of the Alaska Native Review Commission*, makes clear that Alaska Native villagers repeatedly emphasized the centrality of subsistence livelihood to their cultures. See his chapter 2.

10. It is important to note that Native corporations and governments have also invested in cultural continuity (Thornton 194).

11. "In the Tlingit worldview, at.óow . . . represents both natural and supernatural phenomena. . . . At.óow includes the artistic design, which represents either a clan crest animal or spiritual helper, and the physical object on which it is depicted as well as the associated names, songs, and stories. At.óow also embodies the spirits of both humans and supernatural entities, which met sometime in the ancient past, and the geographical site at which the event occurred" (Worl, "Art" 38). This definition helps clarify the work of creating a ritual dance staff in the poem "Reconstruction."

12. The function of display takes place within imposed assimilationist colonial pressures. Dombrowski reports that almost all village people under seventy years of age have English as their first language; few speak their Native languages (xiv). This is true for the speaker of "Reconstruction," who cannot understand the Tlingit language on his uncle's cassette tape (65). It is within this context that the use of Native languages takes on a display function.

13. For an alternative view of government recognition, see Snelgrove and Wildcat.

14. Tommy Orange in the prologue of his distinctly urban novel *There There* notes the ubiquity of urbanization: "Plenty of us are urban now. If not because we live in cities, then because we live on the internet" (9).

15. Friday provides many geographical specifics in his statement in Goldschmidt and Haas 176–78.

16. The more recent federal Alaska National Interest Lands Conservation Act (ANILCA) of 1980 defines subsistence functionally as "the customary and traditional uses by rural Alaska residents of wild, renewable resources for direct personal or family consumptions." Thornton explains that it makes no reference to specific places for subsistence practices since ANCSA had already terminated Native territorial, hunting, and fishing rights. ANILCA, a refinement of ANCSA, partially restored some rights to subsistence use, but for all rural Alaskans and not Native people specifically. Subsistence public policy "typically is not sensitive to the fundamental role of place in Native subsistence economies" (Thornton 116–17; see also Sullivan, "'We Don't Exist'").

Thus Thornton differentiates between the Tlingit understanding of subsistence, "an intricate and profound set of relationships with particular geographic settings where their social groups have dwelled historically," and the government understanding of subsistence as "noncommercial" uses of natural resources (117). Dombrowski emphasizes that it is a livelihood and not just an activity like fishing or hunting (91).

17. Practicing subsistence within the capitalist economy also creates "serious legal jeopardy," Dombrowski notes. Almost all those he knew who depended on a subsistence livelihood had been in court, and many in jail. Some had their equipment confiscated when they could not pay fines (97).

Gender relations have also changed. Women often must do wage work to help pay for equipment, while at the same time their labor is needed in subsistence production. Subsistence living can strain gender relations as women, traditionally playing a special role in maintaining Native identity, now take on a quite different, economic function through wage labor (See Dombrowski 97–99).

18. Dombrowski further notes that material inequality within Native villages is an "unspoken and almost unspeakable" issue within Native studies. Villagers understand this inequality as personal rather than structural (xiv–xv).

19. As in Southwest Alaska, Pentecostalism everywhere has drawn in people who have been marginalized by colonial capitalism (Dombrowski 181). While Dauenhauer notes that these churches have a range of attitudes about traditional Tlingit culture (172), Dombrowski asserts that they all, at least to a degree, stand against it. Pentecostal

churches tend to be against "culture" in general, with its perceived rejection of any belief as absolutely true (5, 174).

In one sense Pentecostal members believe more traditionally, if oppositionally, than do neotraditionalists with their symbolic rather than supernatural form of cosmic apprehension. Pentecostalism, like traditional shamanism, fosters the experience of supernatural powers in everyday life. This contrasts with Hoffmann's explanation of Tlingit neotraditionalist religious apprehensions: "Our Tlingit experience of spirituality was/is immersive, not transcendental. We become. We enter and experience" (email, October 12, 2020). In quite different ways, Pentecostalism and Indigenous neotraditional religious culture are "part of specific social strategies, strategies of making the world meaningful and thus livable" (Dombrowski 151, 10).

CHAPTER 7

1. Charles Taylor explains "fullness": "Somewhere, in some activity, or condition, lies a fullness, a richness; that is, in that place (activity or condition), life is fuller, richer, deeper, more worth while, more admirable, more what it should be. This is perhaps a place of power: we often experience this as deeply moving, as inspiring" (*Secular* 5; see also 8–9). The experience of individual fullness may not have been a goal for aboriginal religious practices. "Fullness," like "belief," has come to mean something different within the modern socioreligious imaginary.

2. Cultural and religious adaptation is not a new Indigenous phenomenon. However, by the second half of the twentieth century, the modern socioreligious imaginary had become much more thoroughly infused throughout Indian Country. As a result, improvisations developed on a more fundamental level. This is reflected in the two novels considered here.

3. Raymond A. Bucko's ethnography of Lakota sweat lodge practices bears this out. He found a proliferation of sweats on the reservation, a place of "great religious pluralism." Within this cultural situation, "not infrequent[ly]" individuals make comparisons of ritual procedures and then choose the one conducted in a way that feels appropriate." However, Bucko adds that participants believe that the basic ritual "faithfully recreates the very ancient past" (12, 202, 13).

Part of Lakota continuity, Bucko explains, is a dynamic relationship between individual and communal religious authority: Early ethnography indicates the "collective interpretation by elder spiritual practitioners, but individual inspiration and interpretation was and continues to be highly valued" (13).

4. One does not determine whether a society is pre-secular or secular by counting the number of religious participants. Taylor observes that in some parts of the United States, church or synagogue attendance is as common as attending a mosque is in Pakistan. Yet the experiential difference of believing within these two contexts is immense when it is an individual option rather than a cultural given (Taylor, *Secular* 3).

5. We see the transition in Erdrich's *Tracks* when Fleur is a young woman. Public and private spheres are breaking apart as the meaning of "land" shifts from spiritual and material

home to saleable commodity. In the present she is still feared as she practices a powerful if finally ineffectual resistance to the tribal loss of both land and the meaning of land.

6. In *Love Medicine* Erdrich uses the name Chippewa but in later books uses Anishinaabe. I use the latter name throughout the paper.

7. The sociological research of Eva Garroutte and colleagues suggests a somewhat different tribal religious landscape, although their study compares one Southwest tribe to two from the Northern Plains. They found that typical religious participation was "sometimes," with about two-thirds of tribal members participating in aboriginal traditions and three-fourths participating in Christian traditions. Clearly it is quite common for tribal members to participate, at least on some level, in both traditions (25, 29–30).

8. McClure published his book in 2007, the same year Taylor's *A Secular Age* came out. While McClure focuses on the experience of contemporary post-secularism, Taylor gets at something more fundamental, the underlying cultural shift that enables this new improvisational religious sensibility. Taylor's explanation of secularity, particularly the third definition, grasps the change in historical conditions of belief and unbelief as well as the resulting shift in sensibility that underlies post-secularism. McClure's explanation of secularism would have benefited from Taylor's more historically situated and conceptually nuanced definitions. McClure uses the common understanding of secularism as the absence of religious belief.

9. Bourdieu is not belittling religion or culture more broadly by using the game metaphor. His point is that these fields have a set of rules, codes, or ways of playing that make sense when one is inside the game but can seem absurd or meaningless outside of it.

In an essay on religion Bourdieu explains, "Religion contributes to the (hidden) imposition of the principles of structuration of the perception and thinking of the world, and of the social world in particular, insofar as it imposes a system of practices and representations whose structure, objectively founded on a principle of political division, presents itself as the natural-supernatural structure of the cosmos" (qtd. in Verter 154).

10. Similarly, Fleur has also lost her sense of the reservation's political game or has chosen to not play. Her subversive attack on the timber company no longer makes sense to the community. In contrast to her direct confrontation, Nector as tribal chair has been traveling to Washington to fight bureaucratically (153).

11. Class needs to be understood relationally rather than as an objective social location. Eric Olin Wright, in "Logics of Class Analysis," distinguished a number of ways to consider class. Most relevant here is "Subjective Salient Groups"—that is, a subjective location in a class hierarchy where a person places him- or herself. This perceived position is part of their identity, what distinguishes the person (331).

12. Herman James, a Pomo informant for *Kashaya Texts*, told a story of Poison Man set "in the old days [when] there were no white men" (Oswalt 213–17). Associated with "the One Below," he made everyone afraid with his deadly but mysterious knowledge and power of poisoning. This was passed on to the children, and James stated in 1958 that "we too are still afraid of what we call poisoning." Elizabeth Colson reported that one of the narrators of *Autobiographies of Three Pomo Women*, in comments from 1939–41, stated that poisoning

had caused "ten deaths in her immediate family" (Colson 223). Fear of poisoning has had an important impact on Pomo culture "by inducing isolation, ensuring strict usage of hospitality rules, and inducing strict rules of etiquette" (Bean and Theodoratus 297). This was important for Pomo well-being within their particular social context. Elizabeth Colson, recorder and editor of *Autobiographies*, observed, "Probably the possibility of 'poisoning' was a major factor in ensuring that people did not trespass upon one another's rights." She adds, "The fear of it, however, locked each small family off by itself" (32).

13. Faye's religious conceptualizations are further discussed in the context of trauma religion in chapter 5.

14. Simon Speck's observation is apropos to Faye's situation: "Fundamentalism is the religion of those left out of the party—it addresses the poor and excluded, those who experience the compulsory individualization that comes with the globalization of free markets and the shriveling of collective provision and welfare protection" (300). What differentiates Faye from other characters is that her failed drive to escape the poverty of Grand Avenue leads her to construct her Pomo fundamentalism rather than accept the resignation experienced by most of the others.

15. The poverty depicted in *Grand Avenue* is historicized in Dyck's afterword for *Grand Avenue* (206–08).

16. Leanne Betasamosake Simpson, for example, takes that position. For her, colonization included "the Christianization of my spirit" (43). "Radical Resistance" seemingly excludes the three-fourths of the citizens of the tribes Garroutte and colleagues researched and found were at least sometimes participating in Christianity. However, Simpson does make a footnote reference to one Native woman who "although a Christian" was also "a resistor" (259, n. 9).

CONCLUSION

1. An Indian Health Service report on health disparities compares American Indian–Native Alaskan mortality rates with those of the US population from 2009 to 2011. The report finds that Native peoples are 2.5 times more likely to die from accidents, 6.6 times more likely to experience alcohol-induced deaths, 1.7 times more likely to commit suicide, and 2.1 times more likely to die from homicide.

2. These include Bonita Lawrence, Renya K. Ramirez, and Donald L. Fixico (Sac and Fox/Muscogee Creek/Shawnee/Seminole), particularly in his *"That's What They Used to Say": Reflections on American Indian Oral Traditions*.

3. See the table of contents or index of any recent critical book related to Indigenous studies.

4. Fixico begins *The Urban Indian Experience in America* by explaining the historical transformation as urban Native peoples shifted from a tribal to a pan-Indian identity (3–7).

5. Another example occurs in Richard Van Camp's (Dogrib) novel *The Lesser Blessed*. The protagonist, ironically within the context of a finally fulfilled sexual connectedness, states to his partner in a post-coital moment, "I have this God-shaped hole in my heart, and I think you do, too" (126).

6. It is worth noting that her series *Children of the Large-Beaked Bird* works in a different direction by annotating photographs of the 1880 Crow Peace Delegation to individualize and recontextualize the isolated subjects.

7. There is so much more that needs to be said about this singing and the religious experiences of contemporary Native peoples. Topics that call for further exploration in relation to the lived religions depicted in Native literature include the role of the Native American Church; powwows as material and spiritual experiences; Christianity, particularly Catholicism and Pentecostalism; the evolving meanings and central position of sweat lodge ceremonies; the significance and ontological status of genres that include enchanted experiences of good and evil, such as horror, fantasy, and science fiction; evolving experiences and conceptualizations of space and place; class and religion (Dombrowski's work provides a useful model); the political implications of various forms of neotraditionalism; Latin American Indigenous experiences, including those of the Maya of Guatemala as a majority Indigenous population; and the intersection of religion and law as a present reality and utopian vision.

WORKS CITED

Alexander, Jeffrey C. "Toward a Theory of Cultural Trauma." *Cultural Trauma and Collective Identity*. Ed. Jeffery C. Alexander, Ron Eyerman, Bernard Giesen, Neil J. Smelser, and Piotz Sztompka. Berkeley: University of California Press, 2004. 1–30.

———. *Trauma: A Social Theory*. Cambridge, UK: Polity Press, 2012.

Alford, C. Fred. "Introduction: Haunted Dialogues: When Histories Collide." *Trans-Generational Trauma and the Other: Dialogue Across History and Difference*. Ed. Sue Grand and Jill Salber. New York: Routledge, 2017. 11–15.

Alfred, Taiaiake. *Wasáse Indigenous Pathways of Action and Freedom*. Toronto: University of Toronto Press, 2009.

Allen, Paula Gunn. *The Sacred Hoop: Recovering the Feminine in American Indian Traditions*. Boston: Beacon Press, 1986.

Anderson, Eric Gary. "Native Horror, Fantasy, and Speculative Fiction." *The Cambridge History of Native American Literature*. Ed. Melanie Benson Taylor. New York: Cambridge University Press, 2020. 431–46.

Angel, Michael. *Preserving the Sacred: Historical Perspectives on the Ojibwa Midewiwin*. Winnipeg: University of Manitoba Press, 2002.

Antonio, Edward P. "Indigenous African Traditions as Models of Theorizing Religion." *Religion, Theory, Critique: Classical and Contemporary Approaches and Methodologies*. Ed. Richard King. New York: Columbia University Press, 2017. 147–54.

Appiah, Kwame Anthony. *In My Father's House: Africa in the Philosophy of Culture*. New York: Oxford University Press, 1992.

Arnal, William. "Critical Responses to Phenomenological Theories of Religion: What Kind of Category Is 'Religion'?" *Religion, Theory, Critique: Classical and Contemporary Approaches and Methodologies*. Ed. Richard King. New York: Columbia University Press, 2017. 421–34.

Auden, W. H. "Lullaby." *Selected Poetry of W. H. Auden*. 2nd ed. New York: Vintage-Random House, 1970. 27–28.

Awiakta, Marilou. *Abiding Appalachia: Where Mountain and Atom Meet*. 1978. Blacksburg, VA: Pocahontas Press, 2006.

Bean, Lowell John, and Dorothea Theodoratus. "Western Pomo and Northeastern Pomo." *Handbook of North American Indians*. Vol. 8: *California*. Ed. Robert F. Heiser. Washington, DC: Smithsonian Institution, 1978. 289–305.

Beck, Ulrich. *A God of One's Own: Religion's Capacity for Peace and Potential for Violence*. Trans. Rodney Livingstone. Cambridge, UK: Polity Press, 2010.

Belcourt, Billy-Ray. *This Wound Is a World*. Minneapolis: University of Minnesota Press, 2019.

Benediktssonn, Thomas E. "The Reawakening of the Gods: Realism and the Supernatural in Silko and Hulme." *Critique* 33.2 (Winter 1992): 121–31.

Berger, Thomas R. *Village Journey: The Report of the Alaska Native Review Commission.* New York: Hill and Wang, 1985.

Berlant, Lauren. "Thinking About Feeling Historical." *Political Emotions: New Agendas in Communication.* Ed. Janet Staiger, Ann Cvetkovich, and Ann Reynolds. New York: Routledge, 2010. 229–45.

Bieger, Laura, Ramón Saldívar, and Johannes Voelz, eds. *The Imaginary and Its Worlds: American Studies After the Transnational Turn.* Hanover, NH: Dartmouth College Press, 2013.

Boulley, Angeline. *The Firekeeper's Daughter.* New York: Holt, 2021.

Bourdieu, Pierre. *The Logic of Practice.* Trans. Richard Nice. 1980. Stanford, CA: Stanford University Press, 1990.

Brooks, Joanna. "Hard Feelings: Samson Occom Contemplates His Christian Mentors." *Native Americans, Christianity, and the Reshaping of the American Religious Landscape.* Ed. Joel W. Martin and Mark A. Nicholas. Chapel Hill: University of North Carolina Press, 2010. 23–37.

Brown, Vinson, and Douglas Andrews. *The Pomo Indians of California and Their Neighbors.* Happy Camp, CA: Naturegraph Publications, 1969.

Bucko, Raymond A. *The Lakota Ritual of the Sweat Lodge: History and Contemporary Practice.* Lincoln: University of Nebraska Press, 1998.

Carpentier, Alejo. *The Kingdom of This World.* Trans. Harriet de Onís. 1957. New York: Farrar, Strauss and Giroux, 1985.

———. "On the Marvelous Real in America." *Magic Realism: Theory, History, Community.* Ed. Lois Parkinson Zamora and Wendy B. Faris. Durham, NC: Duke University Press, 1995. 76–88.

Chavers, Dean. *Racism in Indian Country.* New York: Peter Lang Press, 2009.

Clatterbuck, Mark. *Crow Jesus: Personal Stories of Native Religious Belonging.* Norman: University of Oklahoma Press, 2017.

Clifford, James. "Looking Several Ways: Anthropology and Native Heritage in Alaska." *Current Anthropology* 45.1 (February 2004): 5–30.

Cohen, Anthony P. *The Symbolic Construction of Community.* New York: Routledge, 1985.

Colson, Elizabeth, ed. *Autobiographies of Three Pomo Women.* 1956. Berkley: Archaeological Research Faculty, Department of Anthropology, University of California, 1974.

Coole, Diana, and Samantha Frost, "Introducing the New Materialists." *New Materialisms: Ontology, Agency, and Politics.* Durham, NC: Duke University Press, 2010. 1–43.

Coulthard, Glen Sean. *Red Skin, White Mask: Rejecting the Colonial Politics of Recognition.* Minneapolis: University of Minnesota Press, 2014.

Coviello, Peter, and Jared Hickman. "Introduction: After the Postsecular." *American Literature* 86.4 (December 2014): 645–54.

Crawford, Suzanne J. *Native American Religious Traditions*. New York: Routledge, 2007.

Cvetkovitch, Ann. *An Archive of Feelings: Trauma, Sexuality, and Lesbian Public Cultures*. Durham, NC: Duke University Press, 2003.

Dauenhauer, Richard. "Synchretism, Revival, and Reinvention: Tlingit Religion, Pre- and Postcontact." *Native Religions and Cultures of North America*. Ed. Lawrence E. Sullivan. New York: Continuum, 2003. 160–80.

Dauenhauer, Nora Marks, and Richard Dauenhauer. Introduction. *Haa K̲usteeyí, Our Culture: Tlingit Life Stories*. Seattle: University of Washington Press, Sealaska Heritage Foundation, 1994. 3–121.

———. "Introduction: The Form and Function of Tlingit Oratory." *Haa Tuwunáagu Yís, for Healing Our Spirit: Tlingit Oratory*. Seattle: University of Washington Press, Sealaska Heritage Foundation, 1990. 3–149.

———. "Evolving Concepts of Tlingit Identity and Clan." *Coming to Shore: Northwest Coast Ethnology, Traditions and Visions*. Ed. Marie Mauzé, Michael E. Harking, and Sergei Kan. Lincoln: University of Nebraska Press, 2004. 253–78.

Dawes, Birgit. *Native North American Theater in a Golden Age: Sites of Identity Construction and Transdifference*. Heidelberg: Universitatsverlag Heidelberg, 2007.

de Laguna, Frederica. "Tlingit." *Handbook of Native North American Indians*. Vol. 7: Northwest Coast. Ed. Wayne Suttles. Washington, DC: Smithsonian Institute, 1990. 203–28.

Deloria, Ella Cara. *Waterlily*. Lincoln: University of Nebraska Press, 1988.

Deloria, Philip. Foreword. *Coming Down from Above: Prophecy, Resistance, and Renewal in Native American Religions*. By Lee Irwin. Norman: University of Oklahoma Press, 2008. xi–xii.

———. Preface. *The World We Used to Live In: Remembering the Powers of the Medicine Men*. By Vine Deloria Jr. Arvada, CO: Fulcrum Press, 2006. xiii–xvi.

Deloria, Vine, Jr. *For This Land: Writings on Religion in America*. Ed. James Treat. New York: Routledge, 1999.

———. *The World We Used to Live In: Remembering the Powers of the Medicine Men*. Arvada, CO: Fulcrum Press, 2006.

Denetsosie, Stacie Shannon. "Dormant." *The Missing Morningstar and Other Stories*. Salt Lake City: Torry House Press, 2023. 1–18.

Derrida, Jacques. *The Gift of Death; Literature in Secret*. Trans. David Wills. Chicago: University of Chicago Press, 2008.

Dombroski, Kirk. *Against Culture: Development, Politics, and Religion in Indian Alaska*. Lincoln: University of Nebraska Press, 2001.

Dunn, Carolyn. "The Trick Is Going Home: Secular Spiritualism in Native American Women's Literature." *Reading Native American Women: Critical/Creative Representations*. Ed. Inéz Hernaández-Avila. Lanham, MD: AltaMira Press, 2005. 189–202.

Dunn, Carolyn, and Carol Comfort. Introduction. *Through the Eye of the Deer: An Anthology of Native American Women Writers*. San Francisco: Aunt Lute Books, 1999. ix–xviii.

Duran, Bonnie, Eduardo Duran, and Maria Yellow Horse Brave Heart. "Native Americans and the Trauma of History." *Studying Native America: Problems and Prospects.* Ed. Russell Thornton. Madison: University of Wisconsin Press, 1998. 60–76.

DuVal, Kathleen. *Native Nations: A Millenium in North America.* New York: Random House, 2024.

Dyck, Reginald. Afterword. *Grand Avenue.* By Greg Sarris. Norman: University of Oklahoma Press, 2015. 205–30.

———. Afterword. *Raven Echoes.* By Robert Davis Hoffmann. Tucson: University of Arizona Press, 2022. 93–100.

———. "The Economic Education of Samson Occom." *Studies in American Indian Literatures.* Special Issue: "Indigenous New England." 24.3 (Fall 2012): 3–25.

———. "Practicing Sovereignty in Greg Sarris's *Watermelon Nights.*" *Western American Literature* 45.4 (Winter 2011): 341–61.

———. "When Love Medicine Is Not Enough: Class Conflict and Work Culture on and off the Reservation." *American Indian Culture and Research Journal* 30.3 (2006): 23–43.

Eliade, Mircea. *The Sacred and the Profane: The Nature of Religion.* Trans. Willard R. Trask. Orlando, FL: Harcourt, 1987.

Ellis, Clyde, and Luke Eric Lassiter. Introduction. *Powwow.* Ed. Clyde Ellis, Luke Eric Lassiter, and Gary H. Dunham. Lincoln: University of Nebraska Press, 2005. vii–xv.

Erdrich, Louise. *LaRose.* New York: HarperCollins, 2016.

———. *Love Medicine.* New and expanded version. New York: HarperCollins, 1993.

———. *The Painted Drum.* New York: HarperCollins, 2005.

———. *Tracks.* New York: HarperCollins, 1988.

Evers, Larry, and Felipe S. Molina. *Yaqui Deer Songs, Maso Bwikam.* Tucson: University of Arizona Press, 1987.

Fagan, Kristina. "The Delicate Dance of Reasoning and Togetherness." *Studies in American Indian Literatures* 20.2 (2008): 77–101.

Fixico, Donald L. *"That's What They Used to Say": Reflections on American Indian Oral Traditions.* Norman: University of Oklahoma Press, 2017.

———. *The Urban Indian Experience in America.* Albuquerque: University of New Mexico Press, 2000.

Foucault, Michel. *The History of Sexuality.* Vol. 3: *The Care of the Self.* Trans. Robert Hurley. New York: Vintage-Random, 1986.

———. "Nietzsche, Freud, Marx." *Aesthetics, Method, and Epistemology.* Ed. James D. Faubion. Essential Works of Foucault 1954–1984. New York: New Press, 1998. 269–78.

Furlan, Laura M. *Indigenous Cities: Urban Indian Fiction and the Histories of Relocation.* Lincoln: University of Nebraska Press, 2017.

Gagné, Marie-Anik. "The Role of Dependency and Colonialism in Generating Trauma in First Nation Citizens: The James Bay Cree." *International Handbook of Multigenerational Legacies of Trauma.* Ed. Yael Deneili. New York: Plenum Press, 1998. 355–72.

Galvan, Dennis. "Neotraditionalism." *Britannica Encyclopedia.* August 17, 2015. https://www
.britannica.com/topic/neotraditionalism. Accessed December 17, 2020.

———. *The State Must Be Our Master Fire: How Peasants Craft Culturally Sustainable Development in Senegal.* Berkeley: University of California Press, 2004.

Garfield, Jay L. "Philosophy, Religion, and the Hermeneutic Imperative." *Gadamer's Century: Essays in Honor of Hans-Georg Gadamer.* Ed. Jeff Malpas, Ulrich Arnswald, and Jens Kertscher. Boston: MIT Press, 2002. 97–110.

Garroutte, Eva, et. al. "Religio-Spiritual Participation in Two American Indian Populations." *Journal for the Scientific Study of Religion* 53.1 (2014): 17–37.

Geertz, Clifford. *The Interpretation of Cultures.* New York: Basic Books, 1973.

Geiogamah, Hanay. *Ceremony, Spirituality, and Ritual in Native American Performance: A Creative Notebook.* Los Angeles: UCLA American Indian Studies Center, 2011.

Gerhart, James I., Daphna Canetti, and Stevan E. Hobfoll. "Traumatic Stress in Overview: Context, Scope, and Long-Term Outcomes." *Traumatic Stress and Long-Term Recovery: Coping with Disasters and Other Negative Life Events.* Ed. Kate E. Cherry. Heidelberg: Springer, 2015. 3–24.

Glancy, Diane. *Claiming Breath.* Lincoln: University of Nebraska Press, 1992.

———. "The Naked Spot: A Journey Toward Survivance." *Survivance: Narratives of Native Presence.* Ed. Gerald Vizenor. Lincoln: University of Nebraska Press, 2008. 271–83.

———. "Native American Theater and the Theater That Will Come." *American Indian Theater in Performance: A Reader.* Ed. Hanay Geiogamah and Jaye T. Darby. Los Angeles: UCLA American Indian Studies Center, 2000. 359–61.

———. "Two Dresses." *I Tell You Now: Autobiographical Essays by Native American Writers.* Ed. Brian Swann and Arnold Krupat. Lincoln: University of Nebraska Press, 1987. 169–83.

———. "The Woman Who Was a Red Deer Dressed for the Deer Dance." *American Gypsy: Six Native American Plays.* Norman: University of Oklahoma Press, 20002. 3–18.

Goldschmidt, Walter R., and Theodore H. Haas, eds. *Haa Aaní, Our Land.* Seattle: University of Washington Press, Sealaska Heritage Foundation, 1998.

Gouge, Earnest. *Totkv Mocvse: New Fire: Creek Folktales.* Trans. Jack B. Martin. Norman: University of Oklahoma Press, 2004.

Grand, Sue, and Jill Salber. Introduction. *Trans-Generational Trauma and the Other: Dialogue Across History and Difference.* New York: Routledge, 2017. 1–7.

Hall, David D. Introduction. *Lived Religion in America: Toward a History of Practice.* Princeton, NJ: Princeton University Press, 1997. vii–xiii.

Harjo, Joy. *In Mad Love and War.* Middletown, CT: Wesleyan University Press, 1990.

———. *A Map to the Next World: Poetry and Tales.* New York: Norton, 2000.

Harjo, Joy, and Gloria Bird. Introduction. *Reinventing the Enemy's Language: Contemporary Native Women's Writings of North America.* New York: Norton, 1997. 19–31.

Harper, Anna R., and Kenneth I. Pargament. "Trauma, Religion, and Spirituality: Pathways to Healing." *Traumatic Stress and Long-Term Recovery: Coping with Disasters and Other Native Life Events.* Ed. Katie E. Cherry. Heidelberg: Springer, 2015. 349–67.

Heavener, Mia C. *Under Nushagak Bluff.* Pasadena: Boreal Books, Red Hen Press, 2019.

Hobsbawm, Eric. "Introduction: Inventing Traditions." *The Invention of Tradition.* Ed. Eric Hobsbawm and Terence Ranger. Cambridge, UK: Cambridge University Press, 1983. 1–14.

Hoffmann, Robert Davis. *Raven's Echo.* Tucson: University of Arizona Press, 2022.

———. "Robert H. Davis." *Raven Tells Stories: An Anthology of Alaska Native Writing.* Ed. Joseph Bruchac. Greenfield Center, NY: Greenfield Review Press, 1991. 48–49.

Hogan, Linda. *Power.* New York: Norton, 1998.

———. *Rounding the Human Corners: Poems.* Minneapolis: Coffee House Press, 2008.

———. *Solar Storms.* New York: Scribner, 1995.

———. *The Woman Who Watches over the World: A Native Memoir.* New York: Norton, 2001.

Hokowhitu, Brendan. "Monster: Post-Indigenous Studies." *Critical Indigenous Studies: Engagements in First World Locations.* Ed. Aileen Moreton-Robinson. Tucson: University of Arizona Press, 2016.

Holm, Sharon. "The 'Lie' of the Land: Native Sovereignty, Indian Literary Nationalism, and Early Indigenism in Leslie Marmon Silko's *Ceremony.*" *American Indian Quarterly* 32 (Summer 2008): 243–74.

Howard-Bobiwash, Heather. "Women's Class Strategies as Activism in Native Community Building in Toronto, 1950–1975." *American Indian Quarterly* 27 (2003): 566–82.

Howe, Leanne. Why I Write. n.d. http://www.ileannehowe.com/?s=Choctalking. Accessed February 8, 2021.

———. *Shell Shaker.* San Francisco: Aunt Lute Books, 2001.

Huhndorf, Shari M. *Native Lands: Culture and Gender in Indigenous Territorial Claims.* Oakland: University of California Press, 2024.

Intertribal Friendship House. n.d. https://www.ifhurbanrez.org. Accessed September 28, 2021.

Irwin, Lee. "Native American Spirituality: An Introduction." *Native American Spirituality: A Critical Reader.* Lincoln: University of Nebraska Press, 1997. 1–8.

James, William. *Writings 1902–1910.* New York: Library of America, 1987.

Johnston, Basil. *The Manitous: The Supernatural World of the Ojibway.* New York: Harper, 1995.

Justice, Daniel Heath. *Our Fire Survives the Storm: A Cherokee Literary History.* Minneapolis: University of Minnesota Press, 2006.

———. "The Ragged Edges of Literary Nationhood." *Canadian Journal of Native Studies* 29.1–2 (2009): 24–28.

———. "A Relevant Resonance: Considering the Study of Indigenous National Literatures." *Across Cultures, Across Borders: Canadian Aboriginal and Native American Literatures.* Ed. Paul DePasquale, Renate Eigenbrod, and Emma LaRocque. Peterborough, ON: Broadview Press, 2010. 61–76.

Kellerman, Natan P. F. *Holocaust Trauma: Psychological Effects and Treatment.* iUniverse, 2009.

Kidwell, Clara Sue, Homer Noley, and George E. Tinker. *A Native American Theology.* Maryknoll, NY: Orbis Press, 2001.

King, Thomas. *The Truth About Stories: A Native Narrative*. Minneapolis: University of Minnesota Press, 2003.

Kurtz, J. Roger. Introduction. *Trauma and Literature*. Cambridge, UK: Cambridge University Press, 2018. 1–17.

laFavor, Carole. *Evil Dead Center: A Mystery*. Reprint. Minneapolis: University of Minnesota Press, 1997.

LaPier, Rosalyn R. *Invisible Reality: Storytellers, Storytakers, and the Supernatural World of the Blackfeet*. Lincoln: University of Nebraska Press, American Philosophical Society, 2017.

LaPointe, Sasha taqʷšəblu. *Red Paint: The Ancestral Autobiography of a Coast Salish Punk*. Berkeley: Counterpoint, 2022.

Lassiter, Luke E. *The Power of Kiowa Song: A Collaborative Ethnography*. Tucson: University of Arizona Press, 1998.

Lassiter, Luke Eric, Clyde Ellis, and Ralph Kotay. "Afterward: On the Study of American Indian Christianity." *The Jesus Road: Kiowas, Christianity, and Indian Hymns*. Lincoln: University of Nebraska Press, 2002. 111–19.

Lawrence, Bonita. *Fractured Homeland: Federal Recognition and Algonquin Identity in Ontario*. Vancouver: University of British Columbia Press.

———. *"Real" Indians and Others: Mixed-Blood Urban Native Peoples and Indigenous Nationhood*. Lincoln: University of Nebraska Press, 2004.

Looking Horse, Arval. "The Sacred Pipe in Contemporary Life." Ed. Raymond J. DeMallie and Douglas Parks. *Sioux Indian Religion: Tradition and Innovation*. Norman: University of Oklahoma Press, 1987. 67–73.

Lyons, Scott Richard. "Actually Existing Indian Nations: Modernity, Diversity, and the Future of Native American Studies." *American Indian Quarterly* 35.3 (Summer 2011): 294–312.

———. *X-Marks: Native Signatures of Assent*. Minneapolis: University of Minnesota Press, 2010.

Mackay, James. "Introduction: Red State Poet." *Salt Companion to Diane Glancy*. Cambridge, UK: Salt Publishing, 2010. 1–14.

Maroukis, Thomas Constantine. *The Peyote Road: Religious Freedom and the Native American Church*. Norman: University of Oklahoma Press, 2010.

Martin, Joel W. Introduction. *Native Americans, Christianity, and the Reshaping of the American Religious Landscape*. Ed. Joel W. Martin and Mark A. Nicholas. Chapel Hill: University of North Carolina Press, 2010. 1–20.

Marty, Martin E. *Pilgrims in Their Own Land: 500 Years of Religion in America*. New York: Penguin, 1984.

McAdams, Janet. "'Ways in the World': Formal Poetics in Linda Hogan's *Rounding the Human Corners*." *Kenyon Review* 32.1 (2010): 225–35.

McClure, John A. *Partial Faiths: Postsecular Fiction in the Age of Pynchon and Morrison*. Athens: University of Georgia Press, 2007.

McKegney, Sam. "Beyond Continuance: Criticism of Indigenous Literatures of Canada." *Oxford Handbook of Indigenous American Literature*. Ed. James H. Cox and Donald Heath Justice. Oxford, UK: Oxford University Press, 2014. 409–26.

McLeod, Neal. *Cree Narrative Memory: From Treaties to Contemporary Times*. Saskatoon: Purich Publishing, 2007.

———. "Cree Poetic Discourse." *Across Cultures/Across Borders: Canadian Aboriginal and Native American Literatures*. Ed. Renate Eigenbrod DePasquale and Emma LaRocque. Peterborough, ON: Broadview Press, 2010. 109–21.

McNickle, D'Arcy. *The Surrounded*. 1936. Albuquerque: University of New Mexico Press, 1964.

Merkur, Daniel *Powers Which We Do Not Know: The Gods and Spirits of the Inuit*. Moscow: University of Idaho Press, 1991.

Miller, Susan A. "Native America Writes Back: The Origin of the Indigenous Paradigm in Historiography." *Wicazo Sa Review* 23.2 (Fall 2008): 9–28.

Million, Dian. *Therapeutic Nation: Healing in an Age of Indigenous Human Rights*. Tucson: University of Arizona Press, 2013.

Mitchell, Jon P. "From Ritual to Ritualization." *Religion, Theory, Critique: Classical and Contemporary Approaches and Methodologies*. Ed. Richard King. New York: Columbia University Press, 2017. 377–84.

Momaday, N. Scott. *House Made of Dawn*. New York: Harper, 1966.

———. "Man Made of Words." *Indian Voices: The First Convocation of American Indian Scholars*. San Francisco: Indian Historical Press, 1970. 49–62.

———. *The Man Made of Words: Essays, Stories, Passages*. New York: St. Martin's Griffin, 1997.

Moore, David L. "'The Story Goes Its Own Way': Ortiz, Nationalism, and the Oral Poetics of Power." *Studies in American Indian Literatures* 16.4 (Winter 2004): 34–46.

Morgan, David. "Introduction: The Matter of Belief." *Religion and Material Culture: The Matter of Belief*. New York: Routledge, 2010. 1–17.

———. "Materiality, Social Analysis, and the Study of Religion." *Religion and Material Culture: The Matter of Belief*. New York: Routledge, 2010. 55–74.

Mosionier, Beatrice. *Come Walk With Me: A Memoir*. Winnipeg: Highwater Press, 2009.

Niezen, Ronald. *Spirit Wars: Native North American Religions in the Age of Nation Building*. Berkeley: University of California Press, 2000.

Nu, Jennifer. "City of Kake Celebrates Centennial." *Capital City Weekly*, 11 January 2012.

Ollman, Bertell. *Dialectical Investigations*. New York: Routledge, 1993.

Orange, Tommy. *There There*. New York: Knopf, 2018.

Orsi, Robert J. *Between Heaven and Earth: The Religious Worlds People Make and the Scholars Who Study Them*. Princeton, NJ: Princeton University Press, 2005.

———. "Everyday Miracles: The Study of Lived Religion." *Lived Religion in America: Toward a History of Practice*. Ed. David D. Hall. Princeton, NJ: Princeton University Press, 1997. 3–21.

———. *History and Presence*. Cambridge, MA: Belknap Press of Harvard University Press, 2016.

———. "Introduction: Crossing the City Line." *Gods of the City: Religion and the American Urban Landscape.* Bloomington: Indiana University Press, 1999. 1–78.

———. *The Madonna of 115th Street: Faith and Community in Italian Harlem, 1880–1950.* 3rd ed. New Haven, CT: Yale University Press, 1985.

———. "The Many Names of the Mother of God." *Divine Mirrors: The Virgin Mary in the Visual Arts.* Ed. Melissa R. Katz. Oxford, UK: Oxford University Press, 2001. 3–18.

———. "The Problem of the Holy." *The Cambridge Companion to Religious Studies.* Cambridge, UK: Cambridge University Press, 2012. 84–105.

———. *Thank You, St. Jude: Women's Devotion to the Patron Saint of Hopeless Causes.* New Haven, CT: Yale University Press, 1996.

Ortiz, Simon J. *After and Before the Lightning.* Tucson: University of Arizona Press, 1994.

———. *Fight Back: For the Sake of the Land, for the Sake of the People.* Tucson: University of Arizona Press, 1992. 285–365.

———. *from Sand Creek.* Tucson: University of Arizona Press, 1981.

———. *Out There Somewhere.* Tucson: University of Arizona Press, 2002.

Ortner, Sherry B. *New Jersey Dreaming: Capital, Culture, and the Class of '58.* Durham, NC: Duke University Press, 2003.

Ostler, Jeffrey. *The Lakotas and the Black Hills.* New York: Penguin, 2010.

Oswalt, Robert L. *Kashaya Texts.* University of California Publications in Linguistics. Vol 36. Berkeley: University California Press, 1964.

Parker, Robert Dale. *The Invention of Native American Literature.* Ithaca: Cornell University Press, 2003.

Petrone, Penny, ed. *Northern Voices: Inuit Writing in English.* Toronto: University of Toronto Press, 1988.

Pickering, Kathleen Ann. *Lakota Culture, World Economy.* Lincoln: University of Nebraska Press, 2000.

Piketty, Thomas. *Capital and Ideology.* Trans. Arthur Goldhammer. Cambridge, MA: Belknap Press of the Harvard University Press, 2020.

Porter, Joy. "Historical and Cultural Contexts to Native American Literature." *The Cambridge Companion to Native American Literature.* Ed. Joy Porter and Kenneth M. Roemer. Cambridge, UK: Cambridge University Press, 2005. 39–68.

Power, Susan. *Roofwalker.* Minneapolis: Milkweed Editions, 2002.

Puett, Michael J. "Social Order and Social Chaos." *The Cambridge Companion to Religious Studies.* Cambridge, UK: Cambridge University Press, 2012. 109–29.

Rabine, Leslie. "Romance in the Age of Electronics: Harlequin Enterprises." *Feminisms: An Anthology of Literary Theory and Criticism.* Ed. Robyn R. Warhol and Diane Price Herndl. New Brunswick, NJ: Rutgers University Press, 1997. 976–91.

Rambo, Shelly. "Spirit and Trauma." *Interpretation* 69.1 (2015): 7–19.

———. *Spirit and Trauma: A Theology of Remaining.* Louisville: Westminster John Knox Press, 2010.

Ramirez, Renya K. *Native Hubs: Culture, Community, and Belonging in Silicon Valley and Beyond*. Durham, NC: Duke University Press, 2007.

Rasmussen, Knud. *Across Arctic America: Narratives of the Fifth Thule Expedition*. New York: G. P. Putnam's Sons, 1927.

———. *Intellectual Culture of the Iglulik Eskimos*. Trans. W. Worster. 1929. London: Forgotten Books, 2018.

"Robert Davis Hoffman." *Alaska Quarterly Review* 26.1–2 (2009): 82.

Roemer, Kenneth M. "Silko's Arroyos as Mainstream: Processes and Implications of Canonical Identity." *Leslie Marmon Silko's* Ceremony: *A Casebook*. Ed. Allan Chavkin. Oxford, UK: Oxford University Press, 2002. 223–39.

Sánchez Chan, Feliciano. "Deer." *Words of the True Peoples: Anthology of Contemporary Mexican Indigenous-Language Writers*. Vol 3: *Theater*. Ed. Carlos Montemayor and Donald Frischmann. Austin: University of Texas Press, 2007. 85–91.

Sarris, Greg. "Conversation with Greg Sarris." *Watermelon Nights*. New York: Penguin, 1998. 7–10.

———. *Grand Avenue*. Reprint. Norman: University of Oklahoma Press, 1994.

———. *Keeping Slug Woman Alive: A Holistic Approach to American Indian Texts*. Berkeley: University of California Press, 1993.

———. "Living with Miracles: The Politics and Poetics of Writing American Indian Resistance and Identity." *Displacement, Diaspora, and Geographies of Identity*. Ed. Smadar Lavie and Ted Swedenburg. Durham, NC: Duke University Press, 1996. 27–40.

———. *Mabel McKay: Weaving the Dream*. Berkeley: University of California Press, 1994.

———. *Watermelon Nights*. Reprint. Norman: University of Oklahoma Press, 1998.

Satlow, Michael L. "Tradition: The Power of Constraint." *The Cambridge Companion to Religious Studies*. Ed. Robert A. Orsi. Cambridge, UK: Cambridge University Press, 2012. 130–50.

Schmidt, Leigh E. "On Sympathy, Suspicion, and Studying Religion: Historical Reflections on a Doubled Inheritance." *The Cambridge Companion to Religious Studies*. Ed. Robert A. Orsi. Cambridge, UK: Cambridge University Press, 2012. 17–35.

Schwab, Gabriele M. *Haunting Legacies: Violent Histories and Transgenerational Trauma*. Kindle ed. New York: Columbia University Press, 2010.

Seversted, Per. "Interview with Leslie Marmon Silko." *Conversations with Leslie Marmon Silko*. Ed. Ellen L. Arnold. Jackson: University Press of Mississippi, 2000. 1–9.

Shanley, Kathryn W. "'Born from the Need to Say': Boundaries and Sovereignties in Native American Literary and Cultural Studies." *Paradoxa* 15 (2001): 3–16.

Siebert, Monika Barbara. "Repugnant Aboriginality: LeAnne Howe's *Shell Shaker* and Indigenous Representation in the Age of Multiculturalism." *American Literature* 83.1 (2011): 93–119.

Silko, Leslie Marmon. *Ceremony*. New York: Penguin, 2006.

———. "Language and Literature from a Pueblo Indian Perspective." *Yellow Woman and a Beauty of the Spirit: Essays on Native American Life Today*. New York: Touchstone/ Simon & Schuster, 1996. 25–59.

Simpson, Leanne Betasamosake. *As We Have Always Done: Indigenous Freedom Through Radical Resistance*. Minneapolis: University of Minnesota Press, 2017.

Smith, Andrea. *Conquest: Sexual Violence and American Indian Genocide*. Durham, NC: Duke University Press, 2005.

Smith, Linda Tuhiwai. *Decolonizing Methodologies: Research and Indigenous Peoples*. London: Zed Books, 1999.

Smith, Patricia Clark. "Simon Ortiz: Writing Home." *The Cambridge Companion to Native American Literature*. Ed. Joy Porter and Kenneth M. Roemer. Cambridge, UK: Cambridge University Press, 2005. 221–32.

Smola, Klavdia. *Reinventing Tradition: Russian-Jewish Literature Between the Soviet Underground and Post-Soviet Deconstruction*. Boston: Academic Studies Press, 2023.

Snelgrove, Corey, and Matthew Wildcat. "Political Action in the Time of Reconciliation." *Indigenous Resurgence in an Age of Reconciliation*. Ed. Heidi Kiiwetinepinesiik Stark, Aimée Craft, and Hōkūlani K. Aikau. Toronto: University of Toronto Press, 2023. 237–65.

Spear, Thomas. "Neo-Traditionalism and the Limits of Invention in British Colonial Africa." *Journal of African History* 44 (2003): 3–27.

Speck, Simon. "Contemporary Social Theory and Religion: The Misconstrual of Religion in Theories of 'Second' Modernity. *Religion, Theory, Critique: Classical and Contemporary Approaches and Methodologies*. Ed. Richard King. New York: Columbia University Press, 2017. 297–314.

Staiger, Janet, Ann Cvetkovitch, and Ann Reynolds. "Introduction: Political Emotions and Public Feelings." *Political Emotions*. New York: Routledge, 2010. 1–17.

Stein, Jordan Alexander. "Angels in (Mexican) America." Special Issue: "After the Postsecular." *American Literature* 86.4 (December 2014): 682–711.

Stephens, Nicole, Stephanie A. Fryberg, and Hazel Rose Markus. "It's Your Choice: How the Middle-Class Model of Independence Disadvantages Working-Class Americans." *Facing Social Class: How Societal Rank Influences Interaction*. Ed. Hazel Rose Markus and Susan T. Fiske. New York: Russell Sage, 2012. 87–106.

Stevens, Maurice E. "Trauma Is as Trauma Does: The Politics of Affect in Catastrophic Times." *Critical Trauma Studies*. Ed. Monica J. Casper and Eric Wertheimer. New York: New York University Press, 2016. 19–36.

Straus, Terry, and Debra Valentino. "Retribalization in Urban Indian Communities." *American Indians and the Urban Experience*. Ed. Susan Lobo and Kurt Peters. Walnut Creek, CA: AltaMira Press, 2001. 85–94.

Sullivan, Meghan. "The Modern Treaty: Protecting Alaska Native Land, Values." *Indian Country Today*. June 7, 2021. https://indiancountrytoday.com/news/the-modern-treaty-protecting-alaska-native-land-values. Accessed June 20, 2021.

———. "'We Don't Exist Out Here' Without Subsistence." *Indian Country Today*. October 19, 2021. https://indiancountrytoday.com/news/we-don't-exist-out-here-without-subsistence. Accessed October 19, 2021.

Taylor, Charles. Afterword. *Varieties of Secularism in a Secular Age*. Ed. Michael Warner, Jonathan VanAntwerpen, and Craig Calhoun. Cambridge, MA: Harvard University Press, 2010. 300–21.

———. *Dilemmas and Connections: Selected Essays*. Cambridge, MA: Harvard University Press, 2011.

———. "Modern Social Imaginaries." *Public Culture* 14.1 (2002): 91–124.

———. *A Secular Age*. Cambridge, MA: Harvard University Press, 2007.

Taylor, Melanie Benson. Introduction. *The Cambridge History of Native American Literature*. Cambridge, UK: Cambridge University Press, 2020. 1–14.

———. "Orange Is the New Red " *PMLA* 135.3 (2020): 590–96.

Teuton, Sean. *Native American Literature: A Very Short Introduction*. New York: Oxford University Press, 2018.

Teuton, Sean Kicummah. *Red Land, Red Power: Grounding Knowledge in the American Indian Novel*. Durham, NC: Duke University Press, 2008.

Thornton, Thomas F. *Being and Place Among the Tlingit*. Seattle: University of Washington Press: 2008.

Tinker, George E. "American Indian Theology." *Liberation Theologies in the United States: An Introduction*. Ed. Stacey M. K. Floyd-Thomas and Anthony B. Pinn. New York: New York University Press, 2010. 168–80.

———. "Spirituality, Native American Personhood, Sovereignty, and Solidarity." *Native and Christian: Indigenous Voices on Religious Identity in the United States and Canada*. Ed. James Treat. New York: Routledge, 1996. 115–31.

Tóibín, Colm. "Putting Region in Its Place: Marilynne Robinson." *A Guest at the Feast: Essays*. New York: Scribner, 2023: 211–47.

Trefzer, Annette. "The Indigenous Uncanny: Spectral Genealogies in LeAnne Howe's Fiction." *Undead Souths: The Gothic and Beyond in Southern Literature and Culture*. Ed. Eric Gary Anderson, Taylor Hagood, and Daniel Cross Turner. Baton Rouge: Louisiana State University Press, 2015. 199–210.

Treuer, David. "Reservation Realities and Myths in American Literary History." *The Cambridge History of Native American Literature*. Ed. Melanie Benson Taylor. Cambridge, UK: Cambridge University Press, 2020. 349–64.

———. *The Heartbeat of Wounded Knee: Native America from 1890 to the Present*. New York: Riverhead, 2019.

Tucker, Kenneth H., Jr. *Classical Social Theory: A Contemporary Approach*. Oxford, UK: Blackwell, 2002.

Tucker, Robert C., ed. *The Marx-Engels Reader*. 2nd ed. New York: Norton, 1978.

Van Camp, Richard. *The Lesser Blessed*. 20th anniversary edition. Vancouver: Douglas & McIntyre, 1996.

Vásquez, Manuel A. *More Than Belief: A Materialist Theory of Religion*. Oxford, UK: Oxford University Press, 2011.

Verter, Bradford. "Spiritual Capital: Theorizing Religion with Bourdieu against Bourdieu." *Sociological Theory* 21.2 (June 2003): 150–74.

Vickroy, Laurie. *Reading Trauma Narratives: The Contemporary Novel & the Psychology of Oppression.* Charlottesville: University of Virginia Press, 2015.

Visenor, Gerald. *Manifest Manners: Narratives of Postindian Survivance.* Lincoln: University of Nebraska Press, 1994.

Visenor, Gerald, and A. Robert Lee. *PostIndian Conversations.* Lincoln: University of Nebraska Press, 1999.

Warner, Michael, Jonathan VanAntwerpen, and Craig Calhoun, eds. *Varieties of Secularism in a Secular Age.* Cambridge, MA: Harvard University Press, 2010.

Warrior, Robert. "Native Critics in the World: Edward Said and Nationalism." *American Indian Literary Nationalism.* Ed. Jace Weaver, Craig S. Womack, and Robert Warrior. Albuquerque: University of New Mexico Press, 2005. 179–223.

———. *Tribal Secrets: Recovering American Indian Intellectual Traditions.* Minneapolis: University of Minnesota Press, 1995.

———. "'Your Skin Is the Map': The Theoretical Challenge of Joy Harjo's Erotic Poetics." *Reasoning Together.* Ed. Craig S. Womack, Daniel Heath Justice, and Christopher B. Teuton. Norman: University of Oklahoma Press, 2008. 340–52.

Washuta, Elissa. *White Magic.* Kindle edition. Portland, OR: Tin House Books, 2021.

Weber, Max. "Science as a Vocation." *From Max Weber: Essays in Sociology.* Trans. and ed. H. H. Gerth and C. Wright Mills. Oxford, UK: Oxford University Press, 1946. 129–56.

Welch, James. *Fools Crow.* New York: Penguin, 1986.

———. *Winter in the Blood.* New York: Penguin, 1974.

Whitbeck, Les B., Gary W. Adams, Dan R. Hoyt, and Xiaojin Chen. "Conceptualizing and Measuring Historical Trauma Among American Indian People." *American Journal of Community Psychology* 33.3–4 (June 2004): 119–30.

Whitbeck, Les B., Melissa L. Walls, Kurt D. Johnson, Allan D. Borrisseau, and Cindy M. McDougall. "Depressed Affect and Historical Loss Among North American Indigenous Adolescents." *American Indian and Alaska Native Mental Health Research* 16 (2009): 16–41.

Wilkinson, Charles. *Blood Struggle: The Rise of Modern Indian Nations.* New York: Norton, 2005.

Williams, Joan C. "The Class Culture Gap." *Facing Social Class: How Societal Rank Influences Interactions.* Ed. Susan T. Fiske and Hazel Rose Markis. New York: Russell Sage, 2012. 39–57.

Williams, Raymond. *Marxism and Literature.* Oxford, UK: Oxford University Press, 1977.

Wilson, James. *The Earth Shall Weep: A History of Native America.* New York: Grove Press, 1998.

Wilson, Norma. *The Nature of Native American Poetry.* Albuquerque: University of New Mexico Press, 2001.

Womack, Craig. *Red on Red: Native American Literary Separatism.* Minneapolis: University of Minnesota Press, 1999.

———. "A Single Decade: Book-Length Native Literary Criticism Between 1986 and 1997." *Reasoning Together: The Native Critics Collective.* Ed. Craig S. Womack, Daniel Heath Justice, and Christopher B. Teuton. Norman: University of Oklahoma Press, 2008. 3–104.

———. "Theorizing American Indian Experience." *Reasoning Together: The Native Critics Collective.* Ed. Craig S. Womack, Daniel Heath Justice, and Christopher B. Teuton. Norman: University of Oklahoma Press, 2008. 353–410.

Worl, Rosita. "Art and Atóow." *Celebration: Tlingit, Haida, Tsimshian Dancing on the Land.* Juneau: Sealaska Heritage Institute, University of Washington Press, 2008. 37–41.

———. "History of Southeastern Alaska Since 1867." *Handbook of Native North America.* Vol. 7: *Northwest Coast.* Ed. Wayne Suttles. Washington, DC: Smithsonian Institution, 1990. 149–58.

Wright, Eric Olin. "Logics of Class Analysis." *Social Class: How Does It Work?* Ed. Annette Lareau and Dalton Conley. New York: Russell Sage, 2008. 329–49.

Young Bear, Ray A. Afterword. *Black Eagle Child: The Facepaint Narratives.* Iowa City: University of Iowa Press, 1992. 253–61.

———. *Black Eagle Child: The Facepaint Narratives.* Iowa City: University of Iowa Press, 1992.

———. *Remnants of the First Earth.* New York: Grove Press, 1996.

INDEX